Developing Moral Imagination

Case Studies in Practical Morality

Developing Moral Imagination

Case Studies in Practical Morality

Edward Stevens

Sheed & Ward
Kansas City

Sheed & Ward™ is a service of The National Catholic Reporter Publishing Company.

Library of Congress Cataloging-in-Publication Data
Stevens, Edward, 1928-
    Developing moral imagination : case studies in practical morality / Edward Stevens.
        p.   cm.
    Includes bibliographical references.
    ISBN 1-55612-978-5 (alk. paper)
    1. Ethical problems. 2. Applied ethics. I. Title.
    BJ1031.S75 1997
    170—dc21   97-33535
                                                                     CIP

Published by: Sheed & Ward
                115 E. Armour Blvd.
                P.O. Box 419492
                Kansas City, MO 64141-6492

To order, call: (800) 333-7373
Cover design by James F. Brisson.
This book is printed on recycled paper.

www.natcath.com/sheedward

Contents

1 Introduction

Absolutism fails to offer a convincing account of how opposing people could be both well-informed and good intentioned. It says there is only one answer, and those who do not see it are either ignorant or ill-willed. Relativism fails to offer a convincing account of how people can agree. It says no one is wrong.

There is a third possible response, moral pluralism. Moral pluralists maintain that there are moral truths, but they do not form a body of coherent and consistent truths in the way that one finds in science or mathematics. Moral truths are real, but partial.

         – Lawrence M. Hinman[1]

I invented the word "PO" many years ago. It is derived from words such as hyPOthesis, supPOse, POssible and POetry. . . . They are all provocative . . . ideas put forward to see what effect it will have on our thinking.   **– Edward de Bono**[2]

Theories appear to be the kinds of things that are true or false; but they are also the kinds of things that can be, e.g., useless, arrogant, disrespectful, ignorant, ethnocentric, imperialistic.

     – Maria Lugones and Elizabeth Spelman[3]

---

1.   Laurence M. Hinman, *Contemporary Moral Issues: Diversity and Consensus* (Prentice-Hall, 1996), p. 3.

2.   *De Bono's Thinking Course* (Facts on File Publications, 1985), p. 61. See also logician Edward de Bono, *Po: Beyond Yes and No* (Simon and Schuster, 1972).

3.   "Have We Got a Theory for You!" in Janet Kourany et al. (eds), *Feminist Philosophies* (Prentice-Hall, 1992), p. 385.

ETHICAL PERSPECTIVE:

This is a discussion book about values, not an answers book. "Values" is the current code word for morality or ethics. There are many "my answer is better than your answer" morality books out there. This is only natural. If you have come to some hard won moral conclusions that enhance the values you hold dear, values that work in your experience, you would want everyone to share these values.

So how do you bring about a society of shared values, especially of values that resonate positively in your life? You can't nag, embarrass, shame or intimidate people into agreeing with you. Though certainly people try. The next best thing is to try to legislate your morality, so people, whether they agree with it or not, will have to follow your morality under penalty of fine and imprisonment. So moral debates are fought out in the political arena, in the law courts, and in attempts to amend the constitution as people seek to coercively impose their view of morality on those who disagree. The result is that moral debates get entangled with legal contests, and when disputes arise people's first recourse is to law rather than to persuasion.

This book is about persuasion, not law. It is about enriching and deepening moral life through understanding and dialog, not through indoctrination, dogmatism, or legislation. It starts with the undeniable fact of moral pluralism. There are many different and often contradictory moral views competing for our allegiance. The fact that there are many moralities doesn't mean that one moral view is as good or as correct as another. Moral pluralism does not entail moral *relativism*. For example, there are societies, even in today's world, that see genocide of their unfavorite people, as a right and proper course of action. The moral pluralist doesn't shrug her shoulders with the relativist, and state, "Who am I to say that genocide is wrong?." If she disagrees with moral genocide, she will vigorously explain why. She will try to understand and even dialog with those who think that genocide is good. They may, for example, deem their victims to be worthless subhuman animals, or genetically criminal, or terminally dangerous. Staying committed to her own view, the moral pluralist will show why the opposing view is wrong. And if she truly listens to the opposing view, she may broaden and deepen her own perspective. She may learn that she has a tendency to be naive, for example, about the ethics of war, and about the extreme measures that a society may feel driven to take when defending hearth and home.

✓ So moral pluralism rejects relativism. It also rejects the opposite extreme, *absolutism*, the view that there is only one correct morality, I possess it, and everyone else is wrong. Yes, theories are subject to testing to determine whether they are valid or not, whether they explain what they are supposed to explain. But when a theory takes on an absolutist guise, it can also become dangerous weapon, a moral club with which to bludgeon outsiders. Since moral absolutism imagines itself to be in full possession of the truth, its opponents must be either stupid or bad. Thus absolutism can become arrogant, chauvinistic, disrespectful and imperialistic. Fundamentalist Holy Wars, religious and political, bear sad witness to this danger.

Moral pluralism is an undeniable fact. The globalization of economic life has forced international businesses to hammer out policies for operating in cultural environments whose values are different from and often opposite to the values espoused in the home office. This has spawned a whole literature and field of international business ethics.[4]

---

4.   Thomas Donaldson, *The Ethics of International Business* (Oxford

Business is a latecomer to the problem of global value conflicts. Religions, especially missionary religions, have grappled with pluralism for centuries. This history has often been a story, even in this present day, of attempting to impose religious values coercively through conquest, punishment and intimidation. On the other hand, ecumenical theologians more than any other group have developed tools for respectful dialog. They have shown how to be committed to one's own faith without imperialistically imposing it on non-believers. They point the way to be open to change while faithful to truth and conscience.

Often it is easier to show tolerance and respect for the values of distant peoples than for the person nearby whose values are not that much different from one's own. Liberal and Conservative Catholics alike will cheerfully and with respectful attention participate in a Buddhist-Christian Dialogue, but then return home only to hurl anathemas at each other. The cacophony of radio talk-shows and the litigiousness of our law courts show ethical imperialism to be alive and well within American borders.

University Press, 1989) is a ground-breaking effort to defend specific cross-cultural global rights while at the same time developing ways of operating responsibly when norms of the host country differ from those at home. This has not been easy to implement in the trenches. Foreign managers have been resentful of what they view as American ethical imperialism. See David Vogel, "Is U. S. Business Obsessed with Ethics?" in *Across the Board* (The Conference Board, Inc., 1992) and Andrew W. Singer, "Ethics: Are Standards Lower Overseas?" (*Ibid.*, 1991).

5. See, for example, Harold Coward, *Pluralism: Challenge to the World Religions* (Orbis Books, 1985) outlining how the major world religions can enrich each other while avoiding both fanaticism and relativism. For a Christian standpoint, see, for example, Paul Knitter, *No Other Name? A Critical Survey of Christian Attitudes toward the World Religions* (Orbis, 1985).

√Feminism has shown a similar predilection for including the voices of distant women, while spurning those close by. Feminist Theory grapples with the issues of pluralistic women's voices in interesting and instructive ways. The women's movement has spread from relatively narrow based academic origins into a worldwide campaign to include women of every nation and culture. The global reach of feminism has raised the temptation of ethical imperialism, when women in other cultures embrace values that American feminists abhor. As women in their diversity articulate their views, dialog is opening up and feminism is achieving a deeper and more complex self-understanding. There is an increased sensitivity to listening to these different voices from abroad.[6] But the √women's movement has found it more difficult to embrace divergent voices on the home front. For example, still holding sway are views akin to Andrea Dworkin's stigmatizing of "Right Wing Women" as enemies of feminism and aiders and abettors of patriarchy. Feminist theory is only beginning to reach out to the "I am not a feminist but" voices of women on the American scene. Indeed many self-avowed feminists who diverge from the absolutist line, feel unwelcome at the discussion table.[7] Again, it seems easier to respect the distant neighbor while disdaining the neighbor next door.

This book, then, starts with the well-founded assumption of de facto moral pluralism, as an alternative to both

6.   Maria Lugones and Elisabeth Spelman, "Have We Got a Theory for You! Feminist Theory, Cultural Imperialism and the Demand for 'The Women's Voice'," in *Feminist Philosophies*, edited by Janet A. Kourany *et al.* (Prentice-Hall, 1992), 378-390. Excellent, too, is Laurie Shrage, *Moral Dilemmas of Feminism* (Routledge, 1994).

7.   I am thinking of philosopher Christina Hoff Sommers, maverick academic Camille Paglia, and groups like the Independent Women's Forum.

relativism and absolutism. It parts ways with relativism in that it holds that there *are* moral truths and that these can be defended as true. It parts ways with absolutism in confessing that the moral truths which we hold dear are inevitably *partial* truths.

Moral pluralism is an admission that moral beliefs are limited, partial and incomplete, not that they are wrong. I rightly commit to and defend the truth in my beliefs, even as I stay open to deepening and complementing them in dialog with other moral views. Dialog is necessary because inevitably we are operating with finite minds, cultural filters, and the limits of human language.

Even those who look on the Bible as the literal word of God cannot avoid struggles with language. Witness the controversies over revisionist translations to eliminate sexist language. Similar problems have bedeviled *The New Catholic Catechism.* Indeed, Temple Grandin who grew up afflicted with autism calls into question the adequacy of any language at all in her book *Thinking in Pictures.*[8] Her view is not "a picture is worth a thousand words," but "no number of words can communicate a picture." Engineers call upon her ability to simulate through pictures in her mind how equipment will work when it gets from the drawing page to real life. Her ability to picture equipment simulations has put her in demand as an engineering consultant all over the country when left-brain blueprints fall short or fail. But, alas, this book uses words, not pictures, so *caveat lector.*

---

8.   Temple Grandin, *Thinking in Pictures and Other Reports from my Life with Autism* (Doubleday, 1995).

SELECTION OF ISSUES:

An effort was made to select issues for discussion that are *live* issues. For example, equal opportunity for girls and women to participate in sports used to be a live issue. But now that debate seems to be settled, even though the implementation of the ideal has a way to go. How do you make a case now against such equal opportunity? You don't.

Also an effort has been made to frame the issues in a *non-ideological* way. For example, the abortion debate could have been framed as pro-life absolutism vs. pro-choice absolutism. Rather, we have framed the discussion in non-ideological terms, "Is it possible, without 'selling out' to arrive at a morally responsible middle ground in the abortion debate?." Yes or No?

PRESENTATION OF ISSUES:

Finally, an attempt has been made to overcome the point-counterpoint, either-or, mentality that has overtaken most moral (and political) discussion today. After presenting the issue for discussion, each chapter presents arguments in a tripartite way: (1) YES: the arguments favoring a positive answer to the question under discussion; (2) NO: the reasons for a negative answer to the question under discussion; and (3) PO. Let's explain PO.

"Yes or No" implies that there are only two sides and two answers and two perspectives on any question. The truth of the matter, of course, is that there are a hundred or a thousand sides to every issue.

So in the text, after presenting the YES and the NO, I have borrowed from logician Edward De Bono the concept of PO. PO signals a provocative statement, a new perspective, an idea from left field or out of the blue. It can function as a corrective to left-brain either-or thinking. PO was derived by De Bono from words such as hyPOthesis, supPOse, POssible and POetry, all provocative ideas put forward to jog our thinking out of well worn ruts. Its purpose is to stimulate a fresh look at the question, a possible deepening of moral insight. Understand PO as stating not a defensible position necessarily, but rather a provocation to thought. Understand PO as a shorthand way of saying that statement(s) so labeled are heuristic in intent and do not necessarily reflect the beliefs of the author.

The following discussions and debates – Yes, No and Po – are an opportunity for you to test, strengthen, and modify, if appropriate, your own moral beliefs as you test them against alternative views and arguments. Can you enrich these arguments by bringing to them your own religious and moral insights? Do the views of others point up any incompleteness in your own views, challenging you to evolve toward a broader perspective and wider understanding?

Each chapter concludes by suggesting an "ethics experiment," a real life exercise that might shed some light on the issue just discussed.

PO:

It is salutary to consider what our passionate certitudes of point and counterpoint will look like 150 years from now. In 1855, a number of birth control guides instructed women: "Any exercise calculated to disturb the embryo within twenty-four hours after inception may be sufficient to prevent offspring. . . . But trotting a horse over a rough road would ensure [this effect]." There were, however, mavericks who vigorously contested this view: "The idea of every lady being bound to take a ride on horseback every time she indulges in sexual pleasure is preposterous. . .

Few ladies, espccially among the poor in large cities, have horses at their command; and very few could take violent exercise of any kind every time it became necessary, without annoying others and exposing themselves."[9] How many of the issues proposed in this book will be as moot in the year 2150, as is the impassioned debate about using horses for birth control to us today?

The treatment in this book, it goes without saying, provide only brief outlines of alternative positions. Footnote citations point to fuller discussions and avenues for further research.

On the other hand, the observation of the 6th century Egyptian monk, Dorotheus of Gaza is as pertinent today as it ever was: "We remain all the time against one another, grinding one another down . . . each considers himself right and excuses himself . . . all the while keeping none of the commandments, yet expecting his neighbor to keep the lot."[10]

ETHICS EXPERIMENT:

As a preparation for dealing with the issues in this book, test your tendency to judgementalism. This is an exercise √ of the Buddhist precept of "Right Speech."

The next time you are in conversation with a group of people, at a meal, a party, whatever, see if you can go for thirty minutes without talking about any absent person. It might be interesting to count how many times you are tempted to jump in with your judgments and to watch the judgementalism flying all around you.

---

9. Citations from *The New York Times* (June 2, 1996), on "19th Century Marriage Manuals," p. E7.

10. Cited by Kathleen Norris, *The Cloister Walk* (Riverhead Books, 1996), p. 274.

This book is an effort to make ethical judgments, without judgementalism.

SEX

2 Sex: Who Makes the Rules?

As a matter of fact, there is no reason, not even a most serious one, which can bring it about that what is intrinsically against nature can become consonant with nature and a good act. Since, however, by its very nature the conjugal act is destined for the begetting of children, those who, in making use of it, by their own intervention deprive it of this natural force and power act against nature and do something impure and intrinsically immoral. Pope Pius XI, *Casti Connubii*[1]

Roles in the family are not biologically dictated. . . . No one marital or family pattern is normative, and all others defective in some way. Families do not need to include children. Families need not be based on marriage. Families can be collections of persons who are committed to the physical, moral, spiritual, social, and intellectual development of other members of the collective unit in an ongoing way. Christine E. Gudorf[2]

---

1. This encyclical letter on marriage, written in 1930, was the first letter on sexual morality by a pope to be directed to the Church worldwide.

2. Gudorf in *Body, Sex, and Pleasure: Reconstructing Christian Sexual Ethics* (The Pilgrim Press, 1994), p. 79, summarizes evolving patterns of responsible sex, as people struggle with changing economic and social challenges. Single-heads of family households and extramarital births at times seem more the norm than deviations from the norm. See the discussion by Margaret Cerullo and Marla Erlien, "Beyond the 'Normal' Family: A Cultural Critique of Women's Poverty" in Rochelle Lefkowitz and Ann Withorm (eds.), *For Crying Out Loud: Women and Poverty in the U.S.* (The Pilgrim Press, 1986), 248-261.

1. Sex categories themselves are less unified and stable than everyday thinking admits; 2. Criteria for membership in sex categories can be contested; 3. Sex identity may be experienced by some as transitive and liminal, as genuinely dysphoric and discontinuous. . . Postmodernism supplies a set of ontological commitments needed for a world in which the body appears to be malleable, protean, and constructed through and within discourse. Jacquelyn N. Zita[3]

Few areas of morality are as fiercely contested as sexual and marital ethics. Are we talking about sexual actions or about persons? What are the ingredients of a sexual identity? Of a genuine marriage? Are sexual norms God-given, socially constructed or personally chosen?

Many treatments of sexual ethics focus on the varieties of sexual acts, devising norms and arguments about masturbation, homosexual acts, bisexual acts, heterosexual intercourse, extramarital sexual relations, premarital petting, adulterous acts, premarital contraceptive intercourse, marital contraceptive intercourse, condom use for protection from disease.[4] Often it seems to be a weirdly impersonal world of organs at play in all their various permutations and couplings. After we finish the ethics of sexual organs, are we to go on to the ethics of digestive organs, of olfactory organs? Lost often in the discussion is that these organs belong to people. Morality applies not to organs, but to the free, conscientious, reflective, intelligent choices of human beings.

---

3.   See her "Male Lesbians and the Postmodernist Body" in Claudia Card (ed.), *Adventures in Lesbian Philosophy* (Indiana University Press, 1994), p. 129.

4.   Even relatively liberal and pastorally benign treatments suffer from this focus on such a catalog of sexual acts. See, for example, Philip S. Keane, S.S., *Sexual Morality: A Catholic Perspective* (Paulist Press, 1977).

So this chapter will refrain from enumerating sexual acts and will eschew a catalog of sins' approach, in favor of offering alternative guiding principles for making responsible decisions about the sexual dimension of life. Keep the following definitions in mind, as we deal with these issues.

Identity Category	Oppositional Categories	
SEX Bodies physically sorted into clearly identifiable kinds based on biological criteria.	FEMALE	MALE
GENDER People judged to fit or misfit expected behaviors, functions, personal attributes associated with one sex or the other.	FEMININE	MASCULINE
ORIENTATION People differentiated by their erotic desire or actions with same or "opposite" sex.	MALE MALE FEMALE EITHER	FEMALE MALE FEMALE EITHER
SOCIAL SEX Individual manifests the culturally specific & appropriate combination of the above three identity-categories.	a REAL MAN	a REAL WOMAN

We will look at three different perspectives on sexual ethics, the Premodernist View, the Modernist View, and the Postmodernist View. Each has its strengths and its weaknesses. When you have evaluated these, you will be in a better position to make responsible sexual decisions, and even to devise your own catalog of sexual sins, should you be so inclined. So our question is: *What does it mean to be a sexual human being, and to express this sexuality in a responsible way? Is the answer to these questions: (1) given by*

*nature and/or outside authority (the premodernist approach);
(2) socially constructed by myself and like-minded others (the
modernist approach); or (3) a purely personal choice (the postmodernist approach)?*

(1) PREMODERNISM: NATURE AND/OR GOD MAKES THE RULES:

✓Sexual norms are objective. The body's place, its meaning and use, and therefore the parameters of a responsible sexuality are objective and given by natural law,
which is a reflection of divine law. They are not up-for-
grabs. They are not reducible to personal choices or arbitrary social constructions. Human sexuality is a great
gift to be used in the service of love and life. When this
meaning is distorted or perverted, reality itself is
mocked, and reality exacts its penalty. AIDS, broken
homes, abused children, family violence, unrestricted
abortion, and rampant population explosion are nature's way of protesting the abuse of the realities of sex.

Premodernism as a contemporary view. ✓This view is
"premodern" not in the chronological sense of being
antiquated or outdated. It designates a fundamental
philosophy, a vision of reality that sees nature as informed with intelligence and purpose. At the threshold
of the third millennium, this view may be more alive
and well than it has ever been. People often feel alien-
ated from this view when it is expressed through Bible-
based divine commands and the scoldings of religious
authority figures. Such other-centered, authoritarian
and often dogmatic, extrinsic morality offends people
whose morality is attuned to the promptings of their
conscience, heart and indwelling spirit.

Natural law sexual ethics has been recovered today
not in the autocratic rantings of religionists, but in the

ecological backlash that has shocked us into realizing that we cannot abuse nature with impunity. The "Gaia hypothesis" suggests that the earth and everything on the earth is best viewed as a single interactive organism. The activities in each part depend on and impact for better or worse on the well-being of every other part. Holism is the law of reality; individualism is a lethal delusion.

Holistic sex is the norm. Human sexuality, then, needs to be viewed in this holistic way. Sex is not rightly viewed as an individual pleasure machine. Sex is in the service of life and the continuation of life, expressed and guided by love and the growth of love. A holistic sexual ethic is respectful of human sexuality in all its dimensions. Decisions about sexuality need to be responsive to the biology and physiology of sex, in conjunction with the interpersonal loving dimension of sex, in the context of the social needs that are served, all interacting in an overarching ecology of global population and limited resources. And for the believer, respecting this reality in all its complexity is the path to obeying the divine will that underpins it. This is a far cry from a morality that says "Do anything you want as long as you don't hurt somebody." Every decision affects everybody, even future generations. Let's look briefly at these four dimensions of a holistic view of human sexuality:

A. *The Procreative Dimension:* Let's grant right off that the new reproductive technologies, including IVF, AIH, AID, GIFT, cloning, and varieties of surrogacy show that reproduction can be separated from sexual intercourse. Clearly these technologies serve the procreative dimension of human sexuality. In deciding the ethics of such procedures, we need to ask whether they serve, or whether they violate the other dimensions of sex, namely, the interpersonal, the social, and the ecological. For example, does the impregnation of a wife by a third-party sperm donor violate her committed relationship to her husband? Or if a woman is inseminated artificially with her husband's sperm, is this impersonal procedure a violation of the loving act of intercourse, from which procreation is intended to take place, as some claim? Or does cloning diminish human dignity by turning the conceptus into a manufactured commodity? Or again, is it responsible to artificially multiply births in a world already overpopulated with children with no one to care for them?

But the vast majority of conceptions result from the coupling of sexual organs. While it would be a distortion to reduce sex to procreation alone, clearly sexual intercourse has something to do with procreation, a lot to do with it. Sex education focuses on how procreation occurs. Organs are male and female for a purpose, namely, procreation, the passing on of life. To ignore this is to be sexually irresponsible. A decision that is open to procreation is a decision of responsible readiness to conceive, bring to term and raise a child. If this readiness is not there, a decision not to procreate is imperative.

B. The Interpersonal Love Dimension: But sex is not only organs and procreation. People, not organs, have sex. People have sex to express love, to enjoy pleasure, or both. Procreation is not the only reason, or even the main reason, that people make love. If it were, then a case might be made, and often is made, that homosexual love violates the nature of human sexuality, since procreation cannot come about from homosexual acts. But interpersonal love can be expressed and fostered by homosexual acts, infertile as these may be; in like manner, the sexual love of infertile heterosexual couples, including elder couples, is respectful of that dimension of human sexuality that serves love, even though it cannot serve procreation, the passing on of life.

C. The Physicalist Fallacy: Natural law ethics has often fallen into a fallacy called *physicalism.* This is an ethics of organs rather than of people. Looking at organs apart from people, it asserts that it is the nature of pro-creative organs to procreate. Every sexual act, therefore, must be open to procreation. Artificial contraception, then, is immoral because it violates the nature of the procreative organs (and by extension, for the believer, violates the will of God who created procreative or-gans). Physicalist procreative sexual ethics is the big gun rolled out against contraception and homosexuality. It is fallacious in that it ignores and reduces the complete holistic reality of sex. The acts of sexual organs are in-formed by the intelligent, loving intentions of human beings. To reduce people to organs, and to pretend that nonprocreative sex cannot rightly express and foster love, is to diminish the reality of human sexuality. Pro-creative physicalism is not a conclusion of the natural law, but a violation of it.

The assumption behind the contemporary version of Premodernism, or Natural Law, is that nature is inherently purposeful; it is a total organic system, and is self-regulating. Therefore, we violate it at our peril.

D. The Teaching of the Bible: But Premodernism also ap-pears not only in the physicalist framework we just noted but also in Biblical terms. This is not the place to expound on the Bible's teaching about sex.[5] But a huge amount of teaching and discourse about sexual morality in America alleges to be Bible-based. If one actually reads the Bible, it quickly becomes evident that the sex-

---

5. For some provocative discussion of the Bible and sex, see J. Cheryl Exum, "The Ethics of Biblical Violence Against Women" (pp. 248-271), and Lisa Sowle Cahill, "Sex and Gender Ethics as New Testament Ethics" (pp. 272-295) in *The Bible in Ethics: The Second Sheffield Colloquium,* edited by John W. Rogerson, Margaret Davies, and M. Daniel Carroll Rodas (The Sheffield Academic Press Ltd., 1995).

ual teaching is not that clear or nonproblematic. Jesus
had little to say about sex. There is the account of his
compassion for the woman about to be stoned for adultery, and his admonition to guard one's thoughts
against the intention of committing adultery. And there
is the saying of Jesus about divorce. That's it. The rights
and wrongs of sex were not really a problem in Jesus'
Jewish community. Women were kept under tight rein,
and basically subordinate to men. It is a matter of dis-
pute to what extent Jesus' view of sex and gender ethics
was culture-bound, and to what extent he reformed the
culture. The proper role of women in Christian
churches is debated to this day.

E. The Role of Sexual Pleasure: Love and procreation are
built into the reality of human sexuality. What about
pleasure? Christine Gudorf makes a strong case for
pleasure as a norm for moral rightness in matters sexual.
But isn't the pursuit of pleasure precisely what leads to
licentiousness and immorality? Not so, says Gudorf, if
pleasure is understood in a holistic and comprehensive
way.

---

6.   Exum, *op.cit.,* calmly and meticulously documents the horrifying
pervasiveness of the Old Testament's legitimation of violence against
women. The prophets especially use the image of Israel as a faithless
woman, and have God administering as this woman's proper
punishment the most extreme abuse: God assembles her former lovers
and hands her over to their abuse, "I will give you over to their hand . . .
they will strip off your clothes and leave you stark naked . . they will
stone you with stones and cut you to pieces with their sword." (Ezekiel
16); "They will cut off your nose and ears" (Ezekiel 23); "I [God] will
expose her genitals in the sight of her lovers and no one shall rescue
her from my hands" (Hosea 2); "Because the daughters of Zion are
haughty, glancing provocatively with their eyes, the Lord will make bald
the heads of the daughters of Zion and the Lord will bare their ****
[obscenity for genitals]" (Isaiah 3). Looking to the Bible for normative
sexual and gender ethics has its problems.

The proposed criteria would require, first of all, taking seriously all those obstacles and circumstances which currently prevent sex from being mutually pleasurable. Those include, among others: genital mutilation, fear of pregnancy, fear of AIDS and other STD's, rape and sexual abuse, sexual coercion/harassment, sexual dysfunction, ignorance of sexual biology and technique, and last but not least, poor sexual communication. The criterion of social responsibility would also weigh in . . : conception outside stable, ecologically responsible child-rearing situations; and public policies which support sexual ignorance, sexual dysfunction, sexual abuse, or sexual coercion/harassment. The criterion of respect and care for the partner would at least rule out instrumental understands of partners, including sexual objectification.[7]

When these obstacles to genuine mutual pleasure are all accounted for, we have not a prescription for permissiveness and promiscuity, but a high ideal indeed of sexual morality.

(2) MODERNISM: SOCIETY MAKES THE RULES:

The modernist framework. The scientific revolution stripped the universe of purpose and intrinsic teleology. Nature was considered value-free and intelligible to the extent that it is quantifiable and subject to the hypothetical deductive method of science. Purposes and goals are no longer discovered in nature, but are socially constructed and read back into nature. There is no natural law out there to be discovered and to serve as a moral compass. To the Modernist sensibility and

---

7.   Gudorf, *op. cit.*, pp. 143-144.

mind-set, sexual ethics is not discovered in nature, but socially constructed and read back into nature. Sexual ethics becomes sexual politics.

The sexual body is viewed not as a gift entrusted to my care and demanding respect on its own terms. The sexual body is my property. I see myself free to define it as I please, and to find like-minded others with whom to forge a sexual identity and a sexual ethics. With these like-minded others, I construct a sexual identity and a sexual ethics validated by these others. The norms of sexual morality are not discovered in nature, but constructed by social groups. The challenge then becomes a political one, to have your group's norms validated by the wider society and not consigned to the trash heap of deviancy. Psychological experts arise with authority to distinguish the normal from the deviant, the deviant from the pathological, and the pathological from the criminal. It is a triumph of politics as much as of ethics when, for example, homosexuality is removed from the list of pathologies to become a normal sexual alternative.

Premodernism in a modernist world. Premodernist authorities, church leaders for example, attempt to present objective sexual values based on natural law. This runs head on into the dominant myth of modernism, which enshrines the values of Western science. Human nature's essential characteristics derive from an evolutionary succession of random events and accidental natural selections, without inherent purpose or meaning.[8] So the preachments of premodernists are simply incredible to the modernist sensibility, in which values are constructed, not discovered. Premodernist authori-

---

8. Willis Harmon has an insightful discussion of such alternative paradigms in "Biology Re-visioned," *The Noetic Sciences Review* (Spring 1997), 12-17, 39-42.

ties find their teaching reduced to just one more alternative sexual reality vying for recognition in the marketplace of ideas.

Socially constructed ethics. The winners in the sexual ethics political arena are those who succeed in having their moral sexual codes legitimated. Some of the groups in contention are Right-wing Christians, lesbians, gays, conservative parties, unmarried parents, cohabiting singles, fervent Roman Catholics, swingers and libertines. These groups have succeeded in constructing informal codes that have obtained recognition. Some are readily approved in the wider society, and even become encoded in law. Others remain embattled and can't let down their guard for a moment. There is no commonly agreed upon metaphysical or religious support, such as was enjoyed in premodern societies. These alternative sexual frameworks remain relatively fragile social constructions that in a pluralistic world can never be taken for granted.

Divorce, premarital sex, gay marriage, contraception for kids, man-boy sex: morally right or morally wrong? It depends on whether you can muster a sufficient group of fellow believers to get the behavior recognized, accepted, validated by experts, and best of all, encoded into law. In a world where the meaning of the body and of human sexuality is not given by nature, values need to be socially constructed and imposed upon nature. The Modernist mind-set needs values, but it despairs of *discovering* them. Therefore, it socially *creates* them and uses lobbying, talk shows, propaganda, media outlets, demonstrations, boycotts, votes, bribery, the whole array of political weapons to get them legitimated.

The example of lesbians. For example, in premodernist thought, lesbianism was viewed as a deviation from nature. It was characterized by female bodies and specific sexual acts that deviated from the bipolar sexuality that was "natural" to the human species. In the 1970s, lesbianism came to be defined less by sex acts, and more by a political position against heteropatriarchy. But seen through modernist eyeglasses as an ideological, ethical and political posture, lesbianism is purified of sexual stigma, and becomes a socially constructed role, with its own norms of correct behavior, its own rights and duties, its own legal protections. To go further, a human in a male body can become a lesbian, provided that s/he can get fellow conspirators to welcome her/him into this new identity.[9] Again, the rules of sex for the Modernist are socially constructed.

---

9.   Jacqueline N. Zita, *op. cit.*, carries the argument one step further, showing how even a male can become a lesbian if s/he can persuade others to conspire with her/him in the construction of this self-intended role. So an individual with the "wrong" body (a male) can take up the lesbian role and relate to women as a woman rather than as a man. The challenge is for her/his self-intending attribution as a lesbian to be accepted by her/his hopefully fellow lesbians. What strategies can s/he use to convince the others to extend and attribute to him the lesbian identity s/he claims for her/his self?

Four strategies are used:

(1) transsexual surgery, to persuade the others of the reality and sincerity of her/his lesbian identity;

(2) a trans-gendering strategy: "Please look beyond my male body form to my deep gender identity of a woman trapped in a man's body";

(3) a genital de-essentializing strategy: "Look not at my anatomy but, like other lesbians, consider my ideological political posture against heteropatriarchy as the essence of my lesbian identity." P. 125: "[The penis] remains an appendage, useful perhaps, a location of pleasure like the clitoris, but a perforate clitoris with some optional functions";

(4) a genderf**k strategy: a male can have womanly sex with a female, i.e., (p. 126): "a style of erotic encounter that de-centers attention from the penis and its essentially definitive acts of intercourse," a genetic male "homosexing" with a genetic female. Another example of lesbian genderf**k, would be two genetic females "heterosexing" with each other, butch-femme style.

(3) POST-MODERNISM: I MAKE THE RULES:

The postmodernist framework. Many, younger people especially, feel that in terms of sexual ethics they are living in a clueless wasteland. The postmodernist mind-set suggests the reason for this sense of sexual anarchy. If sexual rules are not objectively based on the nature of reality, if they are merely social constructions, then these constructions can be deconstructed. I don't need fellow believers to tell me who I am in terms of sex and gender and orientation. I can decide for myself and make up my own sexual moral rules. The postmodern mind deconstructs these social moral edifices, and exposes their arbitrariness and fragility.

The deconstruction of sexual codes. The categories of sex, of gender, of orientation and of social sex are all social constructions. They are not "given," or objective, or stable. There are not two sexes. Sexes can range from extreme male to extreme female, and a whole spectrum in between. There are not two genders, masculine and feminine, but all kinds of permutations and commutations that can change from day to day and moment to moment. The same goes for my sexual preferences, which can be ever-variable and ever-changing. Like sex, gender and orientation, the idea of a "Real Man" or a "Real Woman" is a social fiction, parsed and exposed by postmodernist analysis. The rules of sex and gender and orientation are whatever I decide to make them.[10]

Consult again the grid at the beginning of this chapter. The problem both with premodernist and with modernist interpretations is that they try to fit the infinite

---

10. For an entertaining introduction to the postmodernist mind, see Walt Anderson's *Reality Isn't What It Used to Be: Theatrical Politics, Ready to Wear Religion, Global Myths, Primitive Chic, and Other Wonders of the Postmodern World* (Harper Collins, 1992).

variations of sex, gender and orientation into the binary categories of the above grid. Why should we limit ourselves to only two sexes, two genders, two orientations? These are social constructions. De-construct them.

Every human being, not just the "male lesbian," can see her/himself as multiply gendered and polymorphously erotic. Philosophically, there is no need of strategies to persuade others to extend a sexual identity to me. There are no fixed identities to extend.

PO: WHERE DO WE GO FROM HERE?

As we struggle to play the sexual game in a morally responsible way amid the ruins of the postmodernist landscape, we know that something is wrong.[11] We experience broken homes, divorces, affairs, stepchildren, abandoned children, STD's, all lived out under the grim shadow of AIDS. Antidotes to this anarchy and confusion come in the form of bumper-sticker morality: *Do whatever you want as long as you don't hurt anybody; Pet your dog, not your date; Do the right thing, wait for the ring; Just say no; Follow* **The Rules**.[12] Bumper-sticker morality makes good ad copy, but why should it carry any more weight than *Things go better with Coke?* This is a long way from *Thou Shalt Not Commit Adultery* because God said so.

How will you go about forming a post-postmodernist code of sexual ethics that is stable and objective, without being unrealistically dogmatic and rigid?

---

11. For an insightful report on the current state of the sexual landscape, see Katie Roiphe's *Last Night in Paradise: Sex and Morals at the Century's End* (Little, Brown and Company, 1997).
12. Ellen Fein and Sherrie Schneider, *The Rules: Time-Tested Secrets for Capturing the Heart of Mr. Right* (Warner Books, 1996).

ETHICAL EXPERIMENT:

Sit down with your significant other and make a list of Ten Commandments for Responsible Sexual Behavior. These commandments, if followed, would create a world where sexual intimacy would enhance personal loving intimacy, where children would be wanted and cared for, where sex is enjoyed in peace, without fear of disease, where freedom and respect are inviolable, where sexual ignorance is banished, where there is concern for how your decisions affect the wider society and the world.

Imagine sharing these Ten Commandments with your teenage daughter or younger brother. Imagine that they look at you, arms crossed, retorting defiantly: "I'll do anything I want to"? How would you reply? Are your commandments postmodernist bumper stickers? Do they represent a modernist socially constructed consensus? Or do they flow from your judgment that this is the very nature of human sexuality, which demands to be respected on its own terms? What is the basis for your commandments? What makes them true and reliable guides?

3 Gay Sex: Human Right or Moral Wrong?

The Supreme Rabbinical Court, a small group of or-
thodox halachic rabbis, issued a ruling that declared
the lesbian contributors to Nice Jewish Girls, a Jewish
lesbian anthology, "dead" and "non-Jews."[1]

Basing itself on Sacred Scripture, which presents homo-
sexual acts as acts of grave depravity, tradition has al-
ways declared that "homosexual acts are intrinsically
disordered." They are contrary to the natural law.
They close the sexual act to the gift of life. They do not
proceed from a genuine affective and sexual comple-
mentarity. Under no circumstances could they be ap-
proved. **The new *Catechism of the Catholic Church*** [2]

The Bible contains six admonishments to homosexuals
and 362 to heterosexuals. This doesn't mean that God
doesn't love heterosexuals. It's just that they need more
supervision. **Linda Lavner, Comedian** [3]

Is an active homosexual love life morally objectionable
in a way that an active heterosexual love life is not? We
confine the discussion to lesbian and gay (L/G) orientation and behavior, leaving aside other varieties of hu-

---

1.   Lynn Witt, Sherry Thomas and Eric Marcus (eds.), *Out in All
Directions: The Almanac of Gay and Lesbian America* (Warner Books, 1995),
p. 35.
2.   Cited in Gerald D. Coleman, S.S., *Homosexuality: Catholic Teaching
and Pastoral Practice* (Paulist Press, 1995), p. 101.
3.   Witt, *op.cit.*, p. 31.

man sexual desire. The question here is not about the morality of the orientation itself, but its expression in behavior as a regular part of one's sexual life (what people seem to mean by "L/G lifestyle"). Nor is the question whether L/G's are morally reprehensible as persons. If heterosexual desires don't make one a bad person, why should homosexual desires? The question is about behavior – what to do with these desires.

For the postmodernist (see Chapter 1), this is a non-question. Sexual ethics is a personal creation. In the modernist view, this is gradually becoming a non-issue, as gay relationships, and even gay marriages, find social legitimacy and acceptance. But gay sex definitely remains a live ethical issue for the premodernist. The traditional conservative view of morally responsible sexual behavior is that it should occur in the context of heterosexual marriage, open in principle to procreation. So this chapter will consider alternatives available within the premodernist framework. If we grant this for purposes of discussion, then the question becomes: ***are L/G's fated to live celibate lives, morally prohibited from ever expressing sexual love?***

YES:

Natural Law provides the guiding principle for this discussion. Male and female complementarity is the key for moral assessment of human sexuality. Such male-female bipolarity is no accident, but is clearly ordered toward procreation. In humans, this procreative finality demands a stable heterosexual partnership, called marriage. Adultery, fornication, and homosexuality undermine the moral structure built into the very nature of human sexuality, namely the stable procreative heterosexual climate that maximizes spousal love and children's education and growth.

Such stable procreative union is cemented by mutual love and commitment in which husband and wife, through their reciprocal self-giving, transmit life: love in the service of procreative life for the continuation of society.

Homosexual orientation, blameless as its subjects may be, is an objective disorder. It is a sexual orientation closed off by its very nature to the purpose of sex. For example, a diabetic with an orientation for consuming sugar may be blameless for this orientation. But it remains an objective disorder. For diabetics, this orientation undermines nutrition, and it is a moral imperative that they not act on this orientation. As nutrition serves individual survival, so sexuality serves the survival of the species. To act on an objectively disordered nutritional orientation undermines individual survival. To act on an objectively disordered sexuality undermines the survival of the human race.

So, in conclusion, there is no culpability about the orientation. Any condemnation, demeaning of, or violence against L/G's is totally unjust and wrong. Often heterosexuals, because of illness, disability, lack of or death of a marital partner, are called, through no fault or choice of their own, to a life of chaste celibacy. L/G's, through no fault of their own, have a similar moral obligation. Aware of human weakness, people in their better moments show patience and understanding for heterosexuals who fall into adultery or fornication. There is no reason not to extend a similar compassion to L/G's who engage in extramarital sex.

But compassion for weakness does not mean condoning it. It would be just as wrongheaded to legitimate and legalize the "homosexual lifestyle" as it would be to legalize adultery. The sinner is loved, but not the sin.

NO:

Natural law makes the moral demand that we be respectful of the nature of things. So it is imperative that we be very careful in observing the nature of things. Better observations make for more precise and responsible natural law. We have seen the natural law claim that "homosexuality is a moral disorder because it violates the natural procreative complementarity of the female and male sexual organs." Such a simplistic view of human sexuality leads to a reductionistic moral conclusion. The nature of human sexuality is far more complex.

Human sex revolves around personal relationships, not sexual organs. In nonhuman animals, the female is receptive only when she is fertile, and only then are males attracted. Sex is clearly just for procreation. But human sexual attraction is not limited and linked to fertility. Sexual bonding has a purpose beyond bringing about a conception. While other animals at birth have all their survival behaviors preprogrammed, human infants at birth are incomplete and incapable of surviving on their own. They are totally dependent on the care and teaching of adults. Human sexual bonding has the purpose of ensuring a climate where this care will take place.

It is no accident that in humans both sexes are receptive and attracted at all times, not just in fertile periods, but from pubescence to old age, and even during pregnancy. Thus nature assists in creating and maintaining the loving relationship in which the incomplete human newborns can grow and flourish. A partnership that is open to life is much more than two sets of organs creating a zygote. Human life is generated and brought to completion in the matrix of a loving relationship. Beyond the mere act of conception, human sexual relations serve this relationship. In cases of adoption, for example, we have come to recognize that the true parents are those who raised the child, and not just the man and the woman who performed the act of copulation and conception.

This more nuanced view of the nature of human sex yields a natural law where homosexual relations can quite appropriately serve love and life in the bonding and personal growth of L/G lovers, whose relationship can provide the family environment where children can grow and flourish.[4]

So this more respectful look at the complexity of human sexuality leads to natural law, which allows L/G partners to express sexual love in responsible and committed ways, just as do their heterosexual brothers and sisters. L/G's in this view do not form a subspecies of humans morally doomed by nature to a lifetime of sexual repression.

PO:

Can a more flexible look at human ways of interpreting the body help dissolve this problem? Maybe human beings cannot be sorted out so easily into L/G's and heterosexuals. Jacqueline Zita suggests not.[5] JoAnn LouLan suggests not:

> *I believe there are thousands of genders. We have a sense of who we are at a very early age. As the socialization process takes place, we must try to fit into the narrowly defined sex roles that our culture assigns us.*[6]

---

4.   See Robert P. Heaney. M.D., "Sex, Natural Law, and Bread Crumbs," *America* (February 28, 1994), 12-16.

5.   Jacqueline N. Zita, "Male Lesbians and the Post Modernist Body," *Adventures in Lesbian Philosophy*, edited by Claudia Card (Indiana University Press, 1994), pp. 112-132.

6.   "Butch Mothers, Femme Bull Dykes: Dismantling Our Own Stereotypes" in *Dyke Life*, edited by Karla Jay (Basic Books, 1995), p. 253.

For the most part, we can divide female bodies from male bodies: *biological identity*. *Gender identity* is not so clear. In American society, social roles, attributes and behaviors are not so universally linked to biological identity as they used to be. Males are taking on "feminine" gender roles. And humans in female bodies show "masculine" attributes and behaviors.

And either one of the biological *sexes, gendered* in masculine or feminine ways, can be differentiated by the orientation of their erotic desires and actions: *sexual orientation*. Is this orientation a genetic and social given over which I have no control? Or is it a choice? Or a little of both? Or indeed is it a single orientation, or are most of us polyvalent in orientation, polymorphously perverse?

PO: Morally speaking, does it really matter? Might we view orientation like Jewishness? If I am born a Jew, don't I have the right to practice the Jewish lifestyle, even in a Gentile world? And if I convert to Judaism, don't I have the right to practice my chosen religion with the same freedom and responsibilities that I enjoyed before my conversion?

√So this is less an issue about human sexuality and more an issue of social justice, more an issue of respecting the dignity and conscience of each individual. There is no sexual orientation test required to qualify for the just treatment that human dignity requires.[7]

What about the Bible? Unfortunately, it is the perception of most L/G's that the Bible is a resource for gay-bashing, not a source for gay comfort and healing love. The Bible, of course, antedates the modern understandings of sex, gender and orientation that frame our contemporary experience and moral sensibility.[8] Though

---

7.   See Father Richard Peddicord, *Gay and Lesbian Rights: A Question of Sexual Ethics or Social Justice?* (Sheed and Ward, 1995).

the Scriptural words may sound familiar, the reality, experience and meaning to which they point are quite different.

PO: Abraham, Jeremiah and St. Paul had the privilege of tuning into their contemporary experience and conscience without first filtering it through the moral sensibilities of an alien culture, like modern America would be for them. Should we, too, enjoy the privilege of tuning into our own experience and conscience without first filtering it through the lens of an ancient culture alien to the problematic and sensibilities peculiar to our own?[9]

PO: Which is most helpful to L/G's seeking religious support: (1) laying on them St. Paul's blast against homosexual pedophiles? or, (2) helping L/G's to clarify their own experience and the direction in which the spirit is leading their hearts?

Which is truer to biblical teaching: legalistic justice that kills the heart, or fidelity to relationships that stem from the covenant?

ETHICS EXPERIMENT:

Visit a lesbian or gay bar, or attend a lesbian/gay film or film festival, or participate in a meeting of PFLAG (Parents and Friends of Lesbians and Gays). How do the people, the conversations, the behavior differ from or resemble those you are accustomed to in your everyday experience?

---

8.   See John McNeil, *The Church and the Homosexual* (Beacon Press; fourth edition, 1993). See also, Letha Scarezoni and Virginia Ramey Mollenkott, *Is the Homosexual My Neighbor?* (Harper and Row, 1978).

9.   As an excellent example of this modern sensibility, see William Eskridge, Jr., *The Case for Same Sex Marriage: From Sexual Liberty to Civilized Commitment* (The Free Press, 1996).

4 Play of the Sexes: When Flirting Becomes Harassment

Nowhere does the opposition between work and pleasure become more apparent, and at times, absurd, than in the defense of the workplace against the incursions of Aphrodite/Venus in the degraded guise of "sexual harassment." . . . Why must the idea of work be so split from pleasure? Why must eros, beauty, dalliance, frivolity, sweetness, sensuality, seduction, charm, flirtation be marginalized to the singles' bar and the combat zone so that work may be managed by a puritanical order of "suits" in oxford shirts and cordovan shoes?[1]

It's enough to give sexual harassment complaints a bad name: One woman takes umbrage at mistletoe, saying that it creates an abusive atmosphere; another objects to photographs of a colleague's cousin, a Dallas Cowboys' cheerleader, on his desk. But while cases like these abound, often inviting ridicule, they are exceptions to the rule. Most harassment cases reflect clear abuses, or at least much closer calls.[2]

---

1.   James Hillman, *Kinds of Power: A Guide to Its Intelligent Uses* (Currency/Doubleday, 1997), p. 207.

2.   Margot Slade, "Sexual Harassment Stories From the Field," *New York Times* (Sunday, March 27, 1994), Section 4.

> *Shall we allow feminism to become a reign of terror?*
> *We are all – men and women – stumbling human be-*
> *ings. If we can't forgive each other, how can we ever*
> *forgive ourselves? Above all, how can we eradicate sex-*
> *ism without eradicating sex?*   Erica Jong[3]

It goes without saying that sexual harassment is ethically indefensible. It is first and foremost an abuse of power. It violates the human dignity of the victim, reducing her or him to an object. It attacks the core of the victim's identity, overriding the freedom and consent that makes a human being human. It is ethically wrong, in all the ways that rape is wrong, physical rape being the extreme instance of harassment, which can occur in varying degrees of gravity.

It is assumed that this book's readers understand this. If not, there is a whole body of literature in management, education and law enforcement to bring them up to speed. Harassment still flourishes. More than half of my women students say that when they first entered the workforce as teenagers, they were molested on a regular basis. Many male employees, including supervisors, especially in small businesses, still don't have a clue.[4] The situation is infinitely worse for global businesses operating in other cultures, in which the ideal of sexual equality appears as some strange American aberration.[5] The Vatican's jaundiced view of women's ordination is often couched in such terms. In Japan, often led by graduates returning from Western universities, a budding women's movement

---

3. "Fear of Flirting – Bob Packwood Meets Cotton Mather," *The Washington Post National Weekly Edition* (December 14-20, 1992).

4. For examples of cluelessness, see Jan Bohren, "Six Myths of Sexual Harassment," *Management Review* (May 1993), 61-63.

5. See Wendy Hardman and Jacqueline Heidelberg, "When Sexual Harassment is a Foreign Affair," *Personnel Journal* (April 1996), 91-97.

is beginning to make inroads on the subordinate role of women in the workplace and their consequent demeaning treatment. In many less-developed countries, girls as young as 12 and 13 are recruited for the sex trade, or must serve the sexual needs of their bosses under penalty of losing their jobs, which are often a main source of their family's income.

That harassment is wrong is beyond debate. What *can* be debated is what exactly counts as sexual harassment. Sexuality colors the whole identity of most human beings. For most, it is always clear exactly who is a man and who is a woman. Each sex dresses distinctively. Men don't shop for business wear at Talbot's or Anne and Taylor's. Often there are distinct restrooms provided. On business trips, male and female colleagues are assumed to stay in separate hotel rooms. Even if you don't assume that the sexes come from separate planets, the difference is there and yes, attraction too. All this would seem obvious except for the question of sexual harassment. Many talk as if getting rid of sexual harassment means getting rid of sex. Is it necessary to move around the workplace pretending that it is populated with neuters, even though you know very well that you are not a neuter, and even though you know very well that every other man and woman there remains fully conscious all day of himself or herself as a sexual human being? To paraphrase Erica Jong, can we eradicate harassment without eradicating sex? Should we?

So we ask, with James Hillman,[6] how vigorously we must defend the workplace "against the incursions of Aphrodite/Venus in the degraded guise of 'sexual harassment.'" Must the idea of work be cut off from the play of the sexes? Must we stamp out beauty, frivolity, sensuality,

---

6. *Op.cit.* note 1.

sweetness, charm, flirtation? Must we raise a wall of separation between work and pleasure?

Do you agree that in the workplace the play of the sexes must be an ethical taboo?

YES:

Law is not the same as ethics, but the law is a good place to start. Title VII of the *Civil Rights Act of 1964* forbids sexual harassment of employees, as a form of sexual discrimination. Title IX of the *Elementary and Secondary Education Act of 1972* forbids the sexual harassment of students. At minimum, these laws forbid *quid pro quo* harassment – making salary, promotions or discipline on the job conditioned on the granting or not of sexual favors. Some states, such as Massachusetts, extend this protection to college students. And in a far-reaching decision in the case of *Meritor Savings Bank, FSB v Vinson* in June 1986, the Supreme Court broadened the definition of sexual harassment when it unanimously ruled that harassment that results in a hostile or offensive job environment violates Title VII of the *Civil Rights Act*, even if there is no *quid pro quo* discrimination.

Quid quo pro harassment is relatively straightforward and amenable to proof. Behavior that results in an intimidating, hostile, humiliating or offensive job environment is a much vaguer norm. Nonetheless, a work environment should not systematically undermine self-respect and dignity. A person can't just freely walk away from a job. The problem is that we've all met people who are ready and able to take offense at most any word or action. Harassment laws have come to be understood as forbidding be-

---

7.   *Massachusetts General Law on Employment*, chapter 151 B, Section 4, enacted March 10, 1987.

havior that a *reasonable* person would consider offensive. But the "reasonable person" norm is also a can of worms. Do you mean a reasonable man or a reasonable woman? The American Psychological Association conducted an experiment in which workers were shown videos of men and women interacting in everyday situations. The male viewers tended to give sexualized interpretations of behaviors that the women considered neutral. For example, if a woman gave a male colleague a congratulatory pat on the hand, he would interpret this as sexual interest and respond in kind, and be subject then to a charge of harassment.[8]

It is the target of the behavior whose dignity is at stake. A reasonable woman may well be offended by what would not offend a reasonable man. If she is the target, she defines what is unwelcome to her. If something offends her, she needs to say so. If the behavior persists, it becomes harassment. And conversely, the reasonable man has the right to state when behavior is unwelcome to him.

The cleanest and clearest ethical policy is to confine the workplace to work-related words and behavior. The realm of the personal, the interplay of the sexes does not belong in the workplace. Men and women at work interact as gender-neutral, professionally equal colleagues, collaborating in getting the job done. The personal and the sexual are completely inappropriate to the job environment. Save all that for after-hours. So no *quid pro quo* sexual demands (of course!). No grabbing, kissing, sexual touching, sexual propositions (of course!). No dirty jokes, anatomical comments, stories or inquiries about sexual exploits, no "accidentally on purpose" reaching or brushing against or grooming of the other (of course!). It should be obvi-

---

8. M. Roberts, "Understanding Rita," *Psychology Today* (December 1986), 20; 14.

ous that these are demeaning and dehumanizing behaviors.

Not so obvious are the following behaviors, which don"t belong in the workplace since they are not work-related. No social touching, no friendly arm around the shoulder, no stroking the arm or the hand or the back during a conversation, or patting the belly of a pregnant coworker. No staring or leering as colleagues walk by or bend over, no undressing with the eyes, or gratuitous personal comments. No compliments about clothing, hairdo, personal appearance. These are not related to getting the job done. Save your compliments for work-related accomplishments.

NO:

It is a futile and silly enterprise to try to turn the workplace into a unisex environment in the name of preventing sexual harassment. The best efforts of feminism have not been able to abolish sexual differences in every realm of life, including the workplace. Meredith Maron's radical feminist credentials are impeccable. She has been a Marxist union organizer, a women's health collective worker, a hippie and a Vietnam war protester. She really tried to believe that women were no different from men. But her instincts kept saying otherwise:

> *Is it social conditioning, biological inevitability or a combination of the two that makes me feel more "womanly" when I'm planting seedlings in my garden than when I'm chopping wood at my cabin? . . . Our daughters refuse to play with trucks; our sons point the dolls we've given them at us and say, "Bang, you're dead."*

9.   Meredith Maran, *Notes From an Incomplete Revolution: Real Life Since Feminism* (Bantam Books, 1997.)

[She further wonders why women are still more inter-ested in feelings and affection and intimacy than men.] Why most women, even lesbians, still love to dress up and flirt with men? The standard reply of radical feminists to these heretical ideas is that they are proof of patriarchy's enduring strength and symptoms of "backlash." To femi-nist author Karen Lehrman, such observations are not backlash at all, but the simple truth.[10] The whole point of feminism was to give women choices, even the choice to make romance and motherhood top priorities. To sneer at women who choose to make much of female beauty, flirting, romance and the interplay of the sexes can be as condescending and oppressive as patriarchy ever was.

Well-meaning efforts to make the workplace squeaky clean can be just as dehumanizing as an overtly harassing workplace would be.[In the process of eliminating harass-ment, must we also pretend that workers are not human beings, are not sexual, and do not exist in bodies?] Com-puters and other machines can be programmed to work together in an austerely efficient way without "personal distractions." But human beings work best together when they feel comfortable together as persons and personali-ties. And the business of creating a smoothly functioning team out of diverse personalities requires all kinds of schmoozing and stroking and expressions of personal in-terest that are, strictly speaking, irrelevant to the narrowly defined specifics of getting a job done. In this context, conversational exchanges about family and friends, hob-bies and worries, even romantic joys and sorrows – all

---

10. Karen Lehrman, "Truth in Feminism: Reflections on the way women really live vs. the way feminists say they ought to live," *New York Times Book Review Section* (May 4, 1997). Lehrman wrote *The Lipstick Proviso: Women, Sex & Power in the Real World* (Anchor Books, 1997).

ostensibly unrelated to work – play an essential role in shaping a ordered, comfortable work-team environment.

Consider, for example, two companies, one Swiss and one American, offering competing bids to a Japanese negotiating team. The Americans came well-prepared, facts and figures in hand, laying out all the bottom line projections on day one. They were all business. The Swiss, on the other hand, entertained the Japanese for five days. They did not mention business once. On the sixth day they brought up and explained their proposal. The Swiss bid was substantially higher than the American. But the Swiss won the contract. They had presented themselves as human beings who could be worked with in a comfortable way. The longer route is sometimes the shorter path between two points.

[The harassment-free workplace needs to make a space for human beings.] And these human beings come in bodies. So, does a "no touch" rule make any sense? Can reasonable men and women discern the difference between a "friendly" non-sexual touch and a sexual touch? Are reasonable men doomed to interpret a woman's touch as a sexual come-on? Must reasonable women interpret a reassuring hand on a shoulder as an invasive harassment? Are "kissy-kissy, huggy-huggy" sometimes appropriate for workplace greetings or goodbyes, occasions of honor or congratulations or sympathy? Could a firm hand grasp be used to convey seriousness or commitment? Psychological stroking oils the wheels of human commerce. Physical stroking has been shown to be essential for the normal growth of babies. Do adults also need physical touching to flourish and work together as human beings?

So a harassment-free workplace needs to accommodate embodied human beings. But these are sexual bodies. Does this need to be ignored? This, of course, is the most problematic area, most in need of honesty and openness and realism. There is a strong body of opinion that Platonic relationships between the sexes are impossible. So whatever rules and policies are in place, the sexual dimension will remain alive and well. As men and women work more closely together than ever, romance springs up in the workplace, and many marriages are born there. And failed workplace romances can devastate a workplace and end careers. Can reasonable men and reasonable women be lightly flirtatious, exchange compliments in an upbeat way and in a spirit of fun, without being demeaning or compromising or crossing the line into harassment?

PO:

What is to be said of a relatively recent phenomenon, the possibility of virtual harassment, even virtual rape? Sociologist Sherry Turkle, a long-time commentator on the social implications of computers, describes a type of virtual harassment that happens on-line. Assume John and Mary are in a Multi-User Domain [a MUD], engaged in a role-play sexual seduction game. MUDs are an Internet offshoot of video games like Dungeons and Dragons. John's character in the MUD is Satyrman, and Mary's is LovelyEyes. John has no idea who LovelyEyes is in real life. And Mary has no idea who is the real human being playing Satyrman. Satyrman and LovelyEyes, anonymous and in role, engage in a consensual sexual dialogue. Well into the game John, with his computer savvy, contrives to take over the character of LovelyEyes, and Satyrman's role-play words and behavior become harsh and violent. LovelyEyes' replies, manipulated now by John, not Mary, become frightened and perverse. Mary, still anonymous in her real-life identity, can only stare at her computer screen in revulsion or worse as LovelyEyes is abused and raped by Satyrman, under the control of the equally anonymous real-human John. Does this virtual rape of LovelyEyes abuse the real Mary? Are there violations of consent or of human dignity? Or is it all "only words," just a silly game?[11]

Issues of consent are often difficult to define when men and women interact in real life, on an equal basis, face-to-face. The consent situation is murkier when they interact in roles. Roles in computer games put a distance between real humans, and would seem to mitigate a violation. There is a distinct distance between a virtual rape and a real-life rape. But roles in real life "games" can often exacerbate the violation. Consider the military when a male in the role of an officer has "consensual" sex with a female in the role of a trainee. The whole ethos of the military is based on a hierarchical structure that demands obedience to the point of killing and being killed. The role structure renders impossible a free and equal consenting relationship between officer and trainee, all appearances to the contrary.

Or is genuine human consent really so impossible? Are officers presumed to be gods and trainees empty puppets? Even in the Army, doesn't a trainee have the right to conscientiously object to an unjust order? Wouldn't she also have the right to consent to a freely desired relationship? If she needs to be assertive enough to kill an enemy, shouldn't she be assertive enough to say to an officer, "Don't touch me like that"? In an actual court-martial

---

11. Sociologist Sherry Turkle, *Life on the Screen: Identity in the Age of the Internet* (Simon and Schuster, 1995; paperbound 1997), pp. 250-253 recounts examples of virtual abuse on MUDs, and asks whether virtual abuse should be considered abusive to the real humans moving on the Net in these anonymous roles.

case, a 20-year-old trainee, when a sergeant put a hand down her sweatpants while passing her on the stairs, removed his hand, told him to stop it, was never bothered again, and did not consider it to be harassment. Another trainee, when invited by the same man to have sex, said, "No, it's against my beliefs," and she was never bothered again. A third trainee consented, and the officer was convicted of raping her.[12] The fact remains that in relationships between unequal roles, boss and employee, teacher and student, officer and trainee, the burden of proof lies with the superior to prove consent. The unequal roles mean unequal freedom to consent – that's what hierarchy is all about.

≠ freedom to consent
(or Reject)

ETHICS EXPERIMENT: *more than sex - any order*

Do you consider the following to be humane and innocent, or inappropriate and demeaning in a workplace or school environment?

1. Mistletoe in a doorway on the last day before Christmas break.

2. Man, gazing admiringly at coworker, says: "Why don't all women look like you?"

3. Man to woman on St. Patrick's Day: "What a nice green sweater." Woman to man: a similar compliment on his green tie.

4. Grandfatherly boss puts arm around young woman's shoulder as he explains to her an important assignment.

5. A sympathetic hug for a colleague who is "worried to death" about a very sick family member.

---

12. See Elaine Sciolino, "The Army's Problems with Sex and Power," *The New York Times* (May 4, 1997), 4E.

6. Woman boss propositions young male employee, who is surprised but turned on by the idea. Male boss propositions young female employee, who is surprised but turned on by the idea.

7. A second-grade boy unexpectedly kisses his "girl-friend" classmate on the cheek. A high school sophomore boy on the school bus unexpectedly kisses a female classmate.

8. A physics professor uses a sexual intercourse metaphor to help explain the behavior of subatomic particles.

9. A junior-year college woman finds a Renoir nude painting on the library wall offensive and intimidating, and demands that it be removed.

10. Young male to bright young female coworker: "Boy, you look hot today!"

Medicine

5   Infant Transplant Donors: Anencephalics as Organ Banks?

(handwritten margin note: don't we have to wait until the baby dies?)

Imagine that a pediatric heart surgeon skilled in transplantation were on a small Pacific island with two dying babies – an anencephalic and a hypoplastic left heart infant. The latter baby would be dead within hours unless the transplantable heart were immediately procured from the anencephalic baby. . . . Many would agree that the transplant operation is not only morally permissible, but obligatory.

James W. Walters[1]

If use as a donor can be justified by the fact that there is only a limited life span, will we extend this approach to infants who will soon die with other problems such as Tay-Sachs, Werdnig-Hoffman disease, etc.?   **Jacquelyn Bammam, M.D.[2]**

[It is a profound misreading of what it is that gives life meaning, no matter how brief that life may be, to say that the only way that an anencephalic child's life can have significance is if his organs can be transplanted.]

---

1.   James W. Walters, "Anencephalic Organ Procurement: Should the Law be Changed?", *BioLaw: A Legal and Ethical Reporter on Medicine, Health Care, and Bioengineering,* (University Publications of America, 1987), Volume 2 Number 9 (December 1987), pp. S:88-S:89.

2.   Jacquelyn Bammam, M.D., "A Neonatologist's Concern," *Update* (Loma Linda University Ethics Center), Volume 3, Number 4 (November 1987), p. 2.

> *[This] perspective is . . . reducing a person to a func-*
> *tion.*   J.C. Willke, M.D. and Dave Andrusko[3]

There are 2,000-3,000 anencephalic infants born each year in the United States. There is a waiting list of 400-500 newborns who need hearts and kidneys, and 500-1,000 who need livers. What is the ethics of harvesting organs from the first group, which cannot live, to give life to the second group, which can survive? Currently, between 40 and 70% of children under the age of two die before suitable organs can be found for them.

A brain-absent (i.e., an anencephalic) infant is as handicapped as an infant can be. It lacks both cerebral hemispheres, so there is zero possibility of any higher brain function. There is no brain. The face is grotesquely malformed. Eyes bulge from defective sockets. A membrane tops the brain-empty upturned head. But anencephalics do have a lower brain stem, so their hearts and other organs do function.

When a brain-absent baby is born, it is kept as comfortable as possible. It is given food and water before it dies a few days after its birth. When it is allowed to die naturally this way, the vital organs deteriorate and atrophy. So by the time the baby is dead, the organs are useless for transplanting. This raises the ethical problem illustrated by the following two cases.

In February 1988, after one week of life, Baby Evelyn, a Texas anencephalic infant, was taken off life-support equipment at Loma Linda Medical Center. Without machine-assisted breathing, her heart and liver, deprived of oxygen, became useless for transplanting. And she quickly died. Loma Linda's ethical guidelines mandate that life-

---

3. "Personhood Redux," *Hastings Center Report* (October/November 1988), 33. The authors are representatives of the National Right to Life Committee.

support not be used for more than one week in these cases. Since the support is not for the benefit of the hopelessly terminal infant, but for the benefit of the possible organ donees, it is deemed ethically improper to keep such infants indefinitely on life-support.

In October 1987 Baby Gabrielle, born anencephalic in London, Ontario, was put on a respirator and given sugar solution and medication a few hours after her birth, in order to preserve her heart, liver, kidneys and other organs for transplanting. After 48 hours, doctors began to turn off the respirator every six hours to test her breathing reflex. As soon as she failed to breathe on her own for three full minutes, she was pronounced brain-dead and put back on the respirator. Note: at issue here is brain-stem death, as the cerebral hemispheres are missing. So now the return to life-support was so that the organs of the officially dead Baby Evelyn might be maintained sufficiently healthy for transplanting. The infant's body was flown to Loma Linda, where the heart was transplanted to a baby just born by Cesarian section.

The ethical dilemma arises from the conflict between keeping these babies alive so that their organs will be transplantable, and allowing these babies to die, since they have absolutely no hope of survival or of benefit from medical treatment. To put it bluntly, if they are to be useful as organ donors, they have to be dead, but not too dead.[4]

The Baby Evelyn solution was to keep the infant on life support for a week, and if a matching donee could be found, take the baby off life-support, declare her dead

---

4. See "Anencephalic Infants as Sources of Transplantable Organs" (Transplant Policy Center, Ann Arbor), *Hastings Center Report* (November 1988), 28-33. Also Alan D. Shewmon, "Anencephaly: Selected Medical Aspects," *Hastings Center Report* (February 1988), 11-19.

and do the transplant. If no match appeared within a week, the support was removed and the organs were lost. As of this writing, Loma Linda has since ceased to do these transplants because of the ethical uneasiness surrounding them on the part of the medical and social community.

The Baby Gabrielle solution was to keep the baby on supports, except for periodic removals, to achieve a technical death, and then restore supports to what is now an infant cadaver bank maintaining healthy transplantable organs. Under current American law, brain-absent babies are deemed to be born alive. Though higher brain functions are absent, the brain stem functions to maintain spontaneous respiration and circulation. There is discussion about changing the law to declare that individuals born anencephalic be considered as dead at birth. The question of what should be legal is different from the question of what is ethical. Here we focus on ethics. Leaving aside the question of law, *Is it ethical to directly harvest organs from brain-absent babies?*

NO:

The arguments against such use of brain-absent babies concern issues of mercy, and "slippery slope" kinds of issues. And underlying these is concern about redefining the meaning of death.

The basic problem behind the uneasiness that even proponents feel is that these brain-absent babies, though defective and malformed in the extreme, are alive. What

---

5. See President's Commission for the Study of Ethical Problems in Medicine and Biomedical and Behavioral Research, "Defining Death" (U.S. Government Printing Office, 1981), 36-41. Also, Alexander Morgan Capron, "Anencephalic Donors: Separate the Dead from the Dying," *Hastings Center Report* (February 1987), 5-9.

moral claims does such a life make on us? The utter hope-
lessness of the condition and the physical impossibility of
even a theoretical potentiality for a human level of life argues against treatments and support systems to prolong
such a minimal existence. Such treatment and support
cannot possibly benefit the infant. When support and
treatment are given, it is done with a view to *using* the
infant to benefit someone else. This pathetic organism is
being dealt with as a potentially useful product. It violates
the dignity of even such a radically deficient living organism to be reduced to product status. If there ever were a
case where passive euthanasia, i.e., "letting die," is a moral
imperative, it is in the case of anencephalic infants.[6]

Active Euthanasia: On the other hand, if passive euthanasia is a requirement, can we also tolerate active euthanasia? To harvest a vital organ, like the heart or the
liver, from a brain-absent infant is a lethal act. This
radically defective organism is not dead, and as living,
still has a dignity. Like other newborns, it cries, it swal-
lows; it can grasp and puke; it reacts strongly to painful
stimuli, and often also to sound. It will never have more
than such brain-stem functions, but it does have these.
The same dignity which forbids us to support that life as
a useful product also forbids us to actively destroy that
life. The direct harvesting of vital organs from
anencephalics is a double-violation of dignity. It destroys a life in order to reduce it to a product.

Slippery Slope: Slippery slope considerations also argue
against such use of brain-absent infants. The principle
that would justify the sacrifice of anencephalics for the
good of society could be used to justify the sacrifice of

[handwritten margin note: So ... it is someone's child— Baby to hold – other people's needs not Superior—]

6.   Norman Fost, "Organs from Anencephalic Infants: An Idea Whose
Time Has Not Yet Come," *Hastings Center Report* (November 1988), 5-10.

other kinds of defective human life for the good of society. If you are unwilling to extend the principle to other cases, maybe there is something wrong with the principle. [If the radically defective anencephalics can be killed for their organs because they have a short and hopeless life, may other infants who are in terminal severe pain or have severe brain damage also be killed for social benefit? Could you also justify on the grounds of social benefit the killing of terminal adults who have severe brain damage? Can you maintain the morality of this use of anencephalics when you understand how that same principle used to justify it works out in other cases?

[This whole case against the use of living anencephalics as organ banks collapses if it can be claimed that such infants are not alive in any human sense,] if it can be maintained that while they have vegetative life, they are brain-dead. Under this assumption, the harvesting of organs from anencephalics is like using the organs of a cadaver. That is a different matter altogether. What is to be said about such a definition of death?

Slippery slope concerns also are provoked by efforts to declare anencephalics to be equivalently dead, all but dead, dead enough. The often merciless use of medical technology, in the service of prolonging dying rather than of prolonging life, has rightly made us reexamine our definitions of life and death. But the power of these same technologies make it imperative for us to draw a firm line somewhere. In a matter with such wide-ranging implications for society as our understanding of life and death, it is not being too conservative to insist that where there is at least lower brain function, such life has sufficient dignity that it is not ethical to actively kill it, even for the good of society.

YES:

The case in favor of anencephalic organ procurement rests on the <u>extreme</u> need of <u>the donees</u> wh<u>o</u> have the <u>potential</u> for <u>human quality</u> life; this need can be met by brain-absent infants who have no such quality of life potential. In terms of consequences, the <u>benefits</u> outweigh <u>the costs</u>. In terms of human dignity, donee human life is served, while donor human dignity is preserved. Against this, we saw the "slippery slope" argument that the bad consequences outweigh the good, since the use of anencephalic donors would lead to abuse of donors who are defective in other ways. And we saw the "mercy" arguments, that the human dignity of the brain-dead donors was being violated, that their best interests were not being served. Neither argument holds, and here's why.

The fallacy of "slippery slope" arguments is that they substitute psychology for logic. Let the camel's nose under the tent, and next you have the whole camel. Give him an inch, he will take a mile. Granted, there is a legitimate concern that the use of brain-absent infants will set up a psychological momentum in favor of carelessly using infants with other defects as donors. And there is a concern that the proper use of brain-absent donors will improperly be used as a precedent for abusing other classes of donors.

Still, *abusus non tollit usum.* [The fact that something is abused does not mean that there is no legitimate use for it.] Drunken drivers abuse automobiles. Sadistic parents abuse children. The fact of abuse is not an argument against legitimate use for autos or against the right to have children. Abuse or the danger of abuse is a warning to guard against abuse. There is a danger that people will abuse the precedent of using brain-absent infants as donors. Procedural safeguards must be set up to prevent the extension of this precedent to cases where it does not apply, viz., to donors who are not anencephalic. So a clear logical line must be maintained between donors who have no higher brain, and donors who, though defective in other ways, do have a higher brain. Under these conditions, if anencephalic organ procurement is justifiable, the slippery slope argument should not count against it.

Human Dignity: But the question remains, does such use of brain-absent infants respect their human dignity? On the one hand, it was argued that efforts to prolong the life of the donor simply to keep its organs alive does not serve the best interests of the infant. It should appropriately be allowed to die – passive euthanasia. On the other hand, killing the infant by removing vital donor organs – active euthanasia – is equally offensive to its dignity. These concerns can be met in three ways.

First, there is the Baby Gabrielle solution. Baby Gabrielle, as was pointed out above, was sustained on artificial support in order to keep her potential donor organs healthy. But periodically she was removed from the respirator to test her breathing function. When she was found to be unable to breathe unaided, she was declared dead, since the brain stem had ceased to function and she had no higher brain. Then artificial support was restored to what was now officially a cadaver.[7]

This passive, but not active, euthanasia respected her dignity to live out the course of her natural life, insofar as the life was not actively cut short. But was it right to prolong her life by using the respirator at all, when the result and the intention was not the baby's best interests, but the interests of potential donees of the baby's organs? If you take a purely individualistic view of the donor, no, it did

7.   James Walters and Stephen Ashwal, "Organ prolongation in Anencephalic Infants," *Hastings Center Report* (February 1988), 19-27.

not serve her individual interests. But consider that Gabrielle, like other human beings, shares an essentially social, as well as individual, nature. In an act of surrogate altruism, her life and suffering were prolonged in order that she might give life to others. Consider her identity as involving not just herself, but also her relationship to those needful donees who upon her death would receive from her the gift of life. In this wider context, prolonging her life on the respirator serves her best interests as an altruistic social human being. It gives her brief tragic life a meaning that otherwise it would not have had. [And her parents, the surrogates, have the comfort that she had not lived or died in vain.]

Baby Gabrielle's was a case of passive euthanasia. A second approach would be to make a case for active euthanasia and the direct procurement of donor organs from the still living brain-absent infant. The argument from surrogate altruism might be extended to justify active euthanasia. If vital organs are transplanted from the brain-absent baby while it is still "alive," the result, of course, would be the baby's death caused by this direct organ procurement. The death is balanced by the saved lives of the donees, who were in need of these vital organs. The death of the donor was not so much a killing as a loving sacrifice of life for others, accomplished through the intention and decision of the surrogates. Can we honor this sacrifice as we honor the soldier who throws himself on a live grenade that his companions might live? The baby, deciding via the surrogate, dies that others might live.

It can be objected that we would never allow parents to make such a decision for a nondefective infant. The surrogate would have the duty to assist the infant to grow to adult capability in order to make such sacrificial decisions for itself. In response we point out that the brain-dead baby has no such potential for growth. So the surrogate may rightly make the kind of decision on the anencephalic's behalf that the surrogate should never make on behalf of a normal infant.

A third approach to preserving the dignity of the anencephalic organ donor would be to redefine death as the irreversible absence of higher brain function. Then the transplantation of, say, a heart from an anencephalic would involve a vegetative donor death, but not a human death. The American Medical Association now considers it ethical to withhold IV nutrition and hydration from the irreversibly comatose, where brain-stem death has not occurred. Can we logically and properly extend this policy so that we do not insist on brain-stem death when evaluating the human status of brain-absent infants, with a view to transplanting their organs? When the higher brain is absent, can we define lower brain function to be irrelevant to human status at least in these cases? That is the question.

PO:

To sum up, the following four issues need to be resolved:

(1) When we artificially prolong the life of a brain-absent infant, with a view to using its organs, is this equivalent to treating the infant as a useful product rather than as a dignified human life? After all, the infant cannot benefit in any way from this unnatural extension of its existence. Or, on the other hand, should the infant be viewed as sharing a common humanity with the donees in need of organs, so that in prolonging its life you are respecting its social dimension and its ability to help those in need?

(2)   When we cause the death of an anencephalic by transplanting its vital organs, are we reducing it to a mere means to help others, to an organ warehouse, by literally killing it so that others might live? Or do we more correctly view the anencephalic as altruistically (through the surrogates' decision) sacrificing itself so that others might live? "Greater love no person hath than one who lays down their life for their friend."

(3)   Does this use of brain-absent babies set us on a slippery slope of reducing all defectives to become organ banks for a growing population of donees in need? Or should we rather make careful distinctions between ethical and unethical transplant procedures, realizing that the possibility of abuse is no reason to abandon a procedure altogether?

(4)   With the advance of technology so quickly outstripping our ethical categories, do we need to hold fast to a definition of death that insists on whole-brain death, the cessation of both brain-stem and neocortical functioning? Or should brain-absent infants be considered an exception to this strict demand for the cessation of all brain function, since they physically lack a higher brain altogether?

It does seem reasonable to redefine death in the case of anencephalics. Since a higher brain is physically missing, there is no judgement call involved about the potential for future human function. And there is no slippery slope between brain-absent and brain-present. This defect is unlike any other.

ETHICS THOUGHT EXPERIMENT:

Alfred Hitchcock wrote a story about a man who died, except for his brain attached to his eyeball. His brain, sustained in a basin in a nutrient solution, rested in the bedroom. He had hated his wife's smoking. To get even, she would come to the basin and blow smoke in his eyeball, while his pupil would contract in helpless fury staring up at her. This is a story of a brain without a body. The anencephalic baby is a body without a brain. Which of the two is more human?

6 Fetal Tissue Transplants and Research: Use or Abuse?

After all, patients with Parkinson's disease, and those with other diseases potentially treatable via fetal tissues, often suffer terribly, and fetal remains, if not used for transplantation, will probably only be discarded.   Kathleen Nolan[1]

The sale of human embryos for cosmetics production has been reported, and kidneys for transplantation from live donors in Brazil and India have been advertised for sale to physicians in Germany.

Alan Fine[2]

Whosoever saves a single life, it is as if he had saved the whole world.   The Talmud

The ethics of the use of fetal tissue is inextricably bound up with the ethics of abortion. But they are not identical issues. We can still ask whether the pro-choice position on abortion necessarily implies an ethically unrestricted use of fetal tissue for transplants and research. And we can ask whether a pro-life stance on

---

1.   Kathleen Nolan, "Genug ist Genug: A Fetus Is Not a Kidney," *Hastings Center Report*, (December 1988). p. 13.

2.   See Debra MacKenzie, "Third World Kidneys for Sale," *New Scientist*, (March 28, 1985) p. 7, and "Embryos to Lipsticks?", *New Scientist* (October 10, 1985, p. 21, as reported by Alan Fine, "The Ethics of Fetal Tissue Transplants," *Hastings Center Report*, (June/July 1988), p. 7.

abortion necessarily implies that all use of aborted fetal tissue is wrong. The fetal tissue debate tests the limits of the radicals in both camps, pro-choice and pro-life.

It would seem that radical pro-choicers should defend any and all uses of her fetal tissue consented to by a woman. After all, she has absolute dominion over her own body, and over this tissue which is part of her body. So she may ethically dispose of it as she will, be it to throw it away, donate it to research, offer it for use as a transplant, "manufacture" it for transplanting to a relative in need, or sell it for the production of cosmetics. Indeed, it would seem more responsible to use it for the benefit of human-kind than to simply throw it away. Most people do not subscribe to totally unrestricted use of fetal tissue. But radical pro-choicers are challenged to show why unrestricted abortion is ethical, but unrestricted use of the product of abortion is not.

It would seem that radical pro-lifers must reject, as unethical, all uses of aborted fetal tissue, either for transplantation or for research. And indeed many of them do. Fetal tissue, as human, may never be used as a means to an end, even a good end. So even in the case of an unwanted pregnancy, where the mother consents to the use of the fetus for research or transplantation, it is better to reverently dispose of the remains than to direct them to such uses. Pro-lifers are challenged to show why it is better to "waste" the tissue, that was going to die anyway, than to use it to save the life or the health of another. Why is it more "pro-life" to dispose of fetal tissue than to use it for saving life?

Because of their differing views on abortion, we will consider separately the pro-choice and pro-life perspectives on fetal tissue use. It is instructive to see why, even assuming the morality of abortion, pro-choicers might recommend ethical limits on fetal tissue use. And it is equally instructive to consider how, even assuming the immorality of abortion, a pro-lifer might make a case for ethically justifiable uses of aborted fetal tissue.[3]

PRO-CHOICE AND THE ETHICS OF FETAL TISSUE USE
YES:

The medical demand: Fetal tissue transplants can confer great benefit to people in dire medical need. It's a utilitarian argument. Abortion is legal. The products of abortion would otherwise be discarded. When you weigh the benefit of using these products over against the benefits of discarding them, the moral scales come down on the side of transplants.

Potential beneficiaries are sufferers from Parkinson's disease, Huntington's disease, and Alzheimer's. Also spinal cord injury, some types of cortical blindness, bone marrow diseases, like leukemia, aplastic anemia, and marrow failure from radiation are treatable by such transplants. The same goes for hereditary blood and clotting disorders, such as sickle cell anemia, thalassemia, and hemophilia, as well as genetic therapy. Sufferers number in the millions; hundreds of thousands of patients per year could benefit from fetal tissue transplants. And in the face of this demand, there is a supply of tissue to meet it. 80% of induced abortions occur between the sixth and eleventh week, when the tissue is developed sufficiently for useful transplanting.[4]

---

3.   See also George J. Annas and Sherman Elias, "The Politics of Transplantation of Human Fetal Tissue," *The New England Journal of Medicine*, Vol. 320, No. 16 (April 20 1989), 1079-1082; and John A. Robertson, "Rights, Symbolism, and Public Policy in Fetal Tissue Transplants," *Hastings Center Report* (December 1988), pp. 5-12.

4.   Stanley K. Henshaw et al., "A Portrait of American Women Who Obtain Abortions," *Family Planning Perspectives* 17:2, (1985) 90-96.

The legal supply: Finally, the law permits at least limited use of fetal tissue for transplantation. The Uniform Anatomical Gift Act governs transplantation from both adult and fetal cadavers from spontaneous abortions. Fetal cadavers have the same moral and legal standing as do adult ones.[Absent demurrers on the part of the decedents, the next-of-kin may give consent for the medical use of such cadavers.]

What about cadavers from induced abortions? Since abortion is legal, there would seem to be no problem. The ethical issue is this: was the decision to abort completely separate from and unmotivated by any subsequent use of the aborted tissue? This is clearly the case for spontaneous abortions, and also for abortions induced to save the life of the mother. So at least in these cases, a moral calculus can justify the beneficial transplantation of fetal tissue to patients in need. At least in these cases, the arguments in favor of organ donations from adult cadavers would morally justify fetal donations as well.

NO:

Even in a pro-choice perspective, some moral considerations qualify an unrestricted approach to fetal tissue transplantations. Of concern here are: (1) abortions induced for the purpose of contributing tissue and, less acutely, (2) abortions induced for other purposes, but encouraged by the climate of possible use of the abortus for transplantation.

Some radical pro-choicers insist on viewing the fetus as nothing but a product, and abortion as a completely neutral, if not, good procedure. For such, there would be no moral qualms about any and all transplantations of fetal tissue, even that obtained specifically to be used or even sold for transplantation purposes.

Uterus as tissue factory: But moderate pro-choicers and mainstream medical ethics do not view the uterus as a factory and the fetus as a product. (Abortion is not a neutral procedure but a necessary evil,) the responsibility for which the mother must be free to assume. Fetal remains, like adult remains, should be treated with respect and disposed of properly.[5] One can hold to abortion rights for women without demeaning or denying the developing potential of the fetal life interrupted by abortion. Physicians are ethically reluctant to encourage pregnancies entered into for the express purpose of producing tissue as a product for donation. This violates the medical ethical principle of respect for the dignity of human life, both on the side of procreation and on the side of the fetus reduced to be a mere means to an end.[6] Abortion becomes not a necessary evil, but an unqualified good.

Conflict of interest: These ethical misgivings, however, have not been translated into law. Abortion, for any and every purpose, remains legal. And the Uniform Anatomical Gift Act does allow organ donations to specific persons for medical purposes. Wherefore there has been a call to amend the Uniform Act to prohibit such manufacture of tissue for use as a product as a process demeaning both to women and to the potential human

---

5.   Henry T. Greely, et al., "Special Report: The Ethical Use of Human Fetal Tissue in Medicine", *The New England Journal of Medicine*, V 320, No. 16 (April 20, 1989), 1094-1095. The lawyers, doctors and ethicians who cosigned this article make a case for the ethical medical use of fetal tissue, while insisting that it be treated with respect. Some pro-choice adherents see the respectful treatment of fetal remains as the first step to granting the fetus human rights and, thereby, eliminating abortion-choice; they therefore insist that fetal remains be treated as medical waste.

6.   *Ibid.* See also, C. Gorman, "A Balancing Act of Life and Death," *Time* (February 1, 1988), p. 49, and E. Thorn, "Trade in Human Tissue Needs Regulation," *Wall Street Journal* (August 19, 1987), p. 3.

life they procreate. Abortions remain a necessary evil, and physicians should not encourage pregnancies and abortions that would not otherwise take place.

The same misgivings apply, though more speculatively, to abortions which, though induced for other purposes, may have been encouraged by the possibility of contributing the fetal remains to medicine. There is a concern lest the medical use of fetal tissue encourage induced abortions that might not have otherwise taken place. Society encourages the medical use of cadavers. Unlike adult cadavers, fetal cadavers can be legally produced at the will of the mother (the production, at will, of an adult cadaver is called murder). So there is a question as to whether the medical use of fetal tissue may provide an incentive, a "redeeming social value" as it were, for abortion. This is a question of fact. Many say that such incentive to abortion is unlikely to be the case. Even in a perspective of pro-choice, abortion remains problematic, not an unalloyed good. It is unlikely that knowledge about the possible uses for the aborted fetus would motivate an abortion that would not have otherwise been induced.

To guard against a conflict of interest, it is suggested that neither the mother nor the assisting physician at an abortion should have any say about the disposition of the fetal remains. Indeed it has been argued that the mother, by the very act of terminating the pregnancy, has renounced all right to determine disposition of the remains. It is a contradiction for her to undertake the role of a surrogate decision-maker on behalf of the fetus she has destroyed. On the other hand, if the fetus is reduced to a product, like the hair that the hairdresser cuts from her head, then her decision about how to dispose of the fetus would not be the decision of a surrogate. The fetus as the product of her body, like her hair, would be subject to any disposal she cares to make about the product of her body. In this view, a woman producing fetuses for sale would be just like a woman growing hair for sale.

PRO-LIFE AND THE ETHICS OF FETAL TISSUE USE.

YES:

Clearly, a pro-life perspective affirms all the above misgivings and arguments against the unrestricted medical use of tissue from fetal cadavers. Must pro-life, to be consistent, go further and condemn all medical use of fetal tissue from induced abortions, or at least from induced abortions that have not been induced with a view to saving the life of the mother?

Benefits as problematic: We have seen the need of millions of sufferers who could benefit from fetal tissue transplants. We have noted the great potential supply of such tissue from induced abortions. This tissue is especially suitable for transplantation. Fetal tissue grows rapidly, it evokes little or no immune rejection, and it is very adaptable. If not used, it will go to waste: we are talking about tissue from dead fetuses only. Must pro-life forbid the use of dead tissue on behalf of the lives of living sufferers? It would seem that pro-life must forbid such use because of the special nature of this tissue:

> *Biologically, the foetus is not a tissue or an organ, but a body, and morally, the foetus is a developing being and potential member of the human community . . . Perfunctory dicing, shearing, pounding – all perfectly acceptable for an excised tumor or kidney – require special justification when the "tissue fragment" is a fetal corpse.*[7]

7.　Nolan, *op.cit.*, p. 16.

Principles for an imperfect world: Justifying fetal tissue transplants from a pro-life perspective must proceed on the assumption that induced abortion, the source of the tissue, is an evil act in most cases. The morality of such tissue transplants will be governed by traditional moral principles that provide guidelines for being good while doing evil. There is the Principle of Choosing the Lesser Evil, when I am trapped between two evils with no other alternatives. There is the Principle of Double-effect, when my action entails evil effects along with the good consequences which I intend. And finally, there are the Principles for Cooperation in Evil that another commits.

Choosing the lesser evil: balance the evil of letting someone suffer and die, for lack of a transplant, v. the evil of using tissue obtained from induced abortions, tissue that would otherwise serve no benefit for anyone.

Which is the lesser evil? It is morally good, because rational, to choose a lesser evil over a greater evil, when I have no other alternative.

The Principle of Double-effect: The transplanting of aborted tissue is a morally neutral act if I had no part in procuring the abortion. The good effect is the therapy for the donee; the bad effect is the possibility of my action encouraging an abortion mentality. Does the good effect outweigh the bad? If so, I can proceed in good conscience.

Principles for Cooperation in Evil: If I myself do not intend the abortion, and if my part in bringing it about is remote and not necessary to the procedure, then for a good reason I may use the resultant fetal tissue without holding myself complicitous in the abortion act that I condemn. But I am a guilty cooperator if it is my intention to procure the tissue through abortion (making me a formal cooperator), or if the abortion would not happen without me (making me a necessary cooperator), or if I am a hands-on assistant to procuring the tissue from an abortion (making me a proximate cooperator).

I have been speaking about induced abortions, because generally spontaneous abortions generally yield pathological tissue that is unsuited to medical use.

NO:

Fetus as donor, not donation: The clearest case against the medical use of aborted tissue comes from a pro-life perspective that brooks no compromise with the sacredness of fetal life and respect for fetal tissue. The fetus is an individually developing human being in its own right. It is not a body part or product that the mother is free to donate. It is a donor, not a donation. The consent of the mother regarding the "use" of the fetus must be judged accordingly. This is not like the consent she might give for the donation of her kidney, a body part. Since the fetus is not a body part, but an independent organism, her consent is analogous to the consent she might give for an incompetent relative, in this case, her unborn child.

(But the mother who aborts her child by that fact renders herself incapable of acting as a surrogate for the child.) She cannot be said to act on its behalf: she killed it. She has disqualified herself from any legitimate say in the disposal of the victim. To say otherwise would be grotesque. It would be like the parricide who demands help because he is an orphan.

Fetal dignity as overriding value: Since the fetus is a donor and not a donation, it is offensive to human dignity to speak of "using" it. Respect for human dignity is central to medical ethics. No human being may be used as a means, not even as a means to a good end. The end,

however good and praiseworthy, does not justify the reducing of humans to a mere means to that good end.
The use of tissue from induced abortions is the reduc-
tion of something human to a mere means. The offense
to human dignity is an evil that would override any
countervailing good effects from the use of aborted fetal tissue.

PO:

The following are issues to be resolved:[8]

(1) Radical pro-choice views fetal remains as nothing
     more than an excised maternal body part. There-
     fore, the use made of it is no more problematical
     than any other organ donation or disposable excres-
     cence of the mother. Radical pro-life views fetal re-
     mains as worthy of the respect given to the remains
     of any other deceased person; and the mother, as
     the killer of this person, loses all right to speak for
     it. There seems to be no resolution possible between
     these polar opposite valuations of the fetus.

(2) Moderate pro-choice generally favors the medical
     use of fetal tissue, but not in an unrestricted way.
     There are misgivings and qualifications, especially
     concerning the origin of the fetal tissue in question.
     Whatever is legal is not necessarily ethical. On this
     issue, moderate and radical pro-choice part ways.
     Abortions induced with the intention of obtaining
     tissue for transplants are a violation of human dig-
     nity. Safeguards are needed against conflict of inter-
     est, so that tissue transplants do not become an

---

8.   See Mary B. Mahawald, Jerry Silver, and Robert A. Ratcheson, "The
Ethical Options in Fetal Transplants," *Hastings Center Report* (February
1987), 9-15.

incentive for abortion either on the part of women or of their doctors.

(3) For moderate pro-life, the dignity of the fetus is central, and induced abortion (except to save the mother's life) is an unqualified evil. But in the context of this evil, a place can be made for the medical use of aborted tissue. Here is where moderate and radical pro-life part ways. There are moral guidelines for acting in an imperfect world while maintaining a moral distance from the evil. Correct application of the Principle of Choosing the Lesser Evil, the Principle of Double Effect, and the Principles for Cooperation in Evil will show when tissue transplants from abortion are ethical and when they are not, even in a pro-life perspective.

Finally, the issue of fetal transplants is especially vulnerable to the Technological Imperative, i.e., the imperative that whatever *can* be done technologically *should* be done. Legal constraints are not enough. Law lags behind the technology and the ethical judgments that need to be made about the uses of technology. The Legalistic Imperative is an unholy ally to the Technological Imperative: "It's legal, it's feasible, so do it." Until such time as the legal climate on abortion becomes more restrictive and amendments to the Uniform Anatomical Gift Act are in place, only the responsible decisions of human beings will show the way to fetal technologies that do not reduce developing human life to a technological product.

ETHICS THOUGHT EXPERIMENT:

Pro-lifers often compare the medical use of aborted tissue to the use of Nazi research on humans in the death camps. Is it right to make good use of the evil that others do?

But women generally obtain abortions in good faith, whereas it is harder to ascribe good faith to Nazi experimenters. A closer analogy would be the use of organ transplants from cadavers produced by suicide. Can you disapprove of the suicide while using the organs in good conscience? Can you disapprove of abortion while using the tissue in good conscience?

7 Assisted Suicide: Whose Life Is It?

> *Dr. Kevorkian christened his original suicide machine the "Thanatron" (he later decided "Mercitron" had a better ring).*
>
> "A Bedside Manner for Death and Dying"[1]

> *"I'm terrified to go back to that hospital."*
> *"Why?"*
> *"Dad hasn't phoned in five days. It's like he's dead."*
> *"Don't they tell you when someone dies?"*
> *"Of course, I just mean he may be alive, but if he's stopped calling, he's dead."*
> *"Can we pull the plug?"*
> *"You can't pull the plug unless he's plugged in to begin with."*   Delia Ephron, *Hanging Up*[2]

> *There's no such thing as any new right involved. Patient autonomy allows him to ask for anything he wants. . . . Assisted suicide and a patient's right to die could never be immoral or unethical. Any law that prohibits this should be disobeyed.*   Dr. Kevorkian[3]

Is there a right to physician-assisted suicide? To get to our precise discussion, we need first to unmask this question's hidden assumptions.

---

1.   Jeff Stryker, in *The New York Times* (Sunday May 19, 1996), p. E3.
2.   Ballantine Books, 1995, p. 124.
3.   Associated Press, January 1997.

The *moral* right to die is our focus. Legislatures decide on right-to-die laws and assisted suicide laws. Courts review their constitutionality and interpretation. Even Dr. Kevorkian concedes that there may well be no constitutional right to die. Not every legal right is also a moral right. And not every moral right is also legal.

Next, the morality or not of assisted suicide begs the question of whether suicide itself is a moral right. If suicide itself is morally right, then it is an act of virtue to assist a person in exercising this moral right. If suicide itself is morally wrong, then we need to ask under what conditions it is morally permissible to cooperate in a moral wrong. But the prior question is about the act that is being assisted, the morality of suicide itself.

But before we can talk about the morality of suicide itself, we need to define suicide. What counts as suicide? The line between actively killing oneself and allowing the natural dying process to take its course is not always clear.

So, "Is there a right to physician-assisted suicide?" is not a simple question. In this chapter we will first state our definition of suicide. We will treat moral rather than legal issues. Finally, we will note some of the moral considerations involved in committing suicide and in assisting a suicide. So we ask: *(1) What is suicide? (2) Is there a moral right to commit suicide? (3) Is it morally right to assist a suicide?*

The focus will be on clarifying the *meaning* of these questions, rather than on offering alternative answers to these questions. Assisted suicide for the terminally ill is

4.   This is not new territory. "Is there a right to abortion?" is a similarly complex and ambiguous question. What is the definition of abortion? What counts as human life, when does it begin? Is the termination of this life a moral, as well as a legal right? Under what conditions may one assist an abortion? Many doctors, for example, will not be part of "physician-assisted" abortion.

relatively new moral territory. Clarifying the state of the questions will be a step toward the future work of answering the questions so clarified.[5]

(1) WHAT IS SUICIDE?

The interesting moral question is whether I have a moral right freely and deliberately to end my life prematurely, i.e., before its natural conclusion. What is the meaning of "end," and what is the meaning of "prematurely"? I can bring about my premature demise gradually, or I can end it instantly.

Most of us do an implicit cost benefit analysis, and make decisions which will in all probability shorten our lives. We smoke, we get drunk, we jaywalk, we drive without seat belts. These life-shortening decisions are morally justified by the benefits, say, of convenience, relaxation, comfort, time-saving – benefits we judge to balance or outweigh the risks.

The definition of death itself is not an unambiguous concept. Medicine has been guided by the "whole brain standard" articulated by the President's Commission in 1981.[6] Either of two criteria were specified: (1) prolonged absence of circulation and respiration: the irreversible cessation of these vital signs signals the absence of all brain

---

5. Physicians today generally feel that traditional medicine is not meeting the needs of the dying. Hospice or euthanasia seem to be the only alternatives. Other forms of expert palliative care need to be explored. The rush to euthanasia will be slowed when physicians are trained to see end-of-life care (treatment of pain, bedsores, incontinence, depression, psychosis) as an important part of medicine. See John Horgan, "Seeking a Better Way to Die," *Scientific American* (May 1997), 100-105.

6. President's Commission for the Study of Ethical Problems in Medicine and Biomedical and Behavioral Research, *Defining Death* (Washington, D.C.: Government Printing Office, 1981).

function; this is the cardiorespiratory standard; (2) the neurological standard is another test for diagnosing the irreversible loss of entire brain function, including the brain stem. But in practice, these criteria are only an approximation. As many of 20% of patients who are dead, according to these criteria, continue to show activity on their electroencephalograms. And clinicians have sometimes noticed in patients neurologically certified as brain-dead an increase in heart rate and blood pressure during surgical incision to procure organs. These seem to attest to some residual brain stem function.[7]

PO: How dead is dead? Bill gives the following true account of the death of his 95-year-old mother. When did the mother die?

> *Then a nurse came in to suction my mother. Then as she was leaving, she said straightforwardly, clearly and matter-of-factly, "You realize that the only thing going here is the respirator, that without it your mother has no function. See," she said, and she removed the respirator tube, "she turns blue," and then she restored the tube. She then explained how the respirator was now working. It forces the air in, the lungs expand and push the heart, the heart sends out blood, the lungs contract and then expand again, pushing the heart. So a heartbeat is mimicked along with the artificial breathing. Eventually the heart would become so weak that even the lungs pushing it would not move it. I asked, "So she's dead, and just attached to a machine that gives the appearance that she's alive?" She said, "Yes." I said, "Then can the respirator be removed?" She said, "Yes, you'd have to see a doctor." And she left for her other patients.*

---

7.   For an excellent discussion of the problems with defining death, see Robert D. Truog, "Is It Time to Abandon Brain Death?", *Hastings Center Report* (January-February 1997), 20-37.

One nephew said, "You can't remove the respirator, you have to wait till her heart 'stops beating.'" My sister said, "It's awful, weird, like Stephen King." My other nephew said, somewhat nervously and facetiously, "If you remove the respirator, you'll regret it till the day you die." Mostly he was kidding, and assuming that we'd never remove the respirator. I said I had no problem with the respirator being removed. He said, "Oh, I thought we had consensus." He was not pushing a point of view, but just surprised.

Then a blood pressure person came in, and took her blood pressure. He was leaving without saying anything. I stopped him and asked, "It has to be very low, isn't it?" He said yes, he didn't think a stethoscope would be able to detect anything.

So I went to the desk and said, "My Mother is dead and I'd like to see a doctor to remove the respirator." They looked at me like I was an idiot. They said the doctor is at dinner, but that they would call the red team. No explanation of who or what the red team is. I said, "This is a DNR." They told me to go back and wait.

In 15 minutes or so, a little girl, who reminded me of the girl next door when I was in high school, said she was an intern, and what was my problem. I repeated that my mother was dead, that the respirator was moving her lungs, but she had no function. Could the respirator be removed?

She was quite cheerful and perky and said, "Let's see." She took out her stethoscope and seemed unsure if she could hear anything. She tried for a pulse and still wasn't sure. Then she said, "I know how we can be sure." And went off and fetched an EKG machine and administered an EKG – with the respirator on. The EKG was flat. There was no heart function. So she said, "Your surmise is right. Your mother is dead."

(2) IS THERE A MORAL RIGHT TO COMMIT SUICIDE?

[There is no moral imperative to make only those decisions which will prolong our lives as long as possible] So in principle we are all "guilty" of ending our lives prematurely. The moral challenge is to decide when it is reasonable to make such decisions. The challenge becomes more acute when the decision is to end our life more abruptly, by lethal drug, carbon monoxide, or gunshot. When does the benefit of such a foreshortening of life make this kind of decision reasonable?

PO: List some life-shortening behaviors that are part of your life. What would your life today be like if you played it absolutely safe? What values are more important to you than the longest possible life span?

Your judgment about "reasonableness" will depend in large measure on your answer to the question: "Whose life is it anyway?" Is your bodily life a possession, like a car that you own and may dispose of in any way that you choose? I can use my car as I please, and even abuse it, driving it over rough terrain, towing overly heavy loads, neglecting oil changes, trashing it for parts, or just blowing it up. Am I the outright owner of my body to use, abuse or destroy it as I please?

Or is it more correct to say that my bodily life is a gift that I hold in trust, rather than a commodity that I own? Our increasingly fragile global life-support system, and the destructive backlash from environmental abuse, are teaching us that we are not the masters of life but its servants. I can build a new car, but not a new earth. I was born into life. I did not create it. Life is a gift to cherish, use well, and pass on. To pretend to own it is an arrogance that is quickly punished.

My decisions about suicide, both the gradual suicide of living a self-abusive lifestyle, or the instant suicide of a lethal self-destruction, will be a function of whether I view life as a commodity that I own, or as a gift from that which is more than myself.

PO: Are there ways that you take care of your car more responsibly than you take care of your body? If you own your body outright, then you have the perfect moral right to abuse it any way you want to. If your friend owns her body, she has the right to dispose of it as she pleases. If she rationally and voluntarily decides to jump out of a fifth-floor window, would you tell her, "It's your body. You have the right to dispose of it as you choose. Here, let me open the window."

(3) IS IT MORALLY RIGHT TO ASSIST A SUICIDE?

Here is another area of ambiguity. (It is not always clear when assisting a person to die is the same as assisting a person to commit suicide.) There is a lot of gray area between causing death and letting die. What moral line do you draw between injecting a lethal drug or handing a lethal drug to the patient to swallow? Is it assisted suicide to give the patient pain medication that will substantially hasten the end? (Is there a moral difference between withdrawing artificial nutrition and hydration, and shutting off a ventilator or removing a pacemaker?) Is there a moral difference between withdrawing such treatments and never starting them in the first place? What is your view of the following true life scenarios?

---

8. See Ruth Macklin, *Enemies of Patients* (Oxford University Press, 1993), pp. 193-194 – several definitions of euthanasia which look clear and distinct, but which in real life can be very fuzzy.

Scenario 1: Consent: Bill's mother.

My mother, up till a week before her death, was active, watched TV, kept up with the news, including Dr. Kevorkian. She told all of her children again and again, "When I go to the hospital, don't pull the plug on me. I want everything, all possible treatments."

So after "feeling sick all over" and taking to her bed last week, something she never did because she'd always say, "If I stay in bed, I will die," she finally, after four days of resisting, said "I am not getting better, I have to go to the hospital."

What Children told the doctors:

Being very weak, unable to eat, little kidney function, low blood pressure, and an unspecified infection in her abdomen, she was put into ICU, and gasping for breath, was also put on a respirator. My sister informed the staff that "she wanted everything," and a notation to that effect was duly made on her chart.

What Mother told the doctor:

At 11:00 PM on the day of admission, at the end of an exhausting day for family and my mother, an Indian doctor, with my brother present, shouted to my hard-of-hearing mother, still vented and in ICU with a million tubes in her, "You have no kidneys, no liver, are infected, can't breathe and your heart is failing — do you want us to take extraordinary means to treat you?" My mother was confused and didn't know what he was yelling, so he repeated the same again. She answered, "No, don't give me anything extra. I don't want to live like this." The doctor again shouted, verbatim, the same preamble and the same question. Struggling with respirator and agitated, she repeated again, "No, don't give me anything. I don't want to live like this." The doctor shouted at her the same question again verbatim, and she gave the same answer again. My brother, angry at the doctor's "insensitivity," said to the doctor, "That's three times, we know her answer." So the doctor changed her chart to a DNR, maintained all current treatment, but did not schedule any exploratory surgery (which would surely have been fatal), and did not prescribe increased heart medications.

What Mother told her pastor:
I had a pleasant surprise the day of the funeral, talking to her pastor; I discovered that in his monthly visit to my mother at home they spoke about her age, her upcoming death, her health care and the kind of treatment she wanted. She had come to accept that she would be dying soon enough, said she wanted to be on her feet as long as possible, and that when she went to the hospital she would be prepared to die, and did not want to live in bed sustained by tubes and machines. So to her pastor she had given a completely different picture from what she gave to her children, which was "I don't want you to kill me – give me all treatment."

Scenario 2: "Hastening death": semantics or ethics?

Catholic moral theology, relying on the Principle of Double-effect, permits medication for the purpose of alleviating pain, even though this might hasten death. This is a responsible decision as long as the intention is good, i.e., to treat and not to kill, and as long as the intended good effect, pain relief, outweighs the bad effect of hastening death, a result that is tolerated but not intended. Dr. Howard Grossman has little patience for such moral hair-splitting. "It's bullshit."[9] His patient, Willy Barth, with AIDS-related lymphoma, whose brain was ravaged by the disease in spite of chemotherapy and radiation, pleaded, "When will this end?" Do you tell Dr. Grossman that he may not prescribe a lethal medi-

---

9. See David France, "This Doctor Wants to Help You Die," *New York* (January 13, 1997), p. 28.

cine, but he may give a dose that will alleviate pain, though hastening death?

Is this semantics or ethics?

Scenario 3: Causing death.

Increasingly physicians consider it morally praiseworthy to help consenting terminal patients, whose useful lives are at an end, to die. Seconals and Percodans are the most commonly used lethal drugs, according to Dr. Grossman. Derek Humphry's book Final Exit *remains the most popular instruction manual for how to commit suicide.[10] Long before Kevorkian, Betty Rollin wrote a brave account of her dying mother's lonely struggle to end it all.[11] Lingering deaths from AIDS and cancer have made such accounts much more common today. Dr. Timothy E. Quill details nine such cases in his recent book,* A Midwife Through the Dying Process: Stories of Healing and Hard Choices at the End of Life.[12] *A Berkeley physician, Dr. Lonny Shavelson, speaks of all he has learned from the AIDS community in his* A Choice of Death: the Dying Confront Assisted Suicide.[13]

What is your contribution to the moral consensus taking shape around the issue of assisted suicide?

10. Humphry, *Final Exit: the Practicalities of Self-Deliverance and Assisted Suicide for the Dying* (Dell, 1992).
11. *Last Wish* (reprinted by Random House, 1996).
12. Johns Hopkins University Press, 1996.
13. Simon and Shuster, 1995.

8 Children's Rights: Are Kids Different?

I propose that the rights, privileges, duties, and responsibilities of adult citizens be made available to any young person, of whatever age, who wants to make use of them.   John Holt[1]

The mother throws her child out at three-years-old. She has breast-fed it, with some ill humor, and cared for it in some manner for three whole years, and now it is ready to make its own way. . . .

In this environment a child has no chance of survival on his own until he is about 13-years-old, so children divide themselves into two age levels and form age bands. The junior band consists of children between ages of three and seven. The senior band caters for the eight-to-twelve-year-olds.

Colin Turnbull, *The Mountain People*[2]

---

1.   John Holt, "Why Not a Bill of Rights for Children?" in Beatrice Gross and Ronald Gross (eds.), *The Children's Rights Movement: Overcoming the Oppression of Young People* (Anchor Press/Doubleday, 1977), p. 319. For legal trends in children's rights, see Mary Ann Mason, *From Father's Property to Children's Rights* (Columbia University Press, 1994), and Franklin E. Zimming, *The Changing Legal World of Adolescence* (Macmillan/The Free Press, 1982). For the philosophical underpinnings of the Liberationist view, see John Harris, "The Political Status of Children," in *Contemporary Political Philosophy: Radical Studies*, ed. Keith Graham (Cambridge University Press, 1982).

2.   Cited by Laura M. Purdy, *In Their Best Interest? The Case against Equal Rights for Children* (Cornell University Press, 1992), p. 124. Purdy gives an excellent defense of the Protectionist view of children's rights,

> *The crux here is the distinction between power and authority. . . [W]ielding of "naked" power is not at all what telling children what to do . . . is about. Authority is based on acknowledged superiority with respect to some trait relevant to the task at hand, and is directed toward some goal the child would judge desirable were he or she fully informed and rational.)*
>
> Laura Purdy[3]

This is a question about human rights – those rights that you have simply by being born human, regardless of the nation or legal system in which you live. What are the human rights of children? Are they the same as the rights of adults? Or are children's rights more restricted? Are kids different from adults? Yes, says the Protectionist or Caretaker view of children. *The United Nations Declaration of the Rights of the Child* sees children as people to be protected and nurtured, though they are not ready to exercise the full panoply of rights that adults rightly enjoy. The Children's Liberation Movement, on the other hand, views children as no less human than adults, and therefore as enjoying no less rights than adults. So the question we address is as follows: ***Should children, by the fact that they are human beings, have available to them the same full range of human rights that are enjoyed by adults?***

YES:

Autonomy and freedom are the core values that underpin the Liberationist view of children. Under the guise of "protecting" children, Protectionists infringe on the es-

---

while giving full weight and consideration to Liberationist arguments.

3.   Purdy, *op. cit.*, p. 137.

sence of human dignity, namely, the right of a person to have their autonomous freedom respected.

You can understand this more readily if you consider the history of women's rights. Women have been subjected to legislation "protecting" them from lifting heavy weights, from working in environments that might be dangerous to them if they became pregnant, from serving in position dangerous to life, like the military. These well-meaning "protections" have come to be seen by many women as infringements on their autonomy as human beings. To protect women was to diminish women as human beings. It was to render them second-class citizens, with equal opportunities and choices closed off to them.

The time has come, say the Liberationists, to recognize that well-meaning protections for children trample on children's human rights. Children's protection becomes children's oppression. Granted, many children are short-sighted and irrational. But then again, so are many adults. But, aside from criminal violations, we do not take autonomy away from these irrational adults. We recognize their freedom, their right to act in irrational ways, and hence the opportunity to learn from their mistakes. Children are no more irrational than are many adults, and therefore there is no more compelling reason to deprive them of the human rights that we acknowledge in the irrational adults. By exercising these rights, children have the opportunity to exercise free choices, make mistakes and learn from them, and grow in the autonomy that is the basis of their human dignity.

So the Liberationists urge that we take a hard look at restrictions that oppress children in the current state of affairs. Consider housing and living conditions. Adults have the right to some say in where and with whom they will live, within their given economic and social con-

straints⌈ Family arrangements and economic necessity dic-
tate that children are presumed to live with their parents.
And this is only right. Children do not have the right to
greater economic and social freedom than adults enjoy.⌉
But sometimes families are abusive, and there are relatives
or friends who stand ready to shelter the child out of the
abusive situation. Or a child is under extreme tension at
home, and there is a neighbor who would take the child
in for a time out and respite. Or there is a divorce, and a
decision must be made about custody. Adults in such circumstances have the right to choose to move out, to
choose with whom they will live. Why should not the children have the right of their own free choice to leave an
abusive situation, or to take a time out with a neighbor, or
to choose the custodial parent in case of a divorce? Like
adults, children have the right to live as they choose.

   Consider schooling and education. Today, coercion is
the name of the game. Children are forbidden to go to
neighborhood schools in the name of social engineering
schemes. Truancy laws force children to be in school,
often against their wills, with incompetent teachers, desul-
tory and meaningless courses, in dreary buildings, until
the reach the age where they can legally drop out. In fact,
many exercise the option to drop out before the legal age.
Up till the age of five, learning is a joy for children. Why
should that joy and freedom in learning stop at the age of
five? Can we provide the joy of choice and freedom in
what and how and where to learn for the child, even after
the age of five? Like adults, children have the right to
learn as they choose.

   ⌈Consider work and the autonomy to earn money.
Child labor laws rightly restrict the power of employers to
exploit children⌉ Such protective laws against exploitation
are necessary to protect adults and children alike. But, lib-

erationists assert, laws forbidding exploitation often become laws forbidding children to work even when and where they choose to work. Children who are free to earn income will acquire the wherewithal to enjoy other forms of autonomy that are their due. Like adults, children have the right to work as they choose.

Consider sexual rights. Children reach biological sexual maturity earlier than ever before, even before their teenage years. Yet children who complete a mainstream education through college before they get a job and marry to have children must wait later than ever before, often till their late 20s. So they could spend 20 years at the height of their sexual powers, theoretically,in the limbo world of illicit sex. This is an area where children, impelled by overwhelming biological urgencies, are exercising their autonomy outside the strictly legal mainstream. They do practice "illicit" sex. They do have "illegitimate" children. They do seek and obtain abortions. They do even avail themselves of contraception. Clearly, many of these decisions about sex are tragic and devastating, just as are the tragic and devastating sexual decisions made by many autonomous adults. But adults do not to the same extent as children labor under the burden of restrictions on access to birth control or to abortion, or restrictions on the physical and economic infrastructure required to carry on a sexual life. Children would be more likely to learn responsibility in their sexual lives if they could make decisions in this area that are not arbitrarily impeded by society. Like adults, children have the right to autonomy in making decisions about their sexual lives.

NO:

Justice means "Treat equals equally." Equal pay for equal work. Justice also means "Treat unequals unequally." A student with a perfect exam deserves an "A," while another who misses half the questions on the same exam does not deserve an equal grade. Justice enjoins respect for equality, and respect for differences. Women may well claim certain rights linked to pregnancy and lactation, which rights would not be justly claimed by men. So, are children the same as adults, or are they different? They are both, say the protectionists. This is their starting point.

[As human beings, children are the equal of adults and enjoy human rights, as do adults.]This is the basis of the *U.N. Declaration of the Rights of the Child.* Such rights include the right not to be demeaned because of race, color, sex, religion or nationality; the right to adequate nutrition, housing, recreation and medical services; the right to relief in times of disaster; the right to protection against neglect, cruelty and exploitation.

Children are also different from adults. And justice to children demands that these differences be respected. Children are not the "noble savages" that liberationists pretend. [Children are not born with responsible autonomy] They need to be protected, nurtured, disciplined, educated with painstaking care so that they could arrive at the point where they are able to exercise the rights that adults enjoy. Children are not born with the emotional maturity, information, and experiential perspective required to make informed responsible decisions about their education, their living arrangements, their sexual lives, and choosing how to allocate time between work, study and play.

The liberationists make autonomy the value that is central to human dignity in general, and to the dignity and rights of children in particular. This puts the burden of proof on protectionists to show why it is necessary and just to limit the freedom of children. It is not difficult to meet this burden of proof. Children are different from adults. Without nurture and training and education, they are as incapable of responsible choice as they are incapable of driving a truck on the freeway. Adulthood and adult rights are hard-earned and gradually earned achievements. So the specifics of justice for children are different from justice for adults. If autonomy is truly central to human dignity, then protectionist philosophy is the way to lead children to the prerequisites required to exercise responsible freedom and autonomy.

Furthermore, autonomy is not the only value that is central to human dignity. Autonomy is specific to individual dignity. But humans are social as well as individual. The ability to live successfully in society is the social side of humanness. And respect for dignity requires the socialization of the human animal. Socialization puts just and fair limits on unrestricted freedom. True autonomy is exercised in community, and not in opposition to it. Children need to be *socialized* into the responsible exercise of freedom.

PO:

Isn't it interesting that protectionists, who have a heavy investment in the disciplining of children, are often the very ones who, when children break the law in violent ways, call for trying them in court as adults? Protectionists in the education of children become liberationists in the punishment of children.

Winifred Gallagher[4] feels that the nature/nurture debate is at an end. Scientists have discovered that genetic inheritance combines with nurture and socialization to form a "second nature" – the person that you truly are. And this second nature, once formed, cannot be deconstructed, any more than you can separate water and flour out of bread after it comes out of the oven.

Caretakers of homeless kids tell us that three-quarters of runaway children have been abused at home. Should they be returned to abusive environments? And one-third of these were literally pushed out of the home by their parent(s).

Thirty-two states forbid the minor children of drug abusers and alcoholics from getting professional help without their parents' consent. As with abortion, the distribution of condoms and sex education in the schools, is it in the best interests of the child to block children's avenues for solving their problems without parental involvement?

Are we unwittingly conducting an ongoing liberationist experiment? Observe school dropouts, latchkey kids, the teenage STD epidemic, homeless children and runaways.

ETHICS EXPERIMENT:

Interview a prepubescent child about each of the rights here discussed. Which rights does the child claim? What, in their opinion, is the upside and downside of each? Does the child see any practical problems and how would she resolve them?

---

4.   *I.D.: How Temperament and Experience Make You Who You Are* (Random House, 1996).

9 The Elderly Disabled: Who Cares?[1]

Honor thy Father and thy Mother.

The Holy Bible

What do grown children owe their parents? I will contend that the answer is "nothing."

Jane English[2]

When a father gives to his son, both laugh; when a son gives to his father, both cry.

Yiddish proverb

Do adult daughters rightly bear the major ethical duty to care for disabled elderly parents and parents-in-law? Or do they operate beyond the call of duty? There is no question that many women feel "guilty" if they avoid this burden. Should they feel guilty? What ethics governs these health care workers? All of the following issues bear on sons as much as daughters. We focus on daughters, as the ones most imposed upon by American cultural imperatives.

---

1. This chapter is adapted from Edward Stevens, "A Bill of Rights for Adult Daughter Caregivers," *Regis Today* (Winter/Spring 1995).

2. See Onora O'Neill and William Ruddick (eds.), *Having Children: Philosophical and Legal Reflections on Parenthood* (Oxford University Press, 1979). Strict quid pro quo obligations ["Your father put you through college, therefore you owe it to him to go to medical school as he did"] are inappropriate for family relationships, according to English. Mutuality based on caring and gratitude should be the governing principle.

Gerontologist Elaine Brody points out that adult daughter-in-law and adult daughter caregivers (we'll call them *ADCs*) are the primary caregivers to 9 million dependent elders.[3] Only 1 in 20 elderly are institutionalized. √Unpaid care to 90% not in nursing homes is provided by friends and relatives, mostly women. The typical ADC is 45-years-old, female and married, and among children 75% are daughters, 25% are sons, according to Professor Sarah-Vaughan Brakman of Villanova University.[4]

So the question before us is: ***Do ADCs, like other professional caregivers, have a duty to care for elderly disabled parents and parents-in-law?***

NO:

Let's compare the situation of ADCs with other caregivers. Various ethical models govern the duties of other caregivers and their relationships to their clients/patients, viz., the Contract Model, the Covenant Model, and the Pro Bono Model. Do these models provide ethical guidelines for the ADC?

The Contract Model:

Most health care in America today operates on the Contract Model. This is the era of the informed consumer of health services, purchasing specific services from an HMO-like facility, operating under insurance limitations, with litigious lawyers hovering over the shoulder. The caregiver sees her work as a career, a job. She offers for

---

3.   Elaine Brody, "Filial Care of the Elderly and Changing Roles of Women and Men," *Journal of Geriatric Psychiatry* 19, no. 2 (1986): 177-178.

4.   Sarah-Vaughan Brakman, "Adult Daughter Caregivers," *The Hastings Center Report* 24, no. 5 (1994):26.

sale her skills. Buyers of these services self-identify as clients rather than as patients. The expectations and limits of the transaction are spelled out in an explicit or implied agreement between free, informed, consenting adults. This Contract Model of Health Care allows for either caregiver or client to withdraw from the transaction, should they wish to do so, by giving fair warning or making penalty payments. Ask yourself, do you approach your dentist or optician as an educated consumer? Do you expect certain specific skills and services, much as you would from your plumber or automobile mechanic? The Contract Model is an effective way of organizing client-practitioner relationships in an era of consumer-oriented buyers, anonymous physicians and caregiver unions.

This model provides little guidance for the ADC. The Contract Model is driven by economics: no pay, no service. The ADC receives no pay, but she's expected to serve anyway. Why? The contractor signs up to serve. But the ADC never signed up. Typically she is dumped into an emergency situation, her life turned upside down by this unexpected alleged duty to serve as an ADC. Why? The contractor can always back out. But the ADC serves round-the-clock shifts until she or the patient dies. Why?

The Covenant Model:

The Covenant Model of health care is more traditional and idealistic. Here the caregiver views her work as a calling, a vocation. Service recipients present themselves to caregivers as their "patients." Yes, there is a business side to medicine, but much more is it a profession, a sacred trust. Patients feel themselves to be vulnerable human beings, entrusting themselves to caregivers for healing. At stake are precious values of life and health and confidentiality that touch the core of their personhood. They expect an altruistic dedication from the caregiver that they would never expect from their relationship to a plumber or an electrician. This is the world of medicine that your parents and grandparents remember, where the Covenant Model held sway. Ask yourself, do you approach your gynecologist or psychologist in such a spirit of trust or even surrender?

The Covenant Model is closer to the situation of the ADC. Even paying patients, much like the home care patients of ADCs, expect a trust, a dedication, a caring attitude that is not merely dollar-driven. But the situations are not parallel. Even the Covenant Model demands up-front payment. For all its idealism, the bottom line is: no pay, no service. The ADC receives no up-front payment, but she's expected to serve anyway. Why? And even dedicated nurses and physicians can always quit, retire, or change careers, a luxury not afforded to the ADC. She is allegedly duty-bound to serve unto death. Why?

The Pro Bono Model:

Finally, there is the Pro Bono Model. Think of the unpaid dedicated service of Mother Teresa's nuns or Peace Corps Workers or Hospice volunteers. Patients receive care, no money, no questions asked. Pro Bono caregivers serve freely and unreservedly. Is this a satisfactory model for the ADC? Not really. Even the Pro Bono worker freely chooses her calling, and can freely change her mind. Not so the ADC. The adult daughter may have chosen to be a lawyer, a model or a computer wholesaler, but the caregiver role is thrust on her without her consent and she's stuck until death. Why?

The legitimacy of the Contract, Covenant, and Pro Bono Models rests on the fact that the relationship between practitioner and client is freely chosen by both parties, and in the first two models there is also an exchange of money for services, a quid pro quo. Adult children do not choose their patients when their parents become patients.⌋

YES:

The Filial Model:

What is the basis of the ADC's duty to serve? Let's call this the Filial Model. On what does its legitimacy rest? Consider three arguments, based on (1) reciprocity, (2) gratitude, (3) caring.

(1) Reciprocity: Just as parents put their children first and gave them everything they needed in their time of dependency, so children should reciprocate by putting their elder parents first and giving them every needful care in their time of dependency. So goes the argument from reciprocity.

This argument doesn't hold up. Parents have a duty to provide for their children. You don't owe a debt to people for their only doing their duty. And even granting that there were a debt, this would assume that you could pay the debt and then you'd be free. But you can't pay off your parents and then wash your hands of them. You are stuck with them. The emotional and biological bond is a fact. If this is a debt, well, it's impossible to pay it off. There is a maxim in ethics, "No one is obliged to do the impossible." This would be an impossible debt. So reciprocity is not a good argument in favor of the Filial Model of Health Care.

(2) Gratitude: Unlike reciprocity, gratitude does not imply the repayment of a debt. It is not quid pro quo. Gratitude means that the ADC should care for dis-

abled elders out of appreciation for all the goodwill and kindness shown her by these elders throughout her life, and especially her childhood.

Indeed gratitude can make a moral claim on us. But the obligation to show gratitude is not an absolute one. For example, if the ADC was abused by these elders, she may have little to be grateful for. Or indeed she may be morally drawn to grateful service to them, but have competing values that are more morally urgent than gratitude toward her parents, for example, the needs of her children, her husband, or her career. So within limits, gratitude can be the basis for a Filial Model of Health Care.

(3) Caring: Sons and daughters both experience the claims of reciprocity and gratitude. Why does the Filial Model of Elder Care seem to fall more on daughters?

The Filial Model of health care, in conclusion, rests on the obligation of gratitude of children toward their elders. But this obligation is not absolute. It must be balanced off against other obligations that may be equally or more compelling. And in line with Equity Feminism, I suggest that a caring ethic is not gender-specific. It is unjust to assume that the female relatives have the prima facie duty to render care.

Finally and most importantly, like the first three Models of Health Care, the Filial Model must rest on the full, free and informed consent of the caregiver. It is unjust for any ADC to be trapped in this role, or be assigned it by default, or not to be free later to change her mind when her own interests and/or the interests of other loved ones make a more compelling call on her decisions about how to invest her energy and her care. Involuntary servitude is inconsistent with the dignity and humanity of women.

A BILL OF RIGHTS:

I end with a Bill of Rights for ADCs:

1. The right to accept or reject the caregiver role, fully informed of alternatives and of competing obligations in concert with other equally responsible family members;

2. The right not to be emotionally blackmailed or gender-stereotyped into the ADC role;

3. The right to change her mind as she evaluates the impact of the role on her life;

4. The right to give priority to the needs of her children, her spouse and herself, as well as to the needs of the elderly patient;

5. The right not to care for an elder who was abusive of her in earlier life; the Filial Model's duty of gratitude does not apply in such a case.

In conclusion, all studies show that the vast majority of adult children *want* to care for their disabled elders. They have no need to hear about a duty to care. Indeed many, especially women, go far beyond the call of duty. But caregivers also have rights, and maybe they do need to hear about these. I have presented in outline form a very complex and emotionally charged issue. The intention is not to end the discussion, but to begin it.

PO:

"Different voice" feminism may unwittingly play into the stereotype of women as the "caring" gender. Such feminism views woman and man as very different from each other, and in great part at odds. In all spheres of life, women are oppressed by patriarchal structures erected by men that reduce women to victims. In matters of ethics and morality, women speak "in a different voice." The morality of men is objective, abstract and neglectful of relationships. Women's morality focuses on caring and nurturing relationships, and this focus on caring is superior to men's morality. Does this focus on women's special and superior moral charism of caring have the unintentional effect of letting morally inferior uncaring men off the hook in the Filial Model of Health Care?

Equity feminism, on the other hand, sees men and women as more alike than different. Both genders are first and foremost human beings. The goal is that they work together for the full empowerment of every human being, regardless of gender. Neither gender is morally superior to the other. There are nurturing, caring men, as well as abstractly principled women. Women are not doomed to victimhood. A colleague of mine, when faced with a decision to neglect her career so as to care for an elder parent, asked herself this question, "Would Henry Kissinger give up his career to care for a parent?" She concluded that obviously he would not. "Neither will I," she decided, and looked for alternatives.

ETHICS EXPERIMENT:

Ask your mother and your grandmother what care they expect from you and/or their family when and if they become old and disabled. How different are the answers of each generation? What would you tell your daughter?

10 The Poor Need Us: Or Do We Need Them?

Human salvation lies in the hands of the creatively maladjusted. **Martin Luther King, Jr.**

I don't get welfare. . . . I hate those people in there. They make you fuckin' sit and sit and ask you questions that don't make any sense . . . You're homeless, but you have to have an address. They want you to get so fuckin' upset that you get up and walk out. They test you. And if you do get up and walk out, that means you don't really want it.

A homeless New York Woman[1]

When it shall be said in any country in the world, my poor are happy; neither ignorance nor distress is to be found among them; my jails are empty of prisoners, my streets of beggars; the aged are not in want, the taxes are not oppressive. . .; when these things can be said, then may that country boast of its constitution and its government. **Thomas Paine**[2]

Why do people hate "the undeserving poor," what has come to be called the "underclass"? Two reasons: (1) the undeserving poor are perceived to reject main-

---

1. Reported by Gwendolyn Dorick, "Friends among Strangers: Personal Relations Among New York City's Homeless," (Ph.D. dissertation, Columbia University Department of Sociology, 1994), p. 47.

2. Cited by Herbert J. Gans, *The War Against the Poor: The Underclass and Antipoverty Policy* (Basic Books, 1995), frontispiece.

stream values. They don't work for a living. They have children out-of-wedlock, children they cannot afford to raise. They indulge in drugs. They drop out of school. They choose crime as a way of life. (2) This is all bad enough. But worst of all, this socially harmful, self-destructive lifestyle is subsidized on the backs of decent hard-working wage-earners who resent throwing away their hard-earned money on people whose values they despise.

The poor are fellow human beings. Does this entitle them to welfare justice, no matter how "undeserving" they might be? Or do the "undeserving poor" by their irresponsible moral choices forfeit any right to make such just demands? So our question: *Are the undeserving poor deserving of welfare aid?*

NO:

A sense of justice is the earliest ethical concept grasped by kids. "It's not fair: her piece of cake is bigger than mine!" Even children grasp the notion of "Treat equals equally, treat differences differently" – justice as *quid pro quo*. When applying for a job, a young man who stayed in school deserves preference over a dropout. A woman who works hard to earn her living feels cheated to see her nonworking neighbor get a free ride from welfare for doing nothing but watching TV all day. When a teenager gets pregnant, drops out of school and the state sets her up in her own apartment with her own income, how does that look to her former schoolmate who stays in school and lives at home with her family? Does a drug dealer deserve to have welfare provide his food and shelter so he can devote full time to his illegal trade?

Human dignity requires that every person be given equal opportunity to education, work, food and shelter. It is unjust to deny anyone this equality of opportunity. "Treat equals equally." But human dignity does not require equality of result. The result is determined by how I use my opportunity. Those who use it well are rewarded. Those who don't aren't. Those who choose poverty-making behaviors should expect to be poor. "Treat differences differently." This is the fairness that justice requires. The undeserving poor deserve equal opportunity, no more no less.

Society, if it would remedy the lot of the poor, should not focus on the "haves vs. have-nots"; the focus instead should be on the "do-ers vs. the do-not's."[3] It serves neither realism nor justice to just assume that wealth will be magically produced, and all we have to do is redistribute it. Some people produce, and others don't. Let the undeserving poor become the deserving middle class. Let the do-not's become do-er's. The true service of human dignity is based on tough love and respect for justice that is earned.

YES:

Humanitarian justice mandates that the so-called "undeserving poor" receive the basic food, shelter, health care, and income necessary to maintain their human dignity in a society that can afford to give it to them. With few exceptions, the poor are not poor by choice. Let's grant that if school dropouts, drug-dealing, out-of-wedlock pregnancies and crime were free, autonomous lifestyle choices from an abundance of other available choices, then we'd rightly conclude that people should live by the consequences of such free choices, for better or for worse. "The wages of sin is death," says St. Paul. Bad choices create

---

3.   See Thomas Sowell, *Migrations and Cultures* (Basic Books, 1996).

bad karma. [But the main problem is not the individual choices that the poor might make. The problem is the institutions that constrain and confine the range of choices that are available to the poor.]

The problem is institutional or systemic evil, not individual evil. Have you ever felt constrained to make a distasteful decision because you were caught in an unjust system? You find yourself saying, "You can't fight City Hall," or "I hate to do this to you, but those are the rules," or "Yes, it's unfair, but I have no choice; it's company policy." When you are caught in an unjust system, you end up making choices you'd rather not make. To live in systemically unjust institutions is the permanent lot of the poor. Rundown schools, inadequate police and sanitation services, lack of legal occupations, insufficient affordable housing, poor health care support – these are the building blocks of a whole unjust system that undermines the lives and moral possibilities of the poor. Far from being "undeserving," the whole effective world of the poor amounts to an imprisoning of the innocent. The unjust institutions are the prison walls. Such poor are not only "deserving" of humanitarian help and welfare, they rightly demand it in justice.

[The human dignity inherent in every person is itself a moral call for the means to live their life with dignity.] When you are talking about the basic necessities for a life of minimal human dignity, it is irrelevant whether the poor can afford it, or not. You are born with dignity as a human being. You don't have to earn or "afford" it.

And the type of remedy needs to be attuned to type of injustice. When an evil individual assaults your dignity, you need to stop that evil person and punish him. But when an evil institution assaults your dignity, you need to change that evil system into a just system. The distribution of Thanksgiving turkeys, volunteer "cleanup days" in poor neighborhoods, clothing drives for the homeless – these are individual solutions for systemic evils. They are better than nothing. But systemic evils demand systemic solutions: guaranteed food programs for adequate nutrition, regular garbage pickups, and affordable housing for all in need of shelter. The ethical foundation of welfare is the right of every human being to live with the dignity that befits their human condition. It is possible for the poor to be undeserving of aid if they make genuine choices to bring about their own poverty. But the vast majority of the poor are caught in unjust institutions that impoverish them against their wills, and conspire to maintain them in poverty.

PO:

[Talking about the poor as the "underclass" is a politically correct social science type of labeling. Has it become a code word for separating the poor from "normal" society?] Has it become a way not only to designate the poor as a lower economic class, but also to stereotype them as a sub-caste of citizens with less-than-equal human dignity? "The underclass": what overtones does that have for you?

Maybe we should not be reflecting on "the undeserving poor" but on the "undeserving rest of us." Who gains from having poor people around? Certainly not the poor.

---

4.   Kathryn Edin, *Making Ends Meet* (Russell Sage Foundation, 1997), lived for months with the actual poor, working families, and families on welfare, and many both on welfare and working off the books. These people knew who was "deserving" and who was not. They know to the penny where their money goes, what is necessary and what is not. There is no patience for absentee Dads who don't contribute. The working poor do less well than those on welfare. What would welfare reform look like if it was run using the expertise of these practitioners, rather than by the professionals and bureaucrats who staff the poverty industry?

The poor are very useful for the rest of us. Maybe it is to our self-interest to keep the poor in poverty. Herbert Gans points out several functions that the poor serve for better-off Americans.[5]

The poor serve two social functions: (1) by demonizing and stereotyping the poor, we distance ourselves from them and insulate ourselves from having to care for them; (2) by scapegoating the poor, we can relieve our vengeful and punitive feelings in the face of all the evil we feel helpless to cope with.

The poor serve three economic functions: (1) they provide jobs for armies of police, probation officers, welfare officials, shelters, treatment centers, courts, prisons, social workers, and other members of the poverty industry; (2) institutionally excluded from legal occupations, they supply the illegal goods and services demanded by the rest of us, drugs, prostitutes, weapons, and other contraband; (3) they work in the dirty, demeaning, low-paying jobs that better-off Americans don't want to do.

The poor provide three normative functions: (1) they legitimate our sense of "superior" morality. Saints need sinners to look down upon, otherwise how would they know they are saints? (2) they reinforce our values: to "qualify" for aid, they have to give obeisance to mainstream values, pretending to a "work ethic," to "family values," like a welfare mother not living with an unwed partner, to proper respect for poverty officials; better-off Americans have no need not play such charades; (3) they supply popular culture villains, the crime figures, gangs and gangsters, rappers, the staples of eyewitness news and trash TV that mainstream citizens insatiably consume and love to hate.

---

5.   Gans, *op. cit.*, pp. 92 ff.

The poor serve three political functions: (1) they provide a scapegoat for problems that politicians are unwilling or unable to solve; (2) because politicians can safely ignore the stigmatized poor, resources are diverted to better-off citizens, and thus ironically the poor serve to shift power in conservative directions; (3) spaces inhabited by the powerless "underclass" become politically safe areas for drug markets, toxic dumps, red light districts, halfway houses and shelters – all unwelcome in the areas where the better-off live.

Look at all these services and functions supplied by the poor. It seems that it is not the poor who are undeserving. It is the better-off rest of us who are undeserving. Maybe the welfare given to the poor is not merely humanitarian aid. Maybe it should be viewed as strictly earned by all the benefits that the poor confer on mainstream society.

Could better-off citizens survive successfully one week, one month, one year, 10 years in the deprivation created by the systemic evils that shape the lives of the poor? Maybe our job-screening processes are too limited. Maybe the ability to survive *in extremis* should be a job qualifier equivalent to mainstream schooling. Colleges give credit to older students for their "life experience." What credit should we give to poor people for enduring and surviving extreme life experiences?

ETHICS EXPERIMENT:

Lock up your credit cards and checks for 24 hours. Give all your cash away to the first stranger you meet, or leave it on a park bench. If you can't bear to do that, then lock away your cash with your credit cards. Notice what it's like to live for a day and a night "without visible means of support."

11 Racial Justice: Color Blind or Group-Conscious?

When I get big, I'm gonna have blond hair, blue eyes, and I'm gonna be white. I told my mother I don't wanna be black no more. Whoopi Goldberg[1]

Race was once synonymous with community for African Americans. But the rope attached to the anchor has become a noose choking off social growth . . . [it] should be lengthened to allow us to move into other communities . . . [creating] internal coalitions that transcend differences of color, culture, and class as well as those beyond the limits of group identity, to insure political and economic advancement.

Itabari Njeri[2]

The faces of those white women hovering behind that black girl at the Little Rock school in 1957 does not soon leave the retina of the mind . . . It is a source of amusement even now to black women to listen to feminists talk of liberation while somebody's nice black grandmother shoulders the daily responsibility of childrearing and floor mopping. Toni Morrison[3]

---

1. In her stage show and video, *Whoopi Goldberg Live* (1985).

2. Itabari Njeri, *The Last Plantation: Color, Conflict, and Identity* (Houghton Mifflin, 1997). Limited racial definitions, she argues, can create a psychological slavery that turns the mind into the "last plantation." See also, Midge Wilson and Kathy Russell, *Divided Sisters: Bridging the Gap Between Black Women and White Women* (Anchor Books, 1996).

3. *Ibid*, p. 201, from an article by Toni Morrison in *The New York Times Magazine*.

Identity politics, multicultural pride and the politics of difference have challenged traditional notions of justice. Traditionally, justice has been based on the respect demanded by each individual's basic human dignity. Regardless of their differences from one another, human beings were to be viewed as created equal, as children of the same God. Christianity underlined this view of every human being as one in Christ. Secular American society resonates with St. Paul's announcement that "There is no longer Jew or Greek, there is no longer slave or free, there is no longer male and female" [Galatians 3:28]. A person is to be respected not because of their ethnicity, their political-economic status, or their gender. Justice is based not on the group you belong to, but on your equal human dignity under God. This is the ideal of the color-blind society so eloquently proclaimed by Martin Luther King, and of the gender-inclusive society proclaimed by Betty Friedan.

Modern social movements, like multiculturalism and radical feminism, have brought group identity to center stage in the fight for justice. Justice based on equal dignity of human beings has come to be viewed as ineffective and inadequate. The celebration of diversity and the demand for rights based on differences has replaced the egalitarian ideal.[4] The doctrine of "separate but equal" is reappearing in new clothes. The argument for *human* rights gives way to rights based on gender, on ethnicity or on the color of one's skin. Affirmative discrimination replaces

---

4. Nathan Glazer, *We Are All Multiculturalists Now* (Harvard University Press, 1997) examines this phenomenon. Is diversity ethics a positive assertion of one's own causes, celebrations and values? Or is it a new self-chosen apartheid born of frustration caused by the barriers to full assimilation imposed by the dominant white culture?

prohibition against discrimination on the basis of race, sex or ethnic origin.

So we now address the following question: ***Does the primary principle of justice consist in the equal treatment of human beings rather than in diverse treatment based on group differences? Is justice more fundamentally a matter of assimilationist ethics than of diversity ethics?***

YES:

The realities of justice must acknowledge that race distinctions are deeply embedded in American institutions, culture, and ways of thinking. The color of one's skin does not function in American society as does the color of one's eyes. Eye color is irrelevant. Nobody cares. But skin color, specifically non-white skin color, is invested with heavy cultural baggage. And *different* skin color is made to signify *inferior* skin color, inferior human being, to be subordinated and oppressed.

The American legal system has eliminated overt racism, laws and institutions explicitly designed to oppress people on the basis of their race. The basic equal humanity of every race undermines any justification for treating people as less than human on the basis of racial difference.

Covert racism engages in de facto racial oppression, without explicitly using racial criteria for unjustly allocating burdens and benefits. Covert racism is also illegal, but often alive and well. Without mentioning the word race, political gerrymanders, municipal boundaries, economic redlining and zoning regulations are often used for effectively racist ends.

More insidious is the unintentional but effective racism built into stereotyping and ways of thinking that unconsciously oppress and demean. Consider the movie

White Men Can't Jump, ostensibly extolling blacks' athletic supremacy over whites. John M. Hoberman has suggested that there is a stereotypical and unscientific "Law of Compensation" operative in the kind of thinking that admires African-American physical superiority with the covert implication of mental inferiority. Black athlete's physical traits, nerve fiber, muscle fibers, bone density and human growth hormone are acclaimed against a backdrop of *National Geographic* magazine, Tarzan films, and eugenic slavery.[5] There are stores where African American teenagers are presumed to be shoplifters; there are neighborhoods which view the presence of a black male as a physical threat; there are newspapers that will spill copious ink on the drug death of a Caucasian child, while all but ignoring the more horrifying deaths of African American children.

The assimilationist ethical ideal looks to a society in which these odious racist racial distinctions no longer exist, where skin color is irrelevant to the way we think about human beings. What would a society look like where we no longer obsess about differences of race, which inevitably lead to differences of treatment, a society in which our common humanity is the overriding principle of justice, a society which celebrates unity over diversity, and the human dignity that we share rather than the dissimilarities which divide us? Is race an ethically appropriate question when assigning basic rights?

Consider basic political rights, the right to education and health care, the right to vote and to travel, the right to enjoy public lodging and restaurants. Is it ethically appropriate to ask first, "What race are you?" Of course not.

---

5.   John M. Hoberman, *Darwin's Athletes: How Sport Has Damaged Black America and Preserved the Myth of Race* (Houghton Mifflin, 1997), p. 240.

If you are a human being, that is all that is required to exercise these just rights.

Race is no more an appropriate qualifier when looking at non-governmental institutions and benefits. Human beings, regardless of race, should enjoy equal opportunity to live where they choose, to access economic markets, or to marry as they please, all without having to pass any racial identifier tests. It is enough to be a human being to qualify for all these rights.

Finally, the assimilationist ideal sees race as trivial and irrelevant in the area of individual preferences and social interactions. It would be an ethical affront to reject a friend because of her race, to insist on the right to a racially segregated dormitory, to form clubs which assert one racial identity against another, or to forbid interracial adoption of children. The ideal is to respect the dignity of humans as human, with racial differences relegated to the trivial significance they deserve, along with eye color and hair color.

Note that this does not signal the end of diversity. Genuine human diversity is cause for celebration. Let ethnic restaurants flourish, provided that all humans are welcome to the table. But to pit human against human on the basis of physical attributes over which they have no control is an affront to human dignity.

NO:

Diversity ethics and multiculturalism are not only politically correct, they are good science, and they are good ethics. A community which celebrates and supports the full panoply of diverse talents, perspectives, backgrounds and strengths of its members is richer and stronger than a community of clones. There are two ways of viewing racial (and other) differences, essentialist and egalitarian.

When race is perceived as part of a person's essential human nature, then we immediately get into a caste system, with essentially different racial human natures, some races of humans considered superior humans, other races of humans considered and treated as inferior. Assimilationist ethics rightly condemns this view of human diversity as unethical and disrespectful of the common human dignity shared by all. Justice requires that similars be treated similarly. Equal pay for equal work. Equal educational opportunity for equal children.

But there is an egalitarian way of looking at difference, that the assimilationist ignores. Equal human dignity does not always require that people be treated according to the same rules, standards and principles. Yes, justice requires that similars be treated similarly. But justice also requires a respect for differences, that differences be treated differently. An egalitarian view of difference respects the differences among humans without taking anything at all away from respect for their equal humanity.

Egalitarian justice is basic. If respect for differences and different treatment for different races result in a human caste system with inferior and superior races, then such different treatment is unethical and wrong. But if such different treatment does not violate the common humanity shared by every race, then such different treatment for different races can be ethical and just. Ethical debates about race in our society often revolve around the perceived conflicts between equality and difference.

Treating people as equals does not always mean to treat them in the same way. The team that scores the more points wins the prize. While being respected for their equal human dignity, the losers are treated differently and with justice, for they lost, after all. Affirmative action presents a more difficult conflict between respect for equality and respect for difference. If the beginning amateur is to have an equal opportunity to win in a club golf tournament, he or she is given a "handicap," so that even with a worse score s/he could win, the handicap compensating for the worse score. The affirmative action on behalf of the amateur does not take away from the human dignity of the skillful player. It is simply a case of justice – treat differences differently, accommodate and compensate for the lesser skills of the amateur player.

(When assimilationists systematically dismiss group differences as ethically irrelevant, they perpetuate the very oppression they are trying to fight against)The assimilationist goal is to bring all racially disadvantaged groups into the mainstream of society. This apparently well-intentioned goal is arrogant and oppressive for the so-called disadvantaged groups. Who mainstreams whom? What is this mainstream to which the assimilationists are inviting the disadvantaged? (In America it might be loosely characterized as white Euro-American Protestant individualist democratic meritocratic capitalist society). The rules of the mainstream game are well in place, and the current mainstreamers are good at playing this game. By definition, the mainstreamers are the privileged group. They dominate. It is their game, after all, played by their rules. The disadvantaged are disadvantaged because they are coming late to an alien game whose rules they have not learned to play with ease and skill.

The standards of the mainstream game are presented as the common human and ethical ideal. It's like professional soccer players from Brazil or Nigeria trying out for the New York Jets. Soccer in the rest of the world is known as "football." When the soccer "football" players try out for the Jets football team, they are informed that football means the game that is played by NFL rules. "Everybody knows that." If these Nigerian and Brazilian "football" players must assimilate to NFL rules, they will be disadvantaged football players for a very long time. And even with affirmative action, it will not be easy to assimilate into mainstream football. But this is "real football." Similarly, privileged assimilationists tell the disadvantaged, "Our game is the real game," the only game in town. To be a fully functioning member of this community, you need to play by these rules.

When mainstream society is taken to be the universal human norm, when alternative group differences are repressed in the name of assimilation, then the members of the privileged dominating group can easily remain blind to their cultural imperialism. The norms of the privileged group masquerade as universal human norms, enabling the mainstreamers to stay blissfully unaware of the fact that their values are not neutral and universal. Mainstream culture is not a group-neutral humanistic point of view. It is simply one group among many others. Each group, then, has a right in justice that its values be respected. The cultural privilege of the mainstream does not give an ethical privilege for it to impose these values on others.

Finally, this self-deception of the privileged mainstream, that pretends to be a universal human standard, often gets internalized by the disadvantaged groups. Impelled to measure themselves by mainstream norms, they fall short. And demeaned by the mainstream, they often devalue themselves.

In conclusion, assimilationist ethics is correct in rejecting the moral legitimacy of a caste system that would divide different races of human beings into superior and inferior groups. But the world of the assimilationist is not the world for everybody. Different racial groups rightly demand that their differences be respected too. Justice is a matter of diversity ethics, as long as it respects the dignity of every human of every race.

PO:

Anthropologists no longer use the category of "race." Advances in genetics and biotechnology have discredited "race" as a viable objective way of subdividing the human species. Race represents a quite arbitrary, socially constructed way of looking at human variations. Anthropologist C. Loring Brace called race "a social construct derived mainly from perceptions conditioned by the events of recorded history, and it has no basic biological validity."[6] So when you declare your race, it's like declaring which social label you are willing to buy into. Are you a member of the Bloods or the Crips?

Sheila Tobias gives a detailed account of feminism's journey from an all-inclusive Women's Movement to a balkanized assembly of victim groups. First, men were marginalized from the Women's Movement, then married women with children, economically advantaged women, white women, physically abled women, never-abused women, etc.[7] Must a quest for rights become a contest of victimhood? Do victims have rights because they are victims, or because they are human beings?

Mainstream feminists support abortion rights and contraception. African-American women have not been as active as white women in the abortion movement. Black

6.   Cited by David Chamber in *The Boston Globe* (May 11, 1997), p. A30 quoting from Brace's essay in Larry T. Reynolds and Leonard Lieberman (eds.,), *Race and other Misadventures: Essays in Honor of Ashley Montague in His Ninetieth Year* (General Hall, 1996).

7.   Sheila Tobias, *Faces of Feminism: An Activist's Reflection on the Women's Movement* (Westview Press, 1997), p. 256.

women sense the genocidal overtones of efforts to lower the birth rate of Blacks and of poor "welfare moms." To this day, African Americans sense in the abortion movement echoes of Margaret Sanger's goal in birth control: "More children from the fit, less from the unfit."[8]

Mainstream women value breastfeeding. But African American women tend to avoid the "stigma" of breastfeeding. Only 27% of African-American women breastfeed. This compares to 61% of their white sisters who do so. This difference cuts across socioeconomic lines, in reaction perhaps to that time when poverty prevented any alternative to breastfeeding.[9]

A color-blind society based on merit is a quasi-religious belief without rational basis. Duncan Kennedy in "A Cultural Pluralist Case for Affirmative Action" argues against what he calls this new "fundamentalism."[10] Every person is somewhere and coming from somewhere, and is part of a community that is somewhere and coming from somewhere in terms both of achievements and crimes committed. Karma will be served. (It is quite a challenge to form a multi-cultural community when there is "neither a consensual foundation in history nor a myth of human benevolence to make it all seem natural."[11]) Since no one group has the right to demand that every other group assimilate into it, proportional representation is needed in the overall society. Only affirmative action mandating a voice for every group will make this multicultural society viable.

---

8. Wilson, *op.cit.*, p. 207.
9. 1988 National Maternal and Infant Health Survey.
10. See *Campus Wars: Multiculturalism and the Politics of Difference* (eds. John Arthur and Amy Shapiro) (Westview Press, 1995), pp. 153-175.
11. Ibid., p. 175.

ETHICS EXPERIMENTS:

Today, everyone is a minority. White males have long been considered unjust because they used race and gender as entitlements. Now other minorities use race and gender as entitlements. Are they also unjust?[12] Can you think of a sexual minority, or a handicapped minority, or an ethnic minority that needs to be organized to receive their just entitlements? Draw up a charter for this group. How would such a group differ, if at all, from more accepted "minorities"?

The questionnaire used in the decennial federal census reflect's America's obsession with racial labeling. The 1990 census offered people four racial self-identification choices: (1) White, (2) Black, (3) Asian or Pacific Islander, (4) American Indian or Alaskan Native, or they could check "Other." And there was an opportunity to cite Hispanic ethnicity. Are people of mixed race, in being asked to choose one category, implicitly denying the other part(s) of their heritage? Which box would you advise golfer Tiger Woods to check? Suppose you worked for OMB (Office of Management and Budget) and are assigned to revise these classifications. Should they rightly be eliminated all together? Should a box be added for "Multi-Racial"? [From 1960 to 1995, multiracial marriages have increased from 160,000 to 1,400,000.] Justify your decision as the ethically correct thing to do.

---

12. See Shelby Steele, "The Recoloring of Campus Life: Student Racism, Academic Pluralism, and the End of a Dream," in *Campus Wars*, pp. 176-187.

Gender

12 Pregnancy in the Hazardous Workplace

It violates common sense to require an employer to damage unborn children. A manufacturer that creates a hazard has an obligation to protect against injury for that hazard.   Stanley S. Jaspan[1]

Since time immemorial the excuse for keeping women in their place has been because of their role in producing the next generation. The attitude of Johnson Controls is: "We know better than you. We can't allow women to make this decision. We have to make it for them."   Isabelle Katz Pinzler[2]

In the medical setting a person's right to know about risks . . has been recognized under the guise of informed consent. . . . But the headway that has been made in the medical setting is, unfortunately, unparalleled in the workplace. . . . The employer, seeking to augment his profits (the end), may use the employee merely as a means to achieve that end. One way in which he could do this is to fail to inform an employee about hazardous work conditions.

                          Anita M. Superson[3]

1.   Jaspan, lawyer for Johnson Controls, cited by Linda Greenhouse, "Justices Listen to Arguments on Fetal-Protection Policy," *New York Times* (October 10, 1990), p. A20.

2.   Director of Women's Rights at the American Civil Liberties Union, cited in *The New York Times* (September 1, 1990), p. 28.

3.   Anita Superson, "The Employer-Employee Relationship and the Right to Know," *Ethics in the Workplace*, edited by Robert A. Larmer

⌈If fertile women are susceptible to certain workplace hazards, are they rightly excluded from such jobs dangerous to them, though these same jobs are not dangerous to men or to sterile women?⌉Consider, for example, the case of United Auto Workers v Johnson Controls.

Johnson Controls Inc. makes batteries for Sears, Goodyear, and other big companies. The air in its plants is laced with lead and lead oxide in amounts toxic for children and fetuses, but not for adults. Johnson excludes all fertile women from these higher-paying, but hazardous jobs out of concern for fetal damage, should the women become pregnant. These issues extend far beyond the case of Johnson Controls. We will look at the ethical (as opposed to the legal) issues raised by the case.

This case carries one step further the debate already raging on the rights and obligations of pregnant women. Are pregnant women who drink guilty of fetal neglect? Women who smoke? Are third parties duty-bound to stop them, much as they are bound to intervene against the abuse of children after they are born? Does the woman who chooses to bring a child to term lose her autonomy, her right to exercise informed consent, and become a passive ward of her doctor, of her husband, of her parents, of her neighbors and others concerned with her fetus' well-being?

Johnson Controls raises these same questions, but now not of pregnant women but of *possibly* pregnant women. It seeks to paternalistically protect a woman

---

(West Publishing Co., 1996), pp. 177, 179.

4.   See Janet Gallagher, "The Fetus and the Law – Whose Life Is It Anyway?", *Ms.* magazine (September 1984, 62-66, 134-35); and Dawn Johnson, "A New Threat to Pregnant Women's Autonomy," *Hastings Center Report* (August-September 1987), 33-40; and Thomas Mackenzie, Theodore Nagel, and Barbara Katz Rothman, "When a Pregnant Woman Endangers her Fetus," *Hastings Center Report* (February 1986), 24-25.

against her will. It assumes that a fertile woman, even if she intends no pregnancy, must be protected *as if* she were pregnant. Third-party efforts to control the *fetus* have now been extended to control of the *egg.* Fertility becomes the equivalent of pregnancy, and a woman's consequent "perpetual pregnancy" becomes the basis of gender discrimination. A woman's autonomy is violated when third parties usurp her reproductive decisions, and a woman's privacy is violated when her acceptance of a job becomes an announcement that she is sterile.

On the other hand, intervention is justified on humanitarian and economic grounds. A fertile woman is subject to unplanned pregnancy, and without this humanitarian intervention the fetus will be damaged. The employer has a duty not to endanger developing human life. And economically it is unreasonable to demand that the employer make the workplace safe enough for zygotes and embryos, or to pay liability costs if these are damaged. So dignity and utility both argue for intervention that excludes fertile women from these hazardous jobs.

Here, then, is the question: ***Does respect for women's dignity demand a workplace safe enough for zygotes?***

YES:

To sharpen the ethical issue, let's assume certain facts. First, assume that the workplace would threaten significant danger to a fetus. This burden of proof must be met, otherwise discriminatory exclusion of fertile women would be unjust. And assume that all attempted nondiscriminatory solutions have been unsuccessful: for example, that engineering controls cannot be made adequate, that pro-

---

5. George Annas, "Pregnant Women as Fetal Containers," *Hastings Center Report* (December 1986), 13-14.

tective equipment will not sufficiently abate the threat, and that nondiscriminatory work arrangements, like work rotation to shorten exposure time, are not feasible. Assume that fertile women have been warned not to get pregnant if they wanted to keep the job, and that such warnings have not worked. [Clearly, a non-discriminatory solution would be ethically superior to a policy of discrimination.] Finally, assume that exposure to the hazardous workplace does not also affect the reproductive health of males by injuring sperm [the exclusion of women but not men for the same hazard would be clearly unjust]. In summary, when the exclusion of fertile women from the workplace is a policy of last resort, is it ethically justifiable?

The ethical argument in favor of discrimination rests on both deontological and utilitarian grounds: (1) the duty to protect maternal reproductive health and fetal health, and (2) the need to forestall lawsuits that could be ruinous in a litigious climate of "strict liability."

(1) The duty to protect maternal and fetal health.

It would be preferable that fertile women assume responsibility for their own reproductive health and workplace risks. But all women cannot or will not do this. Unplanned worker pregnancies and exposure of fetuses to unacceptable hazards are an unfortunate fact of life. Such

---

6.   Johnson Controls for many years issued warnings for women who planned to become pregnant that they transfer out of these high-risk jobs. But they discovered eight pregnant women in spite of this program. So the new policy directed at all fertile women was instituted out of fear of lawsuits from pregnant women or their offspring. This is not surprising. The National Center for Health Statistics has determined that more than 33% of pregnancies in working women are unplanned. [See Lisa J. Raines and Stephen P. Push, "Protecting Pregnant Workers," *Harvard Business Review* (May-June 1986), p. 29.]

exposure can occur even before the worker knows she is pregnant. In terms of hazardous exposure, the employer, then, must treat the fertile woman as if she were pregnant. Since she will not, and often cannot, protect herself, the employer cannot knowingly allow such harm to reproductive and fetal life. The imperative to intervene rests on this respect for human dignity.[7]

(2) The need to forestall ruinous lawsuits.

American business operates in a legal climate of "strict liability." [The "victim" need not show negligence on the part of the employer. She (or her defective offspring, should they choose to sue) need only show that she suffered harm.]

Employers could be liable, notwithstanding all their warnings and preventative measures. This puts the burden on the employer of forestalling any possibility of fetal harm, at penalty of lawsuits that could destroy the business. A utilitarian calculus could show that the benefit of protecting a business' very survival and well-being out-

---

7.   Does this conclusion imply that the employer also has a duty not to sell cigarettes to fertile women? No. Smoking is not a workplace-related behavior, and the duty to intervene has a different calculus of helps and harms. There needs to be a balancing of the burden that the intervention causes to the mother, over against the burden that nonintervention will impose on the fetus. It may be clear that a heavily smoking mother is hurting her fetus. But to forcibly confine her during her pregnancy so that she can be effectively restrained from smoking is to lay a burden on a mother far out of proportion to the harm she is causing. Indeed, even after they are born, children are harmed by parents who smoke. [Imprisoning the smoking parents would protect children from the smoking. But the intervention would not be proportional.] Neither would it be for pregnant smokers. Intervention in some cases of abuse does not imply that there will be intervention in all cases of abuse, as opponents of intervention argue. There must be a balancing of burdens, of helps and harms.

weighs the cost of fertile women losing their right to perform hazardous work, with its often higher pay.

NO:

As mentioned already, if any of the above-mentioned factual assumptions (that protective gear is insufficient, that
warnings about pregnancy hazards are insufficient, etc.) is
refuted, then the case for discrimination fails, or is weak-
ened. Most humiliating to women is their public categori-
zation into fertile and infertile, and the equation of
"fertile" with "pregnant" for purposes of the job[8] But
even granting the above-mentioned factual assumptions,
excluding fertile women from the hazardous workplace is
unethical: (1) it is contrary to human dignity to oppose
the interests of the fetus to those of the mother, and (2)
the utilitarian costs of excluding all fertile women far outweigh the benefit of protecting business from liability
claims. It is hard to refute the idea that some fertile
women under certain conditions may rightly be excluded
from certain jobs.

*(1) It is wrong to set the fetus's interests in opposition to the
mother's.*

The whole line of thinking in fetal protection policy is
misguided. A fetus during pregnancy, wanted or unwanted, is not to be viewed as a patient, separable from
the mother and whose interests are in competition with
those of the mother. The pregnant worker is one single

---

8.   American Cyanamid, in 1978, the first company to institute a fetal
protection policy, defined as "fertile" any woman age 16 to 50 who has
not been surgically sterilized. But since among women aged 45-50, only
one in 5000 gives birth in a year, there seems little or no justification
for excluding women over the age of 45, even assuming that such
protectionist policies are desirable or required.

symbiotic biological unit. And this biological unit happens to be a person, not a "maternal environment" which contains a baby. It destroys the reality of the person to set her at odds with herself, to divide her into container and contained. The employer must respect his unitary worker, woman-cum-developing fetus, or woman-cum-fertilizable egg. If something is awry with the fetus or ovum, this whole person suffers, and this whole woman must be treated and have her interests served. If something is awry with the worker, this whole woman-cum-ovum/fetus must be treated and have her interests served.

Corporate health directors need to focus on the fertile/pregnant workers, rather than narrowly on the prevention of fetal injury at the expense of equal employment opportunity for the mother. Protect the fetus by protecting the fertile woman: bring to bear engineering controls, warnings, protective equipment, family planning. Deal with her compelling career and economic reasons for wanting to keep the job. Approach this unitary worker in a holistic way. By meeting her medical, economic and social needs, you will best serve the fetus whose interest is bound up with her, just as her interest is bound up with it.

(2) The costs of excluding women outweigh benefits of avoiding liability.

No workplace can be 100% safe, and no policy is lawsuit proof. But even in "strict liability" cases, courts weigh the likelihood of injury and the magnitude of possible harm over against the cost of preventing it. If an exclusionary fetal protection policy is applied only as a genuine last resort, after all non-exclusionary measures have been taken, and applied only to appropriate women, and if care is taken to maintain transferred workers' pay rates, seniority, and benefits, the likelihood of lawsuits is reduced greatly, and the likelihood of unfavorable judgments reduced even more.[9] This is an argument against the unqualified exclusion of all fertile women from hazardous jobs.

May some fertile women under limited conditions rightly be excluded? It's hard to argue that an employer must cooperate in exposing an employee to a likely harm, and then be required under strict liability to remedy that harm that the employer was not allowed to prevent. The law may require this. But it's hard for me to see where ethical justice requires employers to allow workers to recklessly expose themselves to harm that employers will have to remedy.

But such cases should be rare. The harm to business of some liability damage from not enforcing a blanket fetal hazard exclusion policy is outweighed by the far greater harm that would come to women from a heavy-handed application of exclusionary policies. The net effect would be a gender-based resegregation of the workplace, a reversal of Title VII, and a voiding of the Pregnancy Discrimination Act. Hazards are in workplaces everywhere. What level of protection is enough? Such policies could put whole classes of jobs off-limits to every nonsterile woman, irrespective of her age or of her childbearing plans. This wholesale harm to women far outweighs the liability risks that a socially responsible company might face. Unqualified exclusionary fetal protection fails the utilitarian ethical test.

---

9.   DuPont's fetal protection policy, for example, has resulted in the transfer of hundreds of women, and not one of the women has sued. The policy has been applied judiciously and with all the aforementioned safeguards. See Raines, *ibid.*

PO:

Arguments like these are more about the status of women than the status of the fetus. Feminists, including those who are very sensitized about ethical duties toward fetal life, view such duties in a framework of respect for women's dignity and autonomy. Harm to the fetus is first and foremost an injury to the mother. Protection of the fetus means first and foremost the care and protection of the woman. Such feminists recognize their duty toward all life, the life of their fetus, of their family, of their pets, their plants, indeed their duty to their own life. When conflicts arise, as they do for every human being, the autonomy of the pregnant woman in resolving these conflicts must be respected no less than we respect the autonomy of nonpregnant human beings in the face of conflict.

ETHICS EXPERIMENT:

How much responsibility do you take for your own reproductive health? Reflect on the legal substances you ingest: caffeine, nicotine, prescription drugs, alcohol. Illegal substances. Not to get paranoid, but electronic equipment, power lines and the air you breathe are part of your reproductive system. Do you engage in reproductive activities with a significant (or insignificant) other? What is their philosophy of protecting reproductive health?

13 Right-Wing Women[1]: The Enemy Is Us?

This [is] the kind of harm that right-wing women cause. . . . The harm is integrally related to sex roles. Sexist attitudes reflected in sexist behavior express and perpetuate the stereotype that women are fit to occupy only certain roles because of their sex. . . . They include being sex objects, mothers, nurturers, sympathizers, etc. . . . It denies women's autonomy as they cannot do what they . . . would prefer were it not for patriarchy's powerful influence on their beliefs, desires, and values.   **"Right-Wing Women"**[2]

Feminists repeatedly have adopted the strategy of pretending that differences among women do not exist. But of course, denying differences does not abolish them; it simply allows traditional forms of domination to continue unacknowledged. Moreover, avoiding differences prevents women from mining the knowledge and power that are rooted in our racial, ethnic, and religious particularity and from "using difference as a springboard for creative change."[3]

Judith Plaskow[4]

---

1.   See Andrea Dworkin, *Right-Wing Women* (Coward-McCann, 1983).

2.   Anita M. Superson, "Right-Wing Women: Causes, Choices, and Blaming the Victim,' in *"Nagging" Questions: Feminist Ethics in Everyday Life* (Roman and Littlefield Publishers, Inc., 1995), Dana E. Bushnell (ed.), p. 78.

3.   Audre Lorde, *Sister Outsider* (Trumansburg, NY: The Crossing Press, 1984), p. 115.

> *Sisterhood is powerful; . . . so is conservatism, which,*
> *with some unintended help from the sillier reaches of*
> *academe, has half-succeeded in turning "feminism"*
> *into a much mocked anachronism, a mood ring left*
> *over from the bell-bottom epoch.*   Dorothy Wickenden

INTRODUCTION:

Popular literature has a lot to say about women's and
men's different voices. But here we look at the ethical implications for feminism of the different voices among
women themselves. Are the voices and sentiments of the
slave woman, the slave master's wife, the fast-track corporate go-getter, the pro-life advocate, the pro-choice an-
tipornographer, and the happy hooker all to be weighed
and valorized on the same scale of "universal women's experience"?

The short answer is, "Yes, but no." "Women's experience" is the inspiration and foundational core concept of
feminism. Women's experience is a way to challenge "the
objective order of things." Feminists see the so-called "objective order" as not objective at all. Rather it enshrines
the systematic oppression of women. Feminism wants no
part of such rationality. So women's experience becomes a
counterpoint and critique of oppressive rationality.

But women's experience is also an embarrassment to
feminism. What about those women who say to feminists,
"My experience is not like that"? These are those women
who oppose abortion on demand, who see traditional mar-

---

4.   Judith Plaskow, "Transforming the Nature of Community: Toward a
Feminist People of Israel" in *After Patriarchy: Feminist Transformations of
the World Religions*, edited by Paula M. Cooey, William R. Eakin, Jay B.
McDaniel (Orbis Books, 1991), p. 95.

5.   Dorothy Wickenden, executive editor of *New Yorker* magazine,
introducing the 1995 special issue on women.

riage as a benefit, who want to be exempt from the military, who enjoy fashions and cosmetics and the flirting game, who see women as perfectly able to compete on equal terms with men in the workplace, who love to display and even flaunt their sexual attractiveness, and who cheerfully live in a society where women earn more associate, bachelor's and master's degrees than men,[6] and where women outlive men by several years. These are the "right-wing women," excommunicated by feminists from the sisterhood.

The feminist reply goes as follows: it is impossible for such women to be feminists[7] (even if they claim to be). They are "male-identified." They suffer from "false consciousness."

Says who?

Are right-wing women the deluded dupes of patriarchy? Are they unwitting participants in an unethical war against women? Let's state the question in terms of its philosophical underpinning: *Is women's experience an adequate foundation for a feminist defense of women's equal rights?*

---

6. See economist Diana Furchtgott-Roth and historian Christine Stolba, *Women's Figures: The Economic Progress of Women in America* (Independent Women's Forum and American Enterprise Institute, 1997). This comprehensive analysis of the economic status of women, unlike other reports, takes into account life choices made by women, marketforces, employment experience, continuity of workforce participation, and education. See also, Louis Menard (Graduate English Teacher at CUNY), "Everybody Else's College Education," *New York Times Magazine* (April 20, 1997), 48. While college enrollment between 1984 and 1994 has increased by two million, enrollment of white men has declined by 16%, while 71% of the increase is among African-Americans, Asian-Americans, Native Americans, Hispanic-Americans, and the rest among nonresident aliens and white women.

7. Anita M. Superson, "Right Wing Women: Causes, Choices, and Blaming the Victim," *"Nagging" Questions: Feminist Ethics in Everyday Life*, edited by Dana E. Bushnell (Roman and Littlefield Publishers, Inc., 1995), p. 89.

YES:

It is hard to imagine more than three decades after Title VII of the *Civil Rights Act* what the situation of women was before the rise of the Women's Movement. Unjust discrimination was pervasive and taken for granted as the normal state of things. Women's work was confined to the home, or to "pink collar" ghettos, or to low-paying service jobs and piecework manufacturing. Sexual harassment was accepted as normal male behavior, date rape had no name, and marital rape was an unthinkable contradiction. Where women did perform the same work as men, the pay was not the same. The man, assumed to be the breadwinner, earned a "living wage," while the woman, assumed to be earning "pin money," was paid less. Athletics were approached in a genteel fashion as befitted the "weaker sex." The rules of women's basketball, for example, forbade women from running the full length of the court. Women were allowed on golf courses only during off-hours not reserved for men. "Women's nature" made it seem obvious that they could not do construction work, or engage the enemy in the military. And on and on.

All this was "obvious," "women's role," "natural," "normal," suitable for the "weaker sex," the taken-for-granted "order of things," rational, "objectively right and true." The challenge of what was then called the Women's Liberation Movement was to show how what was perfectly logical was also perfectly untrue. These socially constructed "realities" had to be deconstructed to open the way for the alternative reality of women's equal place in the scheme of things. Three core concepts emerged as instruments of women's liberation, and the basis of what came to be known as Feminist Theory.[8]

---

8.   See Judith Grant, *Fundamental Feminism: Contesting the Core Concepts*

The first is the concept of "Woman," and unjust discrimination against women, precisely because they are women. Yes, women and men are discriminated against because of their race or because they are poor. But feminism, for the first time, directed a sharp clear beam of recognition at discrimination against women *precisely as women*. And if you don't see this, you don't "get it." No matter how content you may be as a woman, and no matter how normal and natural you may consider women's situations as a man, if you don't see that women, because they are women, are oppressed in this society, then you have a problem.

And women everywhere did "get it." The light of recognition "clicked" on as words were given to discontent that had been inarticulate. No matter how normal and natural and rational women's place might seem to have been, there was something very, very wrong. "Women's Experience," the second core concept of Feminist Theory, was the proof of the pudding. Women's Experience was the weapon that blew out of the water the comfortable "objective rationality" that legitimated the oppression of women. For example, no matter how many philosophical, theological or psychosocial arguments are mustered to "prove" that women cannot be ordained priests, women's experience says wrong, wrong, wrong! Women's experience gives the lie to the logic.

And these experiences are not just women's private hang-ups. "The personal is the political" became the third core concept of feminism. Traditionally, the public sphere belonged to the man. The private was the realm of the woman. Public issues were played out in the political sphere. Private issues remained personal, to be worked

---

of Feminist Theory (Routledge, 1993), especially chapter 2.

out personally (Feminism politicized women's personal discontents.] "The personal is the political" recognized that women's oppression was a wrong to be dealt with publicly, institutionally, in the political process. Feminist theory and women's studies were not to be insular academic enterprises. Their thrust is political, their validity tested in consciousness raised,[9] and in institutions reformed.

And as is the way of politics, feminists played hardball. Oppression, thy name is woman. You are either with me or against me in this insight. No facet of women's experience could hide from the feminist light revealing the oppression of women. Marriage is legalized rape. Pregnancy is shameful. Hear Anrea Dworkin:

> *Pregnancy is confirmation that the woman has been f**ked [obscenity]: it is confirmation that she is a c**t [obscenity] . . . . The display marks her as a whore. . . . Her belly is proof that she has been used. Her belly is his phallic triumph. . . . The pregnancy is punishment for her participation in sex. She will get sick, her body will go wrong in a thousand different ways, she will die. The sexual excitement is in her possible death.*[10]

The social oppression of women is so utterly pervasive that women are incapable of free consent. Obviously, women do "freely" play the dating game, get married, wear sexy clothes, and sometimes appear in and enjoy pornography. But such consent, though apparently free, is really coerced, since the present oppressive construction

---

9. Consciousness-raising is a political act. See Patricia Ireland, *What Women Want* (Dutton, 1996), p. 75: "Consciousness is a funny thing: once you become conscious you can't just regress. In fact the opposite happens . . . and consciousness is the predecessor of transformation."

10. Andrea Dworkin, *Pornography* (Penguin: Plume Book, 1989), pp. 222-223.

of society closes off alternatives. Consider, for example,
one version of an antipornography law drafted by Andrea
Dworkin and Catharine MacKinnon, making it a civil offense to coerce, intimidate or fraudulently induce anyone
into performing for pornography. According to this law,
none of the following can count as proof that she consented:

> *that she is a woman;*
> *that she is or has been a prostitute;*
> *that she has attained the age of maturity;*
> *that she is connected in any way to anyone making the*
> *pornography;*
> *that she had previously posed for sexually explicit pic-*
> *tures;*
> *that someone else (even a spouse) has given permission*
> *on the person's behalf;*
> *that the person actually consented to the act;*
> *that the person knew the purpose of the act was to make*
> *pornography;*
> *that the person showed no resistance;*
> *that the person signed a contract or stated their willing-*
> *ness to participate;*
> *that no physical force, threats, or weapons were used;*
> *that the person was paid.*[11]

In this view, society's oppressive structures have so far in-
fantilized women that what they experience to be consent
is not consent at all, but false consciousness trapped in
the prevailing patriarchal rationality.[12]

---

11. Mary Kay Blakely's "Is One Women's Sexuality Another Woman's
Pornography? The Question behind a Major Legal Battle," *Ms.* (April
1985): 35-37, and especially 46-47.

12. Since economic discrimination indentures women to men,
heterosexual relationships are always among unequals. So consensual
heterosex is impossible. At best it is like statutory rape. What begins as a
taboo against sexual harassment, for radical feminists, becomes a taboo

If the experience of women is foundational to feminism, do feminists rightly discount the experience of women who inconveniently seem to consent to be involved with pornography? *Is women's experience an adequate foundation for a feminist defense of women's equal rights?*

NO:

The battle for women's liberation is far from won. But a backlash has set in, not all of it sparked by sexism or by excesses of radical feminism. More and more feminists are providing thoughtful critiques of feminism's core concepts. We turn now to this reassessment of feminist theory.[13]

The Concept of Women: The first core concept is that of essential womanhood. Women are oppressed precisely as women. How well does this insight stand up? Why are many women liberationists today reluctant to identify themselves as feminists? An answer lies in the title of Elizabeth Fox-Genovese's latest book: *Feminism is*

---

against heterosexual relations, period. For an interesting reversal following this line of argument, see the case feminist Jane Gallop recounted in her book, *Feminist Accused of Sexual Harassment* (Duke University Press, paperbound edition 1997). She had engaged in an easy, friendly, occasionally flirtatious bantering with two of her male students. When they became disgruntled because of their grades, even though there was no question of an "affair," they sued her for sexual harassment. Because of socially superior position, what all parties had perceived as consensual became "coerced," as feminist logic contends. The criminalization of abuse now becomes the criminalization of heterosexuality.

13. See, for example, Christina Hoff Sommers, *Who Stole Feminism?: How Women Have Betrayed Women* (Simon and Schuster, 1994), and Elizabeth Fox-Genovese, *Feminism Without Illusions* (University of North Carolina Press, 1991), in addition to other citations in this chapter.

Not the Story of My Life.[14] [Many women do not understand "woman" to be their essential identity] Concerns
addressed to them precisely as women are not upper-
most in their consciousness. Some women feel just as
vulnerable or more vulnerable in other parts of their
identity – race, ethnicity, religion, class, sexual preference. The secure and confident "women's voice" of a
white middle class heterosexual WASP professor may
find little resonance with the voice of a poor Jewish
Ethiopian-American lesbian, who has very different self-
identity and vulnerabilities. An essential "women's
voice" is a privilege for those who are not vulnerable in
other ways. For many women, identity is much more
complex. Essential womanhood is a pale abstraction
next to the rich tapestry of real women's identities.[15]

Not all women have the values and priorities of the
theorizers, the insiders of feminism. These other women
were outside the loop when the theory was being invented. The insiders observed themselves and other
women, and there has been a tendency to try to remake
the outsiders in the image of the insiders. The outsiders

---

14. *Feminism is Not the Story of My Life: how today's feminist elite have lost
touch with the concerns of women* (New York: Nan A. Talese, 1996).

15. See the lucid analysis of Elisabeth Young-Bruehl in *The Anatomy of
Prejudices* (Harvard University Press, 1996), pp. 528-529:
*In the past decade, since about 1985, the stasis in American feminist theory, the
pendulum swing between the sameness and the difference theories, has been
challenged by women with "outsider" and critical relations to feminism. Not
surprisingly, women with multiple and complex identities, from whom an
identity can be only approximately mapped out, have articulated an
appropriately complex theoretical stance, off the pendulum course. These women
organize their thought in terms of concerns that surround or cut across the
division between masculine and feminine, the division central to both the sexisms
and the feminisms that are bound up with sexisms. They reject the category,
"Woman," appealing for their rejection either to philosophical attacks on
essentialism and ethnocentrism or to the dilemmas of practical feminist politics,
or both.* Young-Bruehl is the author also of *Anna Freud: A Biography* and
Hannah Arendt: For Love of the World.

quite naturally say, "Wait a minute, that's not me." If the outsider would like to spend more time at home, is ardently pro-life,[16] and finds fulfillment in a religion which has patriarchal origins, who is the insider to say that she is wrong? Feminism is becoming more sensitized to the special problems and priorities of their Third World sisters, and more conscious of the danger of cultural imperialism.

Women's Experience: Feminism is less concerned about cultural imperialism against their neighbor who may live next door, those benighted "right-wing women," likely to be treated at best with condescension, and at worst with arrogance and disrespect. Contrary to the second core concept of feminism, viz. women's experience, the experience of these outsider women is devalued and trivialized.

All women need to become the insiders in reconstructing a theory whose foundation is "women's experience." Unfortunately, as Wendy Kaminer[17] has pointed out, we live in a talk show culture, where one's "liberalism" or "conservatism" has to be ideologically pure. Inviting all women to the theorist table will dilute this purity. But it won't dilute the thoughtfulness of the resultant theory. A theory based on the experience of the privileged few, who use their experience to excommunicate the majority of women they pretend to serve, reduces feminism to a cult. In attempting to marginalize the experience of

---

16. "Without allowing Right-to-Life women to speak the truth as they understand it, without engaging them from a stance that respects their humanity, the possibility for the creation of meaning through uncoerced dialogue . . . we will continue to treat them in distorted, presumptuous and prejudicial ways . . ." See Jean Bethke Elshtain, *Public Man, Private Woman* (Princeton NJ: Princeton University Press, 1981), p. 312.

17. Wendy Kaminer, *True Love Waits: Essays and Criticism* (Addison-Wesley, 1996), pp. 2, 3.

outsider women, they make feminism itself alien to the political process. In contradiction to the third core concept of feminism, "the personal is the political," rather ironically they declare the experience of outsider women to be politically incorrect.

Feminism Reconstructed: We conclude this section with two programmatic statements. If you substitute Womanism for Feminism, says bell hooks, this:

> *radically calls into question the notion of a fundamentally common female experience which has been seen as a prerequisite for our coming together, for political unity. Recognition of the inter-connectedness of sex, race, and class highlights the diversity of experience, compelling redefinition of the terms for unity. If women do not share "common oppression," then what can serve as the basis for our coming together? Unlike many feminist comrades, I believe that women and men must share a common understanding – a basic knowledge of what feminist is – if it is ever to be a powerful mass-based political movement.*[18]

Elizabeth Young-Bruehl states what could be a blueprint for the reconstruction of feminist theory:

> *Beginning from the realization that not all women's experiences, including their experiences of sexism or the types of sexism that they experience, are alike, these [outsider feminist] theorists have sought a new common ground: not the "we are all alike" common ground of sexuality, not the "all women are different from all men" common ground of gender identity, but the multiethnic, multiracial, class-diversified, sexually panoramic, kaleidoscopic terrain of "all women have some experience of sexism, in one or more of its forms and*

---

18. See bell hooks, *Talking Back: Thinking Feminist, Thinking Black* (South End Press, 1989), 22-23.

> *interlocking discourses, but their positions and experi-*
> *ences as often divide them as unite them." And this is,*
> *finally, a framework not determined by male narcissism*
> *and not determined by reactive female (mother-daughter)*
> *narcissism.*[19]

So, by truly listening with respect to all women and to feminist men as well, the women's movement can overcome the stasis of the sameness/difference pendulum in order to arrive at a new synthesis.

PO:

The 90s have seen the birth of Third Wave feminism, cheerfully un-PC, welcoming of all women and lifestyles, with little sense of victimization or grim humorlessness, delighting in romance and femininity, professionally self-confident. Based on the needs of Generation X, this is a varied collection of women, self-described as chicks, gals, babes, girls, grrrls and women. They are an increasing presence on the Web. "Leslie's World O'Chicks" (http://www.fearless.net/woc) give a taste of this movement, wildly diverse, funny, very smart, rude, effortlessly assertive, lightly serious. Check out the grrlzines and newsletters, *Grrowl, The Cyber Mom, the NERVE, Foxy, geekgirl, Stay Free, Women Motorist.*

As feminism broadens its scope to respect the diversity of women, should its women's world widen even further to include the world of men? What hope is there for political revolution if men cannot be assimilated into the theory and methodology that is guiding the revolution? Men who are demonized will act like demons.

Some women have found in The Craft an anarchical identity against established oppression:

---

19. Young-Bruehl, *op.cit.*, p. 529.

WITCH is an all-women Everything. It's theater, revolution, magic, terror, joy, garlic-flowers, spells. . . . Witches have always been women who dared to be: groovy, courageous, aggressive, intelligent, non-conformist, explorative, curious, independent, sexually liberated, revolutionary. . . You are a Witch by saying aloud, "I am a Witch" three times, and thinking about that. You are a Witch by being female, untamed, angry, joyous and immortal.[20]

Is it anti-feminist to have cosmetic surgery? Listen to women's diverse voices:[21]

[status]: "There will be a lot of new faces at the Ball."

[control] "You can keep yourself trim without surgery, but not unwrinkled."

[domination]: "I want a nose that makes a statement."

[gift to self]: "I decided to get a face lift for my 40th birthday."

[economics]: "I can use my breast augmentation as a tax write-off."

[against ageism]: "A teacher who looks like an old bat will get a nickname."

[competitive advantage] Miss America 1986: "I'll admit to a boob job."

---

20. From "New York Coven Statement" in Robin Morgan (ed.), *Sisterhood is Powerful* (Vintage Books, 1970).

21. Based on Kathryn Pauly Morgan, "Women and the Knife: Cosmetic Surgery and the Colonization of Women's Bodies" in Dana E. Bushnell (ed.), *"Nagging" Questions: Feminist Ethics in Everyday Life* (Roman and Littlefield, 1995), p. 312.

ETHICAL EXPERIMENT:

Conduct a cross-generational investigation into the meaning of feminism.[22] Daughters and sons, interview your mothers and grandmothers. Mothers, interview your daughters and mothers, etc. Men, do not exclude yourself from this conversation. Betty Friedan, back at the founding of the official Women's Movement, fought hard to see that NOW would be called the National Organization *for* Women, not *of* Women. The original impetus was all-inclusive. Here are some questions to get this conversation going:

> Are you a feminist? Why? When and why did you decide this? Was there a defining incident or event that affected this decision?
>
> What meaning does feminism have for you?
>
> What values do you consider central to feminism: economic parity? political power? lifestyle choices? abortion rights? child care? equal education? equal career opportunity? having it all? violence against women? sexual freedom? fighting pornography? other?
>
> How do you prioritize feminist values and why?
>
> Can a Republican also be a feminist? Is it a betrayal of feminism to be "pro-life"? Can a man be a feminist?
>
> How do your views of feminism differ from your mother's, your grandmother's, your daughter's, your granddaughter's, from your son's, husband's, father's?

---

22. See the rich insight that can flow from such conversations in Christina Looper Baker and Christina Baker Kline, *The Conversation Begins: Mothers and Daughters Talk About Living Feminism* (Bantam, Doubleday, Dell, 1997). Here 23 prominent feminists describe their experience and life as feminists, together with 23 replies from their daughters, recounting their take on feminist life.

This chapter has discussed one example of identity ethics. Identity ethics can easily move over into exclusionary ethics, as we have seen. Laura Miller puts it well:

> *The worst practice feminism inherited from traditional femininity is the habit of touting an ideal model of womanhood, then ostracizing anyone who deviates from it. Branding a former "sister" as "unfeminist" because she questions doctrine on issues like sexuality, sex roles, or pornography uncomfortably resembles the custom of freezing a disreputable woman out of respectable society.*[23]

Were your intergenerational conversations exclusionary? Or did you find that the generations were able to listen and learn and respect one another?

---

23. Laura Miller, senior editor at the Internet magazine Salon, "Oppressed by Liberation: Feminists, a feminist says, should stop telling feminists how to be feminists," *The New York Times Book Review* (May 11, 1997), p. 11. Miller notes that this sin is a failing of a small number of radicalized Women's Studies professors, and does not represent the view of the vast majority of feminists or women in general.

14   Abortion's Middle Ground: Sell-Out or Compromise?

Unlike the feminist establishment, I recognize that abortion is killing . . . Squeamishly sensitive about their humanitarian self-image, feminists have used convoluted casuistry to define the aborted fetus in purely material terms as inert tissue, efficiently flushed. . . . I am fervently pro-abortion – the term "pro-choice" is a cowardly euphemism.[1]

The Buddhist posture permits – and even encourages – language about the fetus as human life in some sense, but refuses to draw the conclusion that, therefore, abortion is disallowed. It avoids the dualizing dilemma often found in American abortion polemics: namely, that of feeling compelled either to think of the fetus as a life equivalent to that of a fully formed young child, or, alternatively, as so much inert matter or tissue.[2]

The presumption that every fetus should become a human being is glaringly anthropocentric. It ignores the increasing demands made upon the environment by each addition to the developed world. As John Cobb remarks, "It may be . . . that the pro-[fetal] life move-

---

1.   Camille Paglia, *Vamps and Tramps* (Random House Vintage Books, 1994), pp. 40, 38.
2.   William LaFleur, *Liquid Life: Abortion and Buddhism in Japan* (Princeton University Press, 1992), p. 196.

> *ment has been insensitive to the needs of all forms of life except the human."[3]*

The uncompromising passion and extremism that characterizes the abortion debate sets it apart from most other moral issues. Any middle ground is viewed as a betrayal and a sell-out to the other side. [The silent majority who privately hold some middle position are intimidated into standing quietly on the sidelines.] Their voices are never heard.

We consider now not the ethics of abortion, but the ethics of moral absolutism. What is to be said in favor of the moral purity exhibited by the Absolute Pro-Lifers (ALs) and their counterparts, the Absolute Pro-Choicers (ACs)? What is to be said of efforts to discern a middle ground? Does moral compromise imply moral inferiority? Which is the more responsible stance?

Whence our question: *Is it the case that in the matter of abortion rights there can be no middle ground – that any so-called compromise is failure of moral will, a sell-out?*

YES:

Absolutists brook no compromise.

ACs view pregnant women's autonomy in all matters affecting her body, her health, her emotional and economic well-being, and her career and lifestyle as a defining and overriding value. Women's autonomy is a nonnegotiable. Every attempt to nibble away at this autonomy must be fought uncompromisingly, and rejected. This absolutism extends even to the right to choose a partial-birth abortion, though her life is not at stake. If a woman chooses three-quarters of the way down the birth channel

3.   Carol J. Adams, *Neither Man nor Beast: Feminism and the Defense of Animals* (Continuum Publishing Company, 1994), p. 64.

to have the brain sucked out of her infant's head, the right to make that choice must be defended. The pregnant woman's conscientious autonomy is inviolable.

ALs are no less uncompromising. Life from the first moment of conception is sacred and untouchable. The zygote is a unique genetic package, enjoying a specific human identity distinct from either parent's. If the development of this human organism is not interrupted, a human infant will be brought to birth. To kill this entity at any stage of its development is therefore to kill a human being. Morally, it matters not if it is the product of rape or incest. The developing human being that was created is innocent of any crime and does not deserve to be killed. Innocent human life must be protected at all costs. Only the risk of the pregnant woman's life, which is an equally innocent life, could weigh against the human fetus' right to life, which is otherwise inviolable.

Absolutism has several psychological and political payoffs. The first is certitude, the sense of "I'm right and you're wrong." It is the security that comes with absence of doubt that I am in possession of the truth. "How dare anyone try to take away from a woman the right to make decisions about her own well-being?", the ACs righteously ask. How dare society attempt to interfere with her bodily integrity, with her exercise of her own conscience? And ALs counter with equal self-righteous certitude and lack of self-doubt, "How dare you kill an innocent human being, an unborn child who has done no wrong?"

A second payoff is the moral superiority that comes with demonizing the opposition. To venture a doubt, a possible moral limitation, or any qualification of a pregnant's woman's absolute autonomy, according to AC's, puts you in the misogynist camp with abusers of women, domineering patriarchs, and contempt for freedom and choice. Such execrable people will not rest satisfied until they have murdered every abortionist, and jailed every woman who has an abortion. And any Pro-Life lunatic who murders a doctor is living proof of what every Pro-Lifer would like to do if they had the nerve and the opportunity.

And those who defend the right to terminate a pregnancy are killers of unborn human life, and since this unborn life is innocent, they are in the camp of murderers who take innocent life. In this way do AL's demonize those who would compromise or limit in any way or for any reason (other than the mother's life) the right of a zygote or fetus to develop to full term. In fact, choice advocates are worse than murderers. By leaving a whole class of innocent humans unprotected, they are purveyors of genocide, perpetrators of a holocaust.

A third payoff of Absolutism is its political effectiveness. Who wants to be an enemy of freedom, a hater of women, a murderer of doctors? So if you have doubts about the ease, prevalence, or casualness of abortion, keep them to yourself. Or, conversely, who wants to be a murderer of human beings, a proponent of genocide, one who holds in contempt God and God's gift of life? So if you feel that at times a woman's health or emotional or economic needs might rightly be weighed against the claim of the zygote or fetus that is part of this very same woman's body, keep these feelings quiet. Absolutists effectively intimidate those who would seek a middle ground. These latter remove themselves from the debate and stay meekly on the sidelines, while the extremists rage on.

Most important is a final payoff, a sense of moral purity. ALs and ACs are each committed to the defense of a crucial central human value. Life, human life, developing human life is precious, is essential to the survival of the species, represents our most basic instinct and is basic to every other right. If I can devote my own life to the uncompromising defense of life, then I have nothing to be ashamed of. ALs can justifiably take heart that there is no cause more noble than this.

Freedom, autonomy, the right to decide one's own meaning and path are also precious human values. Indeed there is a sense in which freedom is more precious than life itself. "Live free or die," the motto says. If I can devote my life to the uncompromising defense of freedom of conscience, I can look in the mirror and be proud of this commitment. ACs are devoted to a cause as noble, if not more noble, than life itself.

NO:

Absolutism has the appearance of moral purity but at its heart it is irresponsible. Certitude comes at a high price. Absolutists must deliberately blind themselves to important moral values that scream for attention and response. ALs must make themselves deaf to women's cries for autonomy and self-determination. Successfully deafened, they can then smugly indulge their protestations for fetal life. ACs must blind themselves to the living target of their choice to kill. Self-blinded to the value of developing life, they can engage in unfettered moral rhetoric about choice and women's bodies. AL rests on the lie that women's autonomy is trivial or not an issue. AC rests on the lie that fetal life is nothing but an unwanted bodily product like a wart or a tumor. Both are examples not of moral purity but of moral failure.

Absolutists maintain the lie by demonizing the opposition. As in war, when enemies are defined as less than human, it is easier to kill them. So when a lunatic shoots people at an abortion clinic, this is a godsend for AC. It is "proof" that those who care for fetal life are nothing but killers and misogynists. And this "proof" is rendered plausible in that AL polemics are silent about women's choice and women's autonomy. And when AC rhetoric defends any abortion for any reason at any time, right up to partial birth – never admitting to an abortion they didn't like – they are stereotyped as "mass murderers." In their own hearts, ACs are defending conscientious choice, but their silence about the value of the life this choice destroys lends credence to this "proof" of their supposed contempt for life.

So the big weapons are firing. The war goes on. Each side, secure in its self-limited and self-righteous vision, has contempt for the other. There is no dialogue, no conversation, no listening to the enemy. That would be dangerous. I would not be able to cling to the lie on which my certitude and confidence depends. And people who care for the value of life that AC won't permit itself to look at, and those same people who also care for the value of choice that AL won't consider – these people who would seek a middle way, are driven to the sidelines. This is the saddest and most unethical result of moral absolutism. The tactics of intimidation bring an end to dialogue. People of good will are divided from each other and silenced. Absolutism destroys love, destroys compassion, destroys community. That is its biggest sin.

PO:

Consider a suggestion and a moral principle to start the journey toward a middle ground. First a bias check: assume right off that you are biased toward one pole of this debate, be it "choice" or "life," and at least somewhat blind to the other pole. We are in many ways the product of our origins. Kristin Luker has discovered the following AC and AL profiles:

> *The average pro-choice activist is a 44-year-old married woman who grew up in a large metropolitan area and whose father was a college graduate. She was married at age 22, has one or two children and has had some graduate or professional training beyond the B.A. degree. She is married to a professional man, is herself employed in a regular job, and her family income is more than $50,000 [1982 dollars] a year. She is not religiously active, feels that religion is not important to her, and attends church very rarely, if at all.*
>
> *The average pro-life woman is also a 44-year-old married woman who grew up in a large metropolitan area. She married at the age of 17 and has three children or more. Her father was a high school graduate, and she has some college education and may have a B.A. degree. She is not employed in the paid labor force and is married to a small businessman or a lower-level white-collar worker; her family income is $30,000 a year. She is Catholic (and may have converted), and her religion is one of the most important aspects of her life: she attends church at least once a week and occasionally more often.* [4]

Which value in this debate do I tend to minimize or ignore? I determine to give this my full and empathetic attention. My "opponent" is not my enemy, but a friend who speaks for a moral value that I find difficult to listen to and need to hear. Of course, the result is that my easy moral dogmatism is not so easy any more.

---

4. Kristin Luker, *Abortion and the Politics of Motherhood* (University of California Press, 1984), p. 197.

PO:

For *all* sides of this debate, abortion is a reluctant choice. In some cases the decision may be nonproblematic, which means that morality didn't enter the picture. But for most, the decision is emotionally, morally, and sometimes physically painful. The conflicted woman feels caught between two evils, an unwanted pregnancy and an abortion. Traditional morality teaches that when caught between two evils, the right thing is to choose the lesser evil, not the greater. Some view pregnancy as the lesser evil, and go through to term. Others conscientiously judge abortion to be the lesser evil and the responsible choice to make. For the latter the physical evil of ending a developing life is a moral good because in the view of their conscience the alternative was perceived to be far worse. Respect and support for the conscientious decisions of others does not mean that you would have acted the same, either in carrying an unwanted pregnancy to term, or in having an abortion. In other words you may think in either case that though she may have been subjectively right, she was objectively wrong in her decision. You can make judgements for yourself, without judgementalism toward others.

In Western countries, the ratio of male to female infants is roughly 1 to 1. In many Asian countries, the ratio ranges from 106-114 boys for every 100 girls. In populous countries, like India and China, this adds up to millions of "missing" girls. Increasingly, reproductive rights for Third World countries, for which feminists have lobbied so hard, is resulting in abortion for gender selection, specifically for selection of boys over girls. Has the right of a woman to "control her own body" become the right to commit genocide of women?[5]

PO:

Set up ground rules for "debate," in which differences are off-limits. Focus on the common ground. Baby's life or women's choice? – agree to disagree. It's almost never that stark and simple anyway. Ask instead, "How can we work together to bring about all the goals we share?" Preventing unwanted pregnancies, delaying the onset of sexual activity, supporting families, adoption, available day care – such values make up the common ground.[6]

ETHICS EXPERIMENT:

Interview someone whose moral view of abortion is as different as possible from your own. Do not let on your own view, but try to understand the other's view as best as you can. Keep restating that other person's position, asking if you have it right. Can you not only state the other's objective arguments, but also express an empathy and a feeling for the values that are so important to the other person? Can your appreciation for their view be such that the other person could honestly say, "Yes, you understand ex-

---

5. Judith Banister of the U.S. Census Bureau, using Chinese census figures, calculates 1.5 million female fetuses were selectively aborted between 1980-1990. And still female infanticide, abandonment and selective neglect continue unabated. Harvard University researchers Monica Das Gupta and Mari Bhat calculate nearly one million girls aborted in the late 1980s, plus four million who "disappeared" during their first 4-6 years of life. Again, selective abortion is complementing, not substituting for female infanticide. See "No Daughters Need Apply," *Washington Post National Weekly* (May 20-26, 1996).

6. A nonprofit organization based in Washington D.C., Search for Common Ground, was founded in 1982 to develop strategies and tactics for mediating intractable political disputes. This group has supported the formation of the Common Ground Network for Life and Choice to transcend what has become a theater of adversarial violence in abortion politics.

actly where I'm coming from, exactly what I mean"?
Thank them, and say goodbye. How does it feel?

BUSINESS

15 When Does an Economic Plus Become a Human Minus?

Call a thing immoral or ugly, soul-destroying or a degradation of man, a peril to the peace of the world or to the well-being of future generations; as long as you have not shown it to be "uneconomic," you have not questioned its right to exist, grow, and prosper.[1]

Discrimination pays, otherwise it wouldn't have flourished so long. You can bet people say, "We can get her for less than we can get him." You know it goes on.[2]

The fact of the matter is, many women do not wish to go into non-traditional, male-dominated occupations. It is not acceptable in this country to tell nurses and teachers that if they want to make more, they need to choose a different occupation.[3]

Everyone and everything has its price. God bless America. This is a land where economic values trump all other values. *Everything for Sale* suggests the title of economist Robert Kuttner's new book.[4] Two recent box

---

1.   E.F. Schumacher, *Small Is Beautiful: Economics As If People Mattered* (Harper and Row, 1973), pp. 39-40.

2.   Karen Nussbaum, "Education Doesn't Cut Pay Gap," *Mesa Tribune* (November 14, 1991), A1, A7.

3.   Carolin Head, assistant director of the American Association of University Women, *ibid.*

4.   Robert Kuttner, *Everything for Sale: the Virtues and Limits of Markets*

145

office successes underline the triumph of money over all. In 1993 Demi Moore played the wife of Woody Harrelson in *Indecent Proposal*, a "perfect date movie." Down on their luck, they go to Las Vegas to recoup their fortune. There they meet Robert Redford's character, a millionaire who makes them an "indecent proposal," one million dollars for Demi Moore if she will sleep with him for one night. Will she or won't she? Wouldn't she be crazy to refuse such an offer? In 1996, Cuba Gooding, Jr., won an Oscar for his role as a talented young football player with an agent, *Jerry Maguire* (the film's title), played by Tom Cruise, hired of course to win for the athlete the fattest possible contract. The agent received but one instruction from his client, "Show me the money!" Repeated like a mantra throughout the film, this line has entered the American lexicon.

In a conflict between the economic and the human, the economic enjoys presumption of innocence. Those who would question this are relegated to the realm of "special interest" groups out of touch with "reality." Human well-being, it seems, is a "special interest." So the question posed in this chapter, "When does an economic plus become a human minus?" is a loaded question. It is an uphill battle in America to reverse the burden of proof, to demand that the "economic" good must prove itself to be a "human" good before it is embraced. When all the chips are down, it is the market mechanism that controls business decisions. The market remains the controlling paradigm.

To the extent that you buy into the market paradigm, the introduction of humanistic concerns into the business

---

(Alfred A. Knopf, 1997). Kuttner argues for a mixed economy in the face of a libertarian *laissez faire* ideal of a self-regulating free market, which assumes that when market interests are served, human interests will automatically be served as well.

decision-making process will seem like a distortion of that process. A pure socialist economy would put human welfare first. Americans generally reject the welfare state as a controlling paradigm for the distribution of goods and services. Americans generally lack the required rationalistic faith in state planners. Their approach is more experimental: trust the market more than the state to distribute goods and services efficiently.[5] And economic concerns, not humanistic ones, propel the market system. If humanistic concerns are admitted at all, it is marginally, by the back door, hat in hand.

But is it a false dichotomy to set the human and the economic in opposition to each other? We look now at the relationship between marketplace rationality and humanistic rationality. *Is the market the best allocator or human goods and services? Are human values best served by market values?*

YES:

Human beings seek happiness. Even their altruism is self-interested. It satisfies a rational preference. The way you spend your money, choose your occupations, or spend your leisure time is a revelation of your rational preferences. A *laissez-faire* market allows you to rationally maximize benefit for yourself without interference. You get what you want. If what you want is not available, some entrepreneur will rise up to provide it for you. Competition allows you to shop for the lowest prices and the highest-paying jobs.

---

5.   For a classic treatment of these issues that has stood the test of time, see Charles E. Lindblom, *Politics and Markets: The World's Political and Economic Systems* (Basic Books, 1977); also his *Inquiry and Change: The Troubled Attempt to Understand and Shape Society* (reprint edition: Yale University Press, 1992).

Every choice is presumed by definition to be free. If you think you paid "too much" for something, don't be deceived. You enjoyed some payoff, or you wouldn't have paid for it at all. I personally pay "too much" for a Starbucks cup of coffee that I could prepare at home for a fraction of the cost. At some level, in paying "too much" I am satisfying a rational preference. It's not really "too much" at all, or I wouldn't have paid it in the first place. If the government were to put a lower cap on the price of a cup of coffee, Starbucks would go out of business and I would no longer be free to pursue this rational preference. The market model assumes that probably, in such a case, illegal coffee stands would spring up to satisfy my preference. [The flourishing market in illegal drugs is witness to the market's effort to allocate goods and services efficiently even in the face of government interference.] The market always knows best how to maximize human benefit.

You might think that the wages you are paid for your job are "too low." But obviously they're not, or you wouldn't continue to work for these wages. Your work decision reveals your rational self-interest in doing this job for these wages. You prefer this job to the inconvenience of looking for another job, to working at a less satisfying job, to stealing, to starting your own business, or to quitting and standing in a soup line. If the government mandated that your employer pay you more, your job may well be eliminated, or shipped to another country, or the employer could go out of business. The market model is based on human nature's drive toward rational self-interest. Even in the face of government interference, it would expect an underground economy to spring up, employing illegal workers outside the law and off the books. The market is the best determiner of how to efficiently reward work. It does this by leaving you free to auction off your best skills to employers, who will bid the highest wage for you to satisfy their needs. People's rational self-interest operates to maximize human benefit.

By definition, then, *laissez faire* economics best serves human welfare. Coercive paternalistic interference with the market results in higher prices for goods than you should have to pay in a climate of free competition, and loss of jobs when employers are forced to pay more for these jobs than they are worth. The market model is not opposed to human values. On the contrary, the unfettered operation of market forces is the best way to maximize human benefit. Economic rationality and humanistic rationality come down to the same thing. The description of how human nature works becomes an ethical prescription for how to maximize the common good.

Customer Knows Best: Note that the market exists to serve your preferences, not to reform them against your will. It doesn't care, for example, whether people choose to smoke or to quit smoking. But wouldn't it serve rational self-interest for smokers to stop smoking? Not necessarily. I might well make a rational tradeoff that I prefer to risk a shorter life span in favor of the relaxation and stimulation of smoking. Another person may see it in her rational self-interest to quit. The market paradigm allows both smokers and quitters to pursue their happiness in their own respective ways. No need to regulate smoking. Restaurants that allow smoking or forbid it, for example, will go in and out of business depending on how well they respond to customers' preferences in the matter. Insurance companies will charge more for risky smokers, as they do for risky drivers. Mandating smoking areas, or nonsmoking areas in restaurants interferes with the rational pursuit of benefit, and makes for unhappy smokers or nonsmokers.

Keeping insurance for high-risk people artificially low penalizes responsible behavior by rewarding those who pursue self-interest in an irresponsible way. The market will of its own accord discipline the irresponsible and reward the meritorious. Market rationality serves humanistic rationality, if we will only allow it to do so.

Honor Among Thieves: Even those opposed to a controlling market paradigm must grant that the market has its own ethics, a kind of honor among thieves, to use an unkind metaphor. There is a basic responsibility to protect the integrity of the market mechanism. Free enterprise supposes that the consumer be able to make free and intelligent choices in the marketplace. False advertising and price-fixing undermine the ability of the consumer to exercise such choice, thereby crippling the market mechanism itself. Therefore, false advertising and price-fixing are unethical. Unethical, too, would be the falsification of a company's financial position to creditors or shareholders. Such misrepresentation would distort the appropriate allocation of capital, again undermining the market mechanism itself. Also, this mechanism cannot operate effectively unless business is faithful to its contracts with employers and agreements with suppliers. Such fidelity is another fundamental plank in the business ethics platform of the market paradigm. Honesty, fidelity and integrity within the system are the cardinal virtues of free enterprise.

So it is not enough to say that the market model fails because people are deceived by false advertising, or are gauged by monopolistic prices, or are defrauded by broken agreements. All these are violations of the market, not manifestations of it. What is the remedy for these failures of market ethics? Hardliners will claim that the market is self-corrective. People who are deceived and defrauded will punish the offenders by withdrawing their patronage.

And exorbitant prices will cause lower-priced competitors to spring up from underground or, if possible, aboveground. More moderate *laissez-faire* will allow a place for government as the enforcer of market ethics, to ensure genuine competition, honesty in advertising and in financial statements, and the implementing of contracts.

So, are human values best served by market values?

NO:

Market rationality does not come down to the same thing as humanistic rationality. The engine that makes the market model work is the assumption that people are guided in all their decisions by rational self-interest, and that therefore if you leave them alone, the community of rational human beings, under the guidance of the market's invisible yet unerring hand, will, through their free and rational negotiations and tradeoffs, make the decisions that will maximize the well-being of each individual and, therefore, of the community. When each individual's self-interest is well-served, then the community composed of these satisfied individuals is well served. What's wrong with this assumption?

Three things are wrong. First, as a matter of descriptive fact, people are not that rational. Economic self-interest is not their driving concern in all cases. Other values often take priority. Second, many values that are essential to human well-being escape market control, escape the guidance of that invisible hand. Thirdly, human beings are not atomic individuals, and community is more than an aggregate of individuals. The human self is a dialectic of individual and community. Community is more than the sum of its parts. Individual interest can hurt community interest, and thereby backfire to hurt the individual defined by that community.

People Not That Rational: In the market paradigm, "When does an economic plus become a human minus?" is a wrong-headed question. In a freely and efficiently functioning market, guided by rational economic self-interest, an economic plus *is* a human plus. Let's look at this alleged rationality to which the market entrusts the just distribution of goods and services. It is difficult to attack the market assumption on logical grounds, because it rests on a tautology. Any choice that a human makes is by definition rational. For example, as we saw, it might appear that the decision to smoke is against one's rational self-interest. But your very choice to smoke means that you have decided that for you the gains of smoking outweigh its downside. In your framework, you have made a choice in favor of your self-interested pursuit of your own hierarchy of values. While the model may hold up on purely abstract logical grounds, let's enter the messy world of human experience and behavior.

Psychologists like Richard Thaler, Daniel Kahneman, and Amos Tversky have demonstrated the real-life fragility of that rationality that the market model relies on.[6] Consider these experiments. You are going to a show and will purchase your $10 ticket at the door. You arrive and discover that you lost a $10 bill on the way. Would you buy a ticket anyway? Most people said they would. Suppose you prepurchased your $10 ticket and lost it on the way. Would you buy another ticket? In terms of economic self-interest, this is the identical situation to the first. But almost half of the people surveyed said they would not buy another ticket. What is the appeal of Christmas accounts

---

6.   Richard H. Thaler, *The Winner's Curse: Paradoxes and Anomalies in Economic Life* (Free Press, 1992); Amos Tversky and Daniel Kahneman, "The Framing of Decisions and the Psychology of Choice," *Science* 211 (January 30, 1981), 453-458.

at the bank into which people put money that bears no interest? This surely isn't economically rational. Why do I eat a luncheon salad to lose weight, and top this off with a hot fudge sundae, and then pay The Diet Center to help me become slim? The triumphs of human folly undermine the market's assumption of rational economic behavior.

Externalities: A second problem with the market model is that many values important for human well-being (escape market control.) These are so-called economic "externalities." They often exact a high human cost that remains economically nonreimbursed. Environmental pollution is the most obvious example. There is no economic penalty against the person who throws a beer can out of a car window. More seriously, nuclear power plants produce cheap electricity, cheap because the costs of secure and permanent disposal of nuclear waste are not factored into the cost. We still don't even know the cost. And in spite of all the anti-pollution measures, automobiles continue to foul the air we breathe. It would be "too expensive" to make them pollution-free. So the cost to human well-being inflicted by cars is not reimbursed, another case of the market's failure to maximize human well-being. Or consider labor. Companies become profitable, and consumers enjoy clothes purchased at discount, because they are made in sweatshops, often by exploited children.

Pollution of earth and air, plutonium-poisoned energy, or the employment of "wetback" children all become "rational" once the philosophical decision is made that the economic is the norm of what is real and good, and the human costs are factored out of the economic equation. Such spiritual disvalues as threatening future generations or endangering world peace do not weigh in the balance when compared to the metaphysical priority given to the economic. Such metaphysics is bad because it is incomplete. It reduces reality instead of comprehending it. But the dimensions of human well-being that are economically unaccounted for do not disappear. They remain, albeit unacknowledged, to haunt us. Questions of quality and of human purpose remain. Can the purposes of human life and well-being become the measure of economic good, rather than economic good being the measure of the human?

Individualism: A third failing of the purely economic model is its excessive individualism. Family, friendship, shared leisure, education, worship, meditation – human life is so much richer than the pursuit of individual economic utility.[7] We are relentlessly selfish individual entities. Our identities are constituted by a rich web of human relationships that remain priceless but without a purchase price. Our personal investment in community and the resultant social norms forbid a purely market approach to what we most cherish. Should even a very wealthy person feel ethically justified in purchasing a slave, or an infant, or a night with Demi Moore? Buying the votes of public officials is called bribery, not the purchase of services rendered. It is true that the market doesn't know the difference. A million dollars for a vote, or a million dollars for a house: same thing. But human beings know the difference. That is why human beings must not be reduced to economic units. Ethics is more than economic utility. The market model does not ensure the just distribution of goods and services. An economic plus very often is a human minus.

---

7.   See the discussion by social psychologist Robert Lane in his *The Market Experience* (Cambridge University Press, 1991).

PO:

Can the free enterprise system be salvaged? Can it remain true to itself while putting people first? In a conflict between the human and the economic, can business demand (without going "out of business") that the economic serve the human rather than the other way around?

Is bottom-line ethics ever rightly enlisted in the cause of humanistic social values? Consider the following recommendations. Capital punishment should be abolished because it is too expensive – all those appeals. Tobacco smoking should be encouraged because smokers, by dying prematurely, relieve the burden on Medicare.[8] Support abortion of teenage pregnancies because abortion is cheaper than the expenses of childbirth. Slavery should be abolished because it is not cost-effective. All of these arguments have been used in public debate. Americans might dismiss "bleeding-heart" humanism, but the economic argument is well-nigh irresistible.

An uncompromising, unapologetic choice for the human over the economic was issued in November 1996 by the American Catholic Bishops.[9] If you disagree with any of the following principles, how would you reword it, and give your ethical reasoning:

1. The economy exists for the person, not the person for the economy;

2. Economic choices and institutions must be judged on how they protect or undermine the life and dig-

---

8.   "Smokers more than pay their own way . . . by dying early, [they] create future savings in health costs, nursing home care, Social Security and pensions." Robert Samuelson, "A Question of Freedom," *The Washington Post National Weekly Edition* (April 28, 1997), p.5.

9.   U.S. Bishops' *Catholic Framework for Economic Life,* cited in *Woodstock Report* (March 1997), p. 9. The 10 principles are a follow-up on the 10th anniversary of the pastoral letter, *Economic Justice for All.*

nity of the human person, support the family, and serve the common good;

3. A fundamental moral measure of any economy is how the poor and vulnerable are faring;

4. All people have a right to life and to secure the basic necessities of life (e.g., food, clothing, shelter, education, health care, safe environment, economic security);

5. All people have the right to economic initiative, to productive work, to just wages and benefits, to decent working conditions, as well as to join unions or other associations;

6. All people, to the extent they are able, have a corresponding duty to work, a responsibility to provide for the needs of their families, and an obligation to contribute to the broader society;

7. In economic life, free markets have both economic advantages and limits; government has essential responsibilities and limitations; voluntary groups have irreplaceable roles, but cannot substitute for the proper working of the market and the just policies of the state;

8. Society has a moral obligation, including governmental action where necessary, to assure opportunity to meet basic human needs, and pursue justice in economic life;

9. Workers, owners, managers, stockholders, and consumers are moral agents in economic life. By our choices, initiative, creativity, and investment, we enhance or diminish economic opportunity, community life, and social justice;

10. The global economy has moral dimensions and human consequences. Decisions on investment, trade,

aid, and development should protect human life and promote human rights, especially for those most in need, wherever they might live on this globe.

ETHICS EXPERIMENTS:

This chapter could be subtitled *The tyranny of the economic.* Are the following economic decisions fair?

1. Before Christmas, a popular doll is in short supply. A store auctions them off to the highest bidders, rather than selling them at list price, first-come, first-served. Who gains, who loses from each policy? Which is fairer and why?

2. In a time of high unemployment, a business legally fires older employees to make room for younger ones at lower wages, thereby lowering their prices. A competitor stays loyal to senior workers, but charges higher prices.
   Are the firings fair? At which store would you shop?

3. A first-class air passenger pays $1,000 for a coast-to-coast reserved ticket. The man sitting next to her got his seat on standby for $200.
   What explains the different prices? Is it fair?

4. An untimely frost wipes out the Brazilian coffee crop. Anticipating a shortage, the very next day coffee prices go up on the coffee on supermarket shelves.
   Is this fair? What is the alternative?

5. A full-time college student pays twice the tuition for the same course as does a part-time continuing education student.
   Is this fair? If not, what recourse does the full-time student have?

Are you immune to the tyranny of the economic? If there were no economic reward for you:

- would you return a lost wallet, leaving all the contents intact?
- would you return the money to a confused cashier who gave you too much change? Would the amount matter – twenty-five cents too much? Twenty dollars too much?
- would you pick up a piece of trash from the sidewalk and put it in a waste bin?
- on a trip, would you leave the same tip in a restaurant to which you will never return as you leave in one that you visit often?
- would you volunteer to work for a charitable organization when other people are working there for a salary?

Are you for sale? Some "indecent proposals": How much money would it take for you to:

- clean the restrooms in a ballpark 40 hours a week?
- eat a seven-inch raw worm? Cooked?
- work eight hours a day as a call girl or gigolo? As a street walker?
- marry an alien (human being!) so that she or he could qualify for citizenship?
- shoplift a book for a friend?
- buy liquor for an under-aged stranger?
- write a term paper for another student?
- let someone use your car for a day?
- use fake I.D. to take the S.A.T. for someone?

16 Global Business: Ethical Idealism or Ethical Imperialism?

It makes no sense to claim that the Western practice of locking thieves up is preferable to the Moslem practice of chopping off their hands. . . . Americans moralize about freedom, Shiite Moslems moralize about the revealed truths of Islam, and both Jews and Palestinians moralize about the right to a home land. Hence, the most common question . . . about integrating values with international policy is simply whose values should be integrated. **Thomas Donaldson**[1]

One French manager whose company recently had been acquired by an American company, stated: "I resent having notions of right and wrong boiled down to a checklist. I come from a nation whose ethical traditions date back hundreds of years. . . . I don't need to be told by some American lawyers how I should conduct myself in my business activities." **David Vogel**[2]

We discovered that two of our manufacturing contractors in Bangladesh and in Turkey employed underage workers [in] clear violation of our guidelines. . . . It appeared that we had two options: Instruct our con-

---

1. Donaldson describes the relativist view in his *The Ethics of International Business* (Oxford, 1989), p. 14.
2. Adapted from his article in *The California Management Review* (Fall 1992).

> *tractors to fire these children, knowing that many are*
> *the sole wage-earners for their families, and if they lost*
> *their jobs, their families would face extreme hardships;*
> *or continue to employ underage children, ignoring our*
> *company's stance against child labor.*
>
> Robert Haas, CEO Levi Strauss

CROSS-CULTURAL DILEMMAS:

Multi-National Enterprises (MNEs) have been increasingly under the gun for their practices in the Third World, often to the point of being in an apparently no-win position. Richard DeGeorge states well the dilemmas faced by MNEs, even when they try to act responsibly.

> *Third World countries frequently seek to attract American multinationals for the jobs they provide and for the technological transfers they promise. Yet when American MNEs locate in Third World countries, many Americans condemn them for exploiting the resources and the workers of the Third World. [While MNEs are a means for improving the standard of living of underdeveloped countries, MNEs are blamed for the starvation and poverty such countries suffer.] Although MNEs provide jobs in the Third World, many criticize them for transferring these jobs from the United States. American MNEs usually pay at least as high wages as local industries, yet critics blame them for paying the workers in underdevel-*

---

3. "Ethics in the Trenches," *Business Ethics 95/96*, edited by John E. Richardson (Brown and Benchmark Publishers, 1995), p. 169. Levi Strauss persuaded their contractors pay the children salary and benefits while they were going to school, promising them jobs when they became of age. Though this added to the cost of doing business, Haas decided that such a socially responsible decision redounded to the long-run benefit of the company. Burgeoning sales confirmed this judgment.

oped countries less than they pay American workers for comparable work. When MNEs pay higher than local wages, local companies criticize them for skimming off all the best workers and for creating an internal brain-drain. Multinationals are currently the most effective vehicle available for the development of the Third World. At the same time, critics complain that MNEs are destroying local cultures and substituting for them the tinsel of American life and the worst aspects of its culture. American MNEs seek to protect the best interests of their shareholders by locating in an environment in which their enterprise will be safe from destruction by revolutions and confiscation by socialist regimes. When they do so, critics complain that MNEs thrive in countries with strong, often right-wing, governments.

Lack of Ethical Infrastructure: The need for responsible standards is especially urgent in Less Developed countries (LDCs). Developed countries over time, in response to conflicts at the business-society interface, have evolved an infrastructure of institutions and regulations. This infrastructure checks the tendency of the free market to reward cost-effective but unethical behavior. Economic cost-effectiveness can and has exacted a high human price. LDCs are usually lacking in this infrastructure governing minimum wage, consumer protection, pollution control, worker safety, and the like. Such institutions as do exist are often in the service of the economic elite's interest in subordinating the majority. And MNEs, buying into such host-country infrastructure, can become coconspirators in injustice. Lacking the kind of

---

4. Richard T. De George, "Ethical Dilemmas for Multinational Enterprise: A Philosophical Overview," in W. Michael Hoffman, Ann E. Lange, and David A. Fedo (eds.), *Ethics and the Multinational Enterprise: Proceedings of the Sixth National Conference on Business Ethics* (Lanham, MD: The University Press of America, 1986), p. 39. Henceforth, this collection will be referred to as *Proceedings.*

ethical infrastructure that restrains them in their home countries, MNEs have a special responsibility to develop self-imposed standards, lest they become partners in exploitation with host-country elites.

Churches increasingly in the pursuit of social justice are combining preaching with activism in the Third World. Aware that social justice and economic behavior are intimately entwined, and that indeed the Church itself is an economic player, religious leaders, including theologians, are understanding that they must go beyond knee-jerk liberationist nostrums, Marxist jingoism and investment-bashing if they are to be effective. Churches have a unique role to play. They can bring to bear a disinterested economic perspective, a global scope and even economic clout. A sophisticated grasp of multinational business ethics has become a requirement for the effective practice of religion.

Broken Sterotypes: Just as medical ethicians are hard-pressed to keep up with the pace of biotechnology, so business ethicians must scramble to keep pace with the changing face of international business. First versus Third World stereotypes are breaking down. What used to be called the Third World now comprises the traditionally named Less Developed countries (LDCs), as well as a class of Newly Developed Countries (NDCs), NDCs that have emerged from the LDCs. The emergence of NDCs, especially among Pacific rim countries,

---

5.   J. Philip Wogaman shows how failure to develop self-regulatory codes has left MNEs vulnerable to Marxist criticism in the Third World. *See Economics and Ethics: A Christian Inquiry* (Philadelphia, PA: Fortress Press, 1986).

6.   See Timothy Smith, "The Church Corporate Responsibility Movement: Fifteen Years Later," *Proceedings*, pp. 3-24. See also, J. Philip Wogaman, "Reflections on Church Activism and Transnational Corporations," *Proceedings*, pp. 159-162.

Japan, Taiwan, Korea, Hong Kong, Singapore, challenge
liberationist stereotypes about the necessarily destructive
impact of free enterprise on LDCs. Automation, quality
control and knowledge are replacing raw materials and
cheap labor as the most precious natural resources in
the Third World. New technology has created new players in the global business game.[7]

Focus on MNEs: For the kinds of issues to be discussed
here, we will focus on MNEs as opposed to Transnational Corporations (TNCs). MNEs are enterprises that
deploy their assets in two or more countries. They are
managed from headquarters in their parent country, the
home country in which they are legally chartered. To
the extent that their management and ownership are
external to the host countries in which they operate,
their assets in these host countries are subject to expro-
priation. TNCs, on the other hand, are simply exporters
to other countries. If they do business in several countries, their management and ownership remains indige-
nous to the country in which they do business.[8]
Therefore TNCs are not faced with the kinds of cross-
cultural ethical conflicts that bedevil MNEs.

Consider these cases:

> *In Italy, it is a widely accepted practice to substantially
> underestimate and underreport corporate income. An
> American company in Italy is ethically right to interpret
> tax laws according to host norms that would be unac-
> ceptable to the American way of interpreting tax laws.*

> *Facilitating payments (low-level bribery) in certain host
> countries are part of the salary structure, and ethically*

7. See S. Prakash Sethi, "Changing Rules of International Corporate
Behavior," *Proceedings*, pp. 3-24.

8. For a more detailed discussion, see Verne E. Henderson, "Ethical
Criteria for Multinational Consulting," *Proceedings*, pp.133-142.

acceptable in the host land, though unacceptable at home.

A business operating in Kenya would rightly respect local norms for allotting scarce social resources, like health care or employment. The host country would prefer the old to the young, in that the old have forged a complex network of ties to the community and are more important to it than are the young, who are more detached and less essential, and they would prefer a childless young man to one with children, since the one with children has fulfilled his procreative mission and the one without deserves his chance.

And you can think of other examples of cultures with differing views of what constitute morally appropriate gender roles, family privilege, and racial and religious qualifications that differ from current American law and American moral consensus.

Home and host countries can agree on the social and economic facts, but come to a different moral assessment of those facts. The moral principles are different, though the concrete circumstances are the same. This is what Richard Brandt has called "ultimate ethical disagreement."[9] The MNE seems to be caught between imperialistically imposing its own ideals on the host, or conversely, relinquishing its values in favor of the maxim, "When in Rome, do as the Romans do." Whence our question: *In the face of basic value conflicts, should the ethical policies and codes established in the home office be imposed in the host country?*

---

9.   Richard Brandt, "Cultural Relativism" in *Ethical Issues in Business*, T. Donaldson and P. Werhane (eds.) (Englewood-Cliffs, N.J.: Prentice-Hall, Inc., second edition, 1983).

YES:

Thomas Donaldson[10] proposes that a socially responsible corporation in The Home Office must ask these key questions when faced with an ultimate ethical disagreement:

(1) Is the disputed practice really ethically acceptable in the host country?

(2) Is it necessary for doing business there?

(3) Does it violate any basic human rights?

If the problematic practice is genuinely acceptable and necessary in the host country, and does not violate any basic human rights, then the home corporation may practice in the host country what would be ethically offensive back home. But Donaldson stipulates that the home office corporation must ostentatiously hold its ethical nose, as it were, and protest that it finds this necessary practice offensive and would like to see it changed.

The upshot is that MNEs might under certain conditions cooperate under protest with offensive host country practices, like bribery, underreporting of taxes, deviant role distinctions. Bottom line, the home office ethical policies should prevail. The burden of proof rests on those who would deviate from the company's own policies to accommodate a countervailing local practice.

NO:

Is there a chauvinistic ethical imperialism lurking in Donaldson's approach to "ultimate ethical disagreements"? He assumes that the home office's view of human rights should be the arbiter of what counts for genuine human

10. Thomas Donaldson, "Multinational Decision-making: Reconciling International Norms," *Journal of Business Ethics* 4 (1985), pp. 357-366.

rights and ethical practice in the host. Consider his question: "Does it violate basic human rights?" – often the "ultimate ethical disagreement" revolves precisely around just what these human rights are.

And he recommends that the home office protest and try to change the host's practices (nepotism, facilitating payments) that would be offensive in the home culture. Is this idealism, or imperialistic arrogance? The home office does have economic clout. Should this be used as a club to impose an alien ethics? Need the Host countries of the world be made over into the ethical image of the home office?

Alternative Realities: Rather we should understand ultimate ethical disagreements to be just that – ultimate. Human beings and human cultures can look at the same facts and come up with different and even incommensurable moral readings of those facts. MNEs need not become missionaries exporting home country ethics along with their products. MNEs often get a bad rap for abandoning home country standards in favor of host country norms. "When in Rome . . ." can be a maxim of respect for alternate readings of human nature, and not necessarily a sell-out to relativism.

Recall the stance of Ethical Pluralism described in the Introduction of this book. It is different from Relativism. It recognizes that there can come a point where value systems are incommensurate, perhaps even contradictory. It is not just that the same ethical principles are embodied differently in different cultural structures. It is not just that the diverse moral values of cultures represent diverse perspectives on one human moral reality. Pluralism asserts that the ethical myths are ineluctably related to the persons (and persons-in-society) from whom flow choices and judgments about values. There is no absolute ethical standard of weights and measures hidden in a vault somewhere by which to measure one myth against another. Assertions that there is such a standard flow from the myth of the assertor, the myth of having access to some rational superperspective of all perspectives.

Pluralism Not Relativism: Pluralism is not a statement of simple-minded relativism. The assertion of universal relativism, as we all know, is self-contradictory. If all is relative, so is the assertion that "all is relative" relative. Relativism is denied in the very process of attempting to affirm it. Pluralism, on the other hand, is presupposed in the very process of attempting to deny it. Truth, including moral truth, must relate to the individual and/or cultural intellects that affirm it. The doctrine of pluralism underlines the subjective component in the constitution of truth and goodness. Pluralism forbids assertions about absolute truth, which would presuppose relation to an absolute intellect.

Pluralism calls into question the absolutist's pretensions of access to a perspective of all perspectives, as a basis for the claim that my myth is better than your myth, or more strongly, that my truth is better than your myth, or more precisely, that my ideology is better than your myth. Pluralism makes a statement about the incommensurability of world views. Provocative here is the statement made by Raimundo Pannikar in another context. He calls it the Law of Tolerance. "The toleration you have is directly proportional to the myth you live by, and inversely proportional to the ideology you follow."[11] The diverse myths of pluralist ethicians more readily coexist than do the conflicting ideologies of absolutist true believers, with their ethical imperialism.

---

11. Raimundo Pannikar, *Myth, Faith and Hermeneutik* (New York: Paulist Press, 1979), p. 20.

Having given a critique of the pretension inherent in elevating ethnocentric business ethics to an absolute level, the pluralist cannot propose an alternative system as absolute. Proposed, rather, are three modest practical suggestions as an alternative to ethical absolutism:

(1) Live, love, know, and experience your own ethical tradition as deeply and faithfully as possible. Only those who have deeply immersed themselves in one tradition have paid the dues necessary to genuinely respect and listen to an alternative vision. They know of what they speak. Genuine ecumenism is not easy ecumenism. MNEs should be exemplary corporate citizens at home;

(2) Secure in one's own tradition, one is then freed up to be utterly open and attentive, and able to listen and dialogue with alternative cultures. This kind of dialogue is secure enough to be ready to be challenged to the point of change, to the point of being fecundated and enriched by the insights of an alternative vision. It is a dialogue and mutual exchange without end, not a construction of a universal system to embrace both. American business needs economic ambassadors sensitively attuned to the values of host countries more than missionaries hellbent on exporting the American way.

(3) Be confident that goodness, not evil is the universal bottom line, that reality is at its heart love and goodness and truth. While ethical truth will not yield its ultimate intelligible secrets in an absolute package, the partial human discoveries uncovered by the dialogue and interaction of cultures are worth the struggle. As American pragmatist and social psychologist George Herbert Mead suggested, the interactions of humans joined in economic mutual self-interest in

commerce and trade may be a more powerful force for world peace and unity than is religion. Religion, while urging us to love our enemies, often impels us to destroy them. Commerce, while warning us to be suspicious of our enemies, impels us to enter into agreement with them.

PO:

Economic necessity disguised as ethical conflict:

A dilemma of cultural pluralism is to decide which conflicts are ethical and which are assignable to extramoral cultural or economic variables.

Consider the following cases:

(1) Children's pajamas treated with a compound called "tris" are flame-retardant. When tris was found to cause cancer in animals, and the pajamas were withdrawn from U.S. markets, was it ethical to market them in foreign countries which do not act on animal tests and which judge that the fire-proofing benefits of tris outweigh the carcinogenic risks, since living conditions there make open flames more of a hazard to children than is the case in the United States?

(2) A drug developed as the *only* treatment for glaucoma is withdrawn from the U.S. market when it is found to cause cancer in some humans. It is not unethical to market the drug in countries that allow patients a wider latitude in decisions about drugs than is available to patients in the United States.

(3) It is not unethical to market in other countries pesticides which are deemed unsafe for American use, if those countries find the risks acceptable in view of

the severity of their pest problems, of their food shortages, and of the cost-effectiveness of the "dangerous" pesticides.

In cases such as these, why does the host have a different norm? Is it because it disagrees with the ethical ideal of the home country? Or is it because it can't afford to practice the ideal? I.e., is there is a different ordering of priorities due to a lower level of economic development? If the host had the economic luxury of following the home norm, would it do so? If so, then the disagreement at heart is not ethical but economically based. The MNE offers the LDC the alternative of choosing a lesser evil over a greater. Better, perhaps, an imperfect product than no product at all. Home norms may reasonably give way to host norms. The concession is not to moral principles but to their application in different concrete circumstances. A key question that the MNE might ask itself: if the home country were as underdeveloped as the host, would the home country too reasonably change its norm? Could the pajamas, the glaucoma drug, the pesticides be considered examples of this kind of conflict?

ETHICS EXPERIMENT:

Critique the following excerpt from a standard textbook on international business management.[12] Does it represent a morally respectful sensitivity to cultural uniqueness, or is it an ethically irresponsible sell-out? Should you:

accommodate local sensitivity to social status in hiring and promotion?

---

12. Richard D. Robinson, *International Business Management: A Guide to Decision-making* (Hinsdale, IL: The Dryden Press, second edition, 1978), pp. 241-242.

Labor may be recruited on the basis of social status and/or competence. In many societies, quite apart from demonstrated ability, social status is very largely a complex function of family background and ties, wealth (however defined), sex, number of children, race, nationality, regional origin, politics, religion, and former military rank – to mention a few factors. Because of the vast complexity of this subject, in view of the variety of social structures in which the firm may be operating, all one can do is suggest some guidelines that emerge from accumulated experience.

In situations where patterns of dominance-subordination are socially determined, and not a function of demonstrated ability, management should be cautioned against promoting those of inferior social status to positions in which they are expected to supervise those of higher social status (for example, an ex-corporal over an ex-sergeant in societies where this factor is important). A complete breakdown in communication and in morale may be the result.

accommodate nepotism by respecting local preference given family and relatives?

Similarly, nepotism – in the sense of permitting supervisors and foremen to hire kinfolk, fellow tribesmen, or villagers – may result in maximum efficiency, even though the individual worker may not measure up to other candidates for the job in terms of individual ability. In his group, however, the "insider" may be more effective than the "outsider" with superior ability.

adapt to local view of proper gender roles?

Discrimination in employment by sex may also have to conform to traditional practice to gain maximum efficiency. Innovation on this score by a foreign management in a highly traditional society may lead to a variety of difficulties.

adapt to local views of racial preferences?

In a multiracial society, where social status is related to race by both law and prevailing national values, the firm must either conform or withdraw from management responsibility. In determining its policy, the firm should be sensitive to the effect of its behavior in such a society and on attitudes towards the firm in other societies in which it is operating. A relevant query is whether or not, by restructuring itself legally and administratively, the firm can avoid hostility in these other societies. That is, can it insulate itself from being identified with the enterprise in the country that assigns status on the basis of race? Mining companies operating both in the Republic of South Africa and in areas north of "the line," say, in Zambia, have had to face up to this problem. Another relevant query is how long the status quo is likely to last. The conforming firm may find itself trapped by a racial revolution. Total loss of assets may be expected unless the firm is supplying something in terms of skills, external sales channels, and so forth not available from other more acceptable sources.

17 Right Livelihood: Work as Calling or Career?

That by which a follower of the Noble One makes a living, avoiding wrong modes of making a living: this is called right livelihood.

Buddha's Eightfold Path: fifth step

Any time not spent on love is wasted.

Tasso[1]

Professionals are not expected simply to pursue their work as a means to economic well-being. Professions claim to provide services for the public benefit, beyond private gain, or even at its expense. The professional is expected to be "on call" in a way that other workers are not. **William M. Sullivan**[2]

INTRODUCTION:

Do you get the feeling, as I do, that doctors, lawyers, nurses, and even the clergy don't look at you with the same caring eyes as they would not many years ago? I feel that often these professionals see me as a job, a task, a problem, a money source. The last time I had my eyes checked, I reached out with a "hello" to shake my doctor's hand. I had never met him before. He stared at my

---

1. *The Sun: A Magazine of Ideas* (May 1991), p. 40.
2. William M. Sullivan, "Calling or Career: The Tensions of Modern Professional Life," *Professional Ideals,* edited by Albert Flores (Wadsworth Publishing Co., 1988), p. 40.

hand like it was a dead fish, and with a jerk of his head motioned me toward the chair. A half-hour and a half-dozen monosyllables later, I left the office. Case closed, invoice issued and paid. The experience reminded me of a stop I made with my uncle last summer at a "Fresh Corn" stand in Rhode Island. I ventured some "how's business – how's the weather" chit-chat with the young man at the stand. No reply. Nothing. He pointed to the sign: 12 ears of corn – $1. As we walked away, my uncle said, "You're paying him for corn, not conversation." And my uncle was right. Tending a farm stand is a job, and not a very great job at that. Should the same thing be said about the professions, about my doctor: It's a job, and often not a very satisfying one at that?

TWO MEANINGS OF PROFESSIONAL:

This article is about professional ethics, about the very nature of the professions. What does it mean to be a doctor, a lawyer, a nurse, a teacher, an ordained minister? Is a profession to be viewed as a vocation, an honorable trust? Or as just a job, an occupation? I see a movement away from the traditional view of profession-as-calling toward the view of profession-as-career. This is a fundamental shift, a "paradigm-shift," as Dr. Edward Pellegrino[3] calls it. And as for ethics, this paradigm shift means a shift in the way you and I can rightly expect to be treated by the professional. Vocation-minded professionals see themselves as trustees of your welfare. Careerists see themselves hired out to do a job for you. Calling or career? Let's compare the trustees and the careerists, and their different views of

3.   Edmund D. Pellegrino, M.D., "Professional Ethics: Moral Decline or Paradigm Shift?", *Religion & Intellectual Life*, Volume IV No. 3 (Spring 1987), pp. 21-39.

professional ethics. So, our question: *Is a professional occu-pation more rightly approached as a calling to serve the com-mon good, even at personal sacrifice, rather than merely as an income-producing job?*

YES:

The "Traditional Professional" (TP) answers resoundingly in the affirmative. TP resists the paradigm shift away from TP to what we will call the "New Professional" (NP). TP's see their work as "vocation"; NP's see their work as "job."

The TP is professionally devoted to advancing socially shared vital human values: journalistic concern for the truth,[4] medical dedication to the indigent sick, evangelis-tic concern for the salvation of sinners, legal care for the rule of justice, and even investor concern for fair eco-nomic arrangements in society. TP resists temptations to excessive self-interest, careerism, competition, and preoc-cupation with the bottom line.

For TP, a profession is much more than a job. It is set apart from other occupations which are *not* profes-sions. A professional is called to be custodian and trustee of the core values that bind the community together. Pro-fessionals are custodians of truth and culture (the teacher), of social order and internal peace (the lawyer), of physical health and life (the physician and the nurse),

---

4. Note that the TP ideal is not limited to doctors, lawyers and teachers. Social workers, engineers, auto mechanics, journalists, and many other occupations often aspire, individually and as groups, to the ideal of traditional professionalism. For example, Jack Fuller (publisher of *The Chicago Tribune,* lawyer, ex-reporter) in *News Values: Ideas for an Information Age* (U of Chicago Press, 1996) states:
The crucial thing for journalists to recognize is that their trade does not exempt them from the basic moral imperatives that guide all other human relationships. If they depart from the general standard, they must have good and precise reason to do so. Pursuit of truth is not a license to be a jerk.

of spiritual well-being and healing (the minister of God). Around such core values the professional community takes shape as society's Board of Trustees. These trustees share a distinctive set of ideals and standards, a shared moral ethos in favor of the common good.

TP is a beautiful ideal, and so is the ideal of society on which it rests. (Maybe too beautiful, NP will say). TP assumes that we really do share a concept of "common good," that atheists and believers, poor and rich, Jews and Christians, blacks and whites, women and men actually do have core values that they hold in common. TP assumes that we individuals in society each see our own good bound up with the common good. People are naturally social. In such a society, the professional is at the service of the fundamental shared values - truth, law, health, salvation -that hold society together. This altruistic calling to assist the common good is an ideal that overrides professionals' temptation to view themselves in terms of narrow self-interest.

Which brings us to professional ethics.

THE ETHICS OF TP:

Health, knowledge, salvation and justice are essential to human well-being. When these values are violated, humanity itself is wounded. TP sees the professional as altruistically dedicated to the service of these central human needs. Thus ill health or unjust treatment hurt us humanly in ways that a broken car or a losing sports team do not. So in TP, medicine and law are professions. Auto mechanics and pro sports not. Accordingly, TP will tolerate the self-interested mechanic or shortstop, but condemns the egotistic pastor or self-serving research scientist.

The TP client rightly or wrongly counts on such idealism and dedication. She does expect a "servant of humanity." She presents herself to the professional when she is wounded in a particularly human way. The client approaches the physician, the lawyer, the pastor usually in a state of intimate need, dependency, and peculiar vulnerability. This trust renders a client especially open to being exploited.

Such vulnerability lays on the professional a moral claim to a special trustworthiness over and above what would be expected from other occupations. No amount of "informed consent" or signing of papers can do justice to the act of faith in the integrity of the professional that is required on the operating table or in the courtroom or in the confessional. In TP, the guarantee of such trustworthiness is a covenant, not a contract, that springs from a calling, not a job.

THE PRIVILEGES GRANTED TO TP:

Traditionally, society has endowed the professional with special privileges and immunity, with scope for personal discretion in the execution of their services. These grants were certainly not given for the self-aggrandizement of the professional. The assumption was that the professionals, faithful to their calling, would use these privileges in the service of the precious human values entrusted to their care. So religious enjoy tax exemptions; lawyers enjoy privileged communication; physicians may experiment on humans – all in the service not of private profit, but of the common weal.

NO:

NP's, however, do not perceive themselves functioning in the idealized world of the TP. And so of necessity they live by a very different code. NP sees the mark of the professional not so much to be a custodian of values but a master of techniques. NP is first and foremost an expert rather than a trustee. As expert and technician, NPs view themselves as worthy of their hire. They do not shrink from "professing" for profit. The NP is quite openly self-interested. Self-effacing altruistic devotion is not a key value. The physician, for example, who might be inclined to perform C-sections rather than vaginal deliveries in the interest of convenience and profit is in the same professional bed as the baseball free agent. Both are professional by reason of their expertise and skills; both use their expertise to advance their own careers. NP is the profession understood as special-interest group. NP is the world of nurses on strike, unionized professors, and publicity-seeking clergy.

This is not a noble vision of how the world works, but perhaps it is more hard-nosed and accurate than TP. NP does not see a society bound by shared values. It sees, rather, an uneasy alliance of primarily self-interested individuals and special interest groups. We cannot assume that doctors and lawyers, men and women, blacks and whites, young and old, Midwest and far West all subscribe to a core of goods and goals entrusted to the care of professionals. Professionals themselves form special-interest groups, often at odds with other professional groups. Society is not natural to human beings. We must make contracts and agreements to help us to live together. "You scratch my back, and I'll scratch yours." To the extent that NP succeeds, it serves the "Public Interest." Note that "Public Interest" is different from TP's "Common Good."

NP has faith that the public interest will be served if private interests conspire together for mutual advantage. Suppose you are too poor or powerless to scratch the professional's back? Well, that's just too bad. NP is a world of AIDS patients left to die, of disadvantaged students allowed to drop out, of poor people languishing in jail, unable to post bond. NP serves the qualified consumer. TP reaches out without qualification to serve every needful human being.

Professionals are much more comfortable with the paradigm shift than is the public. Often there is public outrage at trust violated and expectations unmet. And in response, there is professional bewilderment and protestation that such expectations are wrong, that professionals are acting in good conscience, and that the name of the game has changed. The evangelist finds no embarrassment in saying "I'm worth $1.2 million per year," or the physician in declaring, "I can make more money elsewhere," or the lawyer, "The best way I can get mine is by helping you get yours." Vocational ethics gives way to amoral economics as the prime motivator. So the journalist does whatever is required to get the scoop; the investment analyst amorally weighs the potential profits of rule-bending over against the risk of getting caught.

Let's admit right off that neither TP (the Traditional Professional) nor NP (the New Professional) exists in pure form. But there is a major shift in the direction of NP. Is this an entirely bad thing? What are the implications for professional ethics?

THE ETHICS OF NP:

For NP, on the other hand, the professional is not the servant of humanity, but the technical problem-solver. In a climate of moral skepticism and pluralism, we cannot

agree on the very meaning of human. Values are rela-
tivized, and so are human needs. The human needs of TP
become the technical problems of NP. Whether I have a
broken limb or a broken fuel pump, I seek out the "professional," i.e., the one with the expertise to fix it.

Pursuit of due process replaces pursuit of shared values. There *are* no shared values. Pluralism is the norm.
The professional strives to protect those social arrangements and institutions that make for an orderly society in
the pursuit of mutual advantage. Such a society, for example, would place more faith in an enforceable Patient's
Bill of Rights than in the dedication of the health care
professional.

Last week I attended a discussion by nurses who were
ready to shed the "Florence Nightingale" image and face
up to the fact that they are technicians: give the shots,
read the instruments, document the symptoms, work your
shift and then go home. "I'll do my job, but spare me the
guilt trip of being the servant of humanity."

The NP client views herself as a rational consumer of
technical services. The client has no special moral claim
on the professional over and above the expectations for
the performance that the client would have of any other
nonprofessional practitioner. In this view, the psychiatrist
who breaks a confidence would be judged by the same
moral ruler as the car salesperson who sells you a lemon.
If either broke a contract, they can be sued. The contract
completely defines the relationship. Beyond that, *caveat
emptor.*

THE END OF PROFESSIONAL PRIVILEGE?

The shift to NP is causing society to take a second look at
the privileges accorded to the professions. The public has
shown great consternation at scandals like those alleged

below. It is a picture of privileges abused, of trust betrayed.

⎣ I am suggesting that the fault may lie with society,
not with the professional⎦ The professional, often quite
deliberately, is playing by new rules – NP. Many of the old
privileges might not be appropriate to the new game.
Many of the traditional expectations of the professions are
unrealistic in the new paradigm. As society catches up
with the new paradigm, we may increasingly see social accountability as a check on professional discretion, detailed
regulations hedging professional privileges, and legal contractual obligations replacing vocational obligations which
no longer apply in the new paradigm. Churches may be
forced to open their books, and physicians forced to treat
the poor. Coercion replaces dedication when professions
become careers.

PO:

Are the following trends a betrayal of professionalism?

> *Item:*
> Televangelical rhetoric these days about a calling
> from Jesus as often as not is echoed by a call for
> a personal jet plane.

> *Item:*
> Some physicians today are prepared to abandon
> their "vocations" rather than treat Medicaid pa-
> tients, or even AIDS patients.

> *Item:*
> The legal profession, which once viewed advertis-
> ing as demeaning to the profession, today quite
> readily drums the airwaves with the beat of "am-
> bulance-chasing" commercials.

Item:
College Deans who formerly appealed to their faculty using accents of service and dedication, now appeal for carefully written syllabi as a buffer against liability suits.

ETHICS EXPERIMENT:

Think back to an activity or job in which you did exactly the minimum required: no more, no less. What feelings and implicit ground rules made you act this way? What meaning did this activity have for your life and values? Can you imagine yourself repeating this activity, but this time going beyond the call of duty? Why or why not?

Think back to an activity or job in which you went beyond the call of duty, even at some cost to yourself. What feelings and implicit assumptions made you act this way? What meaning did this activity have in your overall life? Can you imagine yourself repeating this activity, but this time doing just the minimum required? Why or why not?

18   Product Liability: *Caveat Emptor?*

Where the seller at the time of contracting has reason to know any particular purpose for which the goods are required and that the buyer is relying on the seller's skill or judgment to select or furnish suitable goods, there is . . . an implied warranty that the goods shall be fit for such purpose.[1]

In today's world it is often only the manufacturer who can fairly be said to know and to understand when an article is suitably designed and safely made for its intended purpose. Once floated on the market, many articles in a very real practical sense defy detection of defect, except possibly in the hands of an expert after laborious, and perhaps even destructive, disassembly. . . . We are accordingly persuaded that from the standpoint of justice as regards the operating aspect of today's products, responsibility should be laid on the manufacturer.[2]

[The Holy Bible – Disclaimer of Liability] All beings, places and events depicted in this work are fictional, and any resemblance to actual beings, places and events past, present or future is purely coincidental. Some of the actions performed in this work are danger-

---

1.   Section 2-315 of the Uniform Commercial Code.

2.   *Codling v. Paglia*, 32 New York 2nd 330, 298 Northeastern 2nd 622, 345 New York Supplement 2nd 461 (1973), a New York Court decision replacing the doctrine of *caveat emptor* with *caveat vendor.*

> *ous and should only be attempted by professionals fa-*
> *miliar with the action in question. Some randomly oc-*
> *curring points of light appearing in the sky at night*
> *are comets. In no way should these be construed as*
> *hiding UFO's or other vehicles of salvation.*[3]

Product liability is a matter of responsibility and accountability. If you make a purchase with your eyes wide open,
should you be responsible for the consequences of how
you use that product? This is an issue where ethics inter-
sects in a special way with law and economics. Is present
liability law in line with the ethical principles of justice, or
does it assign responsibility to all the wrong people? Is
there anything ethically repugnant in putting a price tag
on safety, weighing the costs of making a safe product
over against the likelihood of harm from its use?

Consider that notorious hot cup of coffee that the
woman bought from McDonald's. Seated behind the
wheel of her car, she put the cup between her legs. Of
course, the coffee spilled and burned her. The fact that
coffee is designed to be consumed in the mouth and not
between the legs did not protect McDonald's from having
to pay a bundle of money to this woman. And now coffee
cups everywhere have labels on them warning you that
your hot cup of coffee may actually be hot. Who should
be ethically responsible for drinking a cup of coffee in a
safe way, the coffee drinker or the coffee maker?

As for the economics of safety, consider the equally
notorious case of the Ford Pinto which, because of the location of its gasoline tank, tended to blow up if struck
from the rear. Ford had to decide whether the costs of
modifying the design were worth the benefits of the harms

---

3. Adapted from *The Bible's Copyright*, Internet Newsgroup
"rec.humor.funny" – Subject: Lost in the translation.

that would be prevented from future accidents. The cost of modifying over 12 million cars and trucks at $11 per vehicle comes to a total of $137 million. Statistically, this modification would save 180 burn deaths (at an estimated saving of $200,000 liability awards per death), 180 serious burn injuries (at $67,000 per injury), and 2100 burned vehicles (at $700 per vehicle), for a benefit of $49.15 million in savings. Cost: $137 million; benefit: $49 million.[4] It's a no-brainer. Economically, the costs of modifying the gas tank far outweigh the benefits. The economic imperative is to make no changes. What is the ethical imperative?

Finally, consider the case that has become a rallying cry against big jury awards. Birmingham doctor Ira Gore, Jr., sued BMW for not telling him that his new car's paint had been damaged and retouched before he bought the car. BMW had repaired acid rain damage to the finish of the car. It was nine months before Dr. Gore noticed anything amiss. How much should BMW be punished for the doctor's anguish over his BMW? An Alabama jury said $4 million.[5]

As far as possible, we will focus on the ethical issues at stake, but with attention to the legal and economic contexts in which such ethical decisions take place. We will hang the discussion on the following question: ***In the safe use of products, should the consumer bear the burden of risk?***

---

4.   Ford Motor Company's internal safety memo on the Pinto is cited in Marianne Moody Moore, *Case Studies in Business Ethics* (West Publishing Company, 1996; second edition), Case 5.9.

5.   BMW in 1000 other cases had not disclosed such paint touch-ups, so the punitive award was to deter BMW from such behavior in the future. An appeals judge reduced it to $2 million. The US Supreme Court called even this amount grossly excessive. And eventually $50,000 was the penalty BMW actually paid. See Associated Press story (May 10, 1997).

YES:

Automobiles, computers, tampons, and peanut butter make America the consumer paradise that it is. But every consumer product comes with risks attached. I just bought an anti-theft device for my car. So who was the first person to be locked out of the car? You guessed it: not the thief, but me. Computer keyboards occasion hundreds of cases of carpal tunnel syndrome year after year. Now users of tennis racquets, cash registers, and wheelchairs are lining up to get compensated for repetitive stress injury (RSI). Since the late 1970s, the U.S. Center for Disease Control (CDC) estimates that between 1 and 17 per 100,000 menstruating women suffer from a potentially fatal bacterial illness, Toxic Shock Syndrome (TSS), a disease associated with the use of tampons containing rayon.[6] And even pretzels may not be safe. In November, J&J Snack Foods Corp. had to recall their cheese-filled SUPERPRETZEL[R] SOFTSTIX[R] when a peanut-based ingredient accidentally found its way into the filling, posing a potentially life-threatening reaction to people allergic to peanuts. It's dangerous out there!

Hard Core *Caveat Emptor:* If your view of society is a dog-eat-dog world, a Hobbesian war of everyone against everyone else, then your ethics will reflect this. A hardline doctrine of *caveat emptor* would guide your view of product liability. So a rational person will assume that the seller or producer of a product is likely to try to cheat and deceive the buyer so as to maximize their own gain. Be hard-nosed, crafty and skeptical. In all such transactions, proceed at your own risk, because when it is done and you go home, you and you alone

---

6.   A study released at the 1994 convention of the American Society for Microbiology demonstrates the propensity of rayon fibers to amplify the production of the TSST-1 toxin responsible for TSS.

will have to live with the risk and consequences. *Caveat emptor.*

Soft Core *Caveat Emptor:* If you view human nature and society as a community of people who are cooperative as well as competitive, then your ethics will reflect this kinder view. You will expect a certain good faith on the part of sellers and buyers alike. It will be as important for the buyer to *be aware* as to *beware.* This is a softer version of *caveat emptor.*

Contract theory and tort theory are the twin pillars for assigning liability for unsafe products. Both theories are well-founded in ethics.

Contract Theory: Contract theory says "Keep your agreements." Its deontological basis is *quid pro quo* justice. For a consideration, usually money, the seller contracts to deliver the product that the buyer wants. There are three moral constraints: (1) both parties must be fully aware of the nature of the agreement; (2) neither should intentionally deceive the other; and (3) they must enter into the agreement freely. When these conditions are met, then the contract is binding. The buyer now is fully responsible for the product and the risks associated with its use. Contract theory says, *caveat emptor,* make sure you know what you're doing. If you have regrets afterwards, your only recourse is to prove that the seller did not live up to the contract. If you contract for an ice cream cone and receive an ice cream cone, and then drop it between your legs, that's your problem. The same goes for a cup of hot coffee.

Traditionally, common law recognized the "privity of contract" rule. If you bought a bottle of cola with a dead mouse in it from a convenience store, your quarrel would be with the convenience store, not the cola company. In the case of a defective product – you presumably didn't intend to buy a dead mouse – your recourse is only to the party with whom you had a direct contract, i.e., the store to whom you gave your money. Early in the 20th century, the privity doctrine began to erode, and contracts were interpreted to extend to the producers of products as well as the immediate retailers. The cola producer becomes an indirect party to the contract, and liable if you received a defective product. An ethically and legally binding contract assumes knowledge by all parties, and the convenience store owner cannot be assumed to be fully knowledgeable about all the products in the store. The privity doctrine was seen to fall short of assuring an ethically fair contract.

The buyer, too, needs to be confident that she is fully aware of what she is buying. This contractual knowledge on the part of the buyer is assured by means of warranties. An express warranty is clearest. It states the explicit claims for the product made by the producer. If you buy frosted double-fudge diet brownies, alleged to contain only 50 calories, and later discover they have 500 calories, the producer has violated the express warranty, and is liable for breech of contract.

Implicit Warranty: And a warranty doesn't have to be express and explicit. There is an implicit warranty. A contract, if it is not to be deceptive, assumes that the product is fit, usable, and safe for its reasonably intended purpose. This is the "implied warranty of merchantability" doctrine. So the cola producer does not have to expressly claim that the cola is mouse-free. The buyer has the right to assume implicitly that her reasonable intention to buy a refreshing drink implies among other things that it does not contain dead rodents. The producer does have the ethical right to disclaim all warranties, and to sell a product "as is." Many states legally restrict such disclaimers, since they leave gullible consumers open to deception.

The buyer is responsible for the safe use of her purchases, provided that they result from honest agreements knowledgeably and freely entered into by all parties honoring express and implied warranties. An unhappy consumer's recourse is to show breech of contract or violation of warranty. This is the ethical basis of contract theory.

Tort Theory: The second ethical and legal basis of product liability rests on tort theory. Tort means harm. If the provider of a product is negligent, and this negligence causes harm for the user of the product, then the user has a right to have that harm reimbursed. Again, this is the deontological duty of *quid pro quo* justice. If my negligence has caused damage, I have the duty to repair the damage I have caused. The burden of proof for the dissatisfied consumer is to show that the producer was negligent and that the negligence caused harm to the consumer. Negligence means that the producer did not show "due care" in the production and marketing of a product. The producer did not foresee and prevent the harm that a reasonable person should have foreseen was liable to occur.

Soft Core *Caveat Vendor:* This duty to reimburse harm from negligence might be called a soft form of *caveat vendor,* i.e., a weak version of "let the seller beware." The annual list of dangerous toys that comes out every Christmas is fodder for possible product liability suits, based on harm stemming from vendor negligence. Does the marketing of the following toys represent a lack of due care on the part of producers to foresee harm to children that a reasonable person should foresee? The PIRG list[7] of dangerous toys include:

---

7.   These toys are taken from the Public Interest Research Group's list, issued in November 1996.

Osh Kosh B'Gosh's Soft Cow Pull Toy, which has a 28-inch cord, and Tomy's Big Fun Chuffa Train with a 39-inch cord, these cords posing a strangulation risk, according to PIRG, which recommends cords no longer than 8 inches long;

Catchin' Shark Game by an unknown manufacturer in China poses a laceration hazard from sharp edges and pointed shark teeth;

Pentech's NBA Squirt Balls, less than 1.75 inches in diameter, pose a choking hazard for small children, though the toy is labeled not for children under four-years-old;

Similarly posing choking hazards from an unknown manufacturer in China are Fun Novelty Erasers, under 1.25 inches in diameter, and easily fitting into a choke tube.

Other targets for possible tort are bicycle helmets that fail head-impact tests, portable playpens that can collapse and strangle a baby, and infant swings that don't lock securely and turn into baby ejection seats. The ethical and legal question is to determine who is negligent. Would a reasonable person say that these are products that consumers should be able to use in a safe manner, or should the vendors exercising due care foresee that these products will cause harm to consumers? The penalty for tort is to repair the damage. The question is: Whose negligence caused the damage? If the consumer, then the consumer assumes the burden of risk. If the vendor, then the vendor bears the burden.

We arrive now to the doctrine of "strict liability." *In the safe use of products, should the consumer bear the burden of risk?*

NO:

Strict Liability: The doctrine of strict liability puts the whole burden of forestalling harm onto the backs of manufacturers, *even when there is no negligence on the part of the manufacturer!* This really seems unfair. Consider the example of a man who injured his hand in the blades of a lawnmower. The manufacturer had put a hand guard or shield on the lawnmower precisely to prevent such an injury. The man deliberately removed the shield, and his stupidity or negligence resulted in an injury. He wasn't even the original owner of the mower, but had bought it second-hand. Nonetheless, under strict liability, the manufacturer of the lawnmower was found liable. Manufacturer liability from negligent tort we labeled a "weak" version of caveat vendor. Manufacturer liability from non-negligent tort is certainly a strong version of *caveat vendor.* What is the ethical reasoning behind the doctrine of strict liability?

Hard core *caveat emptor:* Strict liability is a way of dealing with social costs of the harms that consumers experience from the products they buy. Contract Theory and Due Care Theory sound good in the abstract.[8] When manufacturers honor their contracts, fulfill their warranties, and show due care against foreseeable harm, their job is done. Responsibility for avoiding harm then rightly rests on the shoulders of consumers. So the theory goes. But in the real world, it's not so simple.

---

8.   For a fuller analysis of these concepts, see Manuel G. Velasquez's excellent treatment, Chapter 6, "The Ethics of Consumer Production and Marketing," *Business Ethics* (Prentice Hall, 1988; second edition). Softer and stronger versions of *caveat emptor* and *caveat vendor* are categories devised by Velasquez, which I summarize here.

Contracts are not enough: Contract theory is wrong in assuming that seller and buyer enter into a contract as equal partners. The average consumer doesn't have the time, the wherewithal or the knowledge to evaluate products in a comprehensive and rational way. The manufacturer knows the inside story, the plans and recipes, the trade secrets, the strengths and weaknesses of the product. Only a very small, highly polished image of all this information is shared with the prospective buyer, usually in the form of upbeat advertising which ignores and plays down any problems. The consumer is reduced to reading limited mandated labels and warranties written in legalese tilted toward the manufacturer's interest. A tiny minority of activists might consult consumer interest magazines. This is a long way from two parties giving equally informed consent to a contract. The consumer simply doesn't have enough knowledge to assume with the manufacturer an equal share of the risks of the product. Therefore, in most cases it is unjust to treat buyer and seller as equal parties to a contract in terms of liability.

Also contracts are less able to protect against product harm because of economic constraints. Safety comes at a price. The buyer might quite happily, without full awareness of the risks, accept a less safe product at a lower price. In a penny-wise, pound-foolish mood, the buyer might contract to waive warranty rights to save money. And a seller in a contract may explicitly disclaim that a product is reliable or safe. People do buy and sell "as is," and this doesn't prevent consumer harm. And people do trade safety for savings, buying a light, more dangerous and cheaper small car, for example, over a larger, safer and much more expensive one.

Due Care by manufacturer not enough: Due Care Theory also has problems guarding against social costs that comc from product harm. Contracts at least have the virtue of being relatively clear about mutual obligations. "Due care" is much more difficult to determine. How much due care is reasonable? There's no such thing as an absolutely safe product. The safer a product is, the more expensive it is to produce it, and the more it will cost. There always will be a point when the costs of safety outweigh the benefits of safety. This was the question Ford Motor Company had to face when deciding whether to pay for a safer gas tank design on the Pinto.

And due care is patronizing. Maybe the consumer prefers to have less airline safety if safety means long airport delays and much higher ticket prices. Maybe I prefer to buy my medications in a little cardboard box, rather than in plastic jars with fail-safe tops that no adult can open. And if I am very, very ill, shouldn't I be free to use experimental drugs that may well harm me, but might help too?

Finally, it is hard to exercise due care before you launch your product and discover experimentally what happens with it in the real world. Play dolls have been created that will talk and sing and nurse and pee. This year, dolls were made that could eat. Who knew that they would start eating the hair of the little girls who owned them? Who predicted with the invention of desktop computers that carpal tunnel syndrome would become a major liability issue? Who had the due care to foresee that so many computer software programs would become universally defective in the year 2000, programmed as they were to identify the year by using only the last two digits? Due Care Theory is not an effective guarantee against social harm from defective products.

So enter "strict liability." This strong version of *caveat vendor* makes manufacturers liable for harm that no reasonable person could have foreseen. Companies are ordered to pay up even though they have not been negligent. The victim of product harm has a relatively simple burden of proof: (1) show that the product had a defect that harmed the user, even though this harm could not have reasonably been foreseen; (2) show that a better design would have protected even stupid and unreasonable consumers from accidents not reasonably foreseeable. Doesn't it seem unfair to penalize companies for not making their products idiot-proof? What is the ethical justification for this?

Benefits Outweigh Costs: The clearest argument is a utilitarian one. We live in a complex technological society. It is for the greater benefit of the common good that we all be protected from harmful products. Yes, there are fools and misfits among us who find a way to misuse just about anything; but there are normal people like you and me who don't always take the time and care to use products in a reasonable way; and there are good intelligent people who are technologically naive. We need to be protected from ourselves. The cost of that protection is assigned to the manufacturers of these products that so many of us unreasonably misuse. We turn the manufacturers into insurance providers for society at large. This is not an unjust thing to do, since we all pay the bill for this insurance by way of higher prices for these fail-safe products. The fail-safe price built into the cost of products has been called the "Tort Tax." You could look at it as an insurance premium. This premium accounts for 30% of the price of a stepladder, 25% of the price of a tour bus, 33% of the price of a small airplane.[9]

---

9. For a discussion of the economic and legal side of liability, see Peter W. Huben, *Liability: The Legal Revolution and Its Consequences* (Basic Books, Inc., 1988). See also, Anna J. Bray, "Why Have Tort Costs Exploded?", *Investor's Business Daily* (January 20, 1995), A1-2.

The utilitarian calculus weighs the benefits of strict liability against its cost. The benefits are that all of society's members have a way to be reimbursed for harm that products cause, even unwittingly. And this system motivates manufacturers to make safer products, even fail-safe products, as far as possible.

The costs of this system lie in the higher prices paid by all of us, and the perceived unfairness of making one sector of society – manufacturers – responsible for the irresponsibility of the rest of us. And there is another cost. This system inhibits innovation. For example, Immune Systems Response has withdrawn from AIDS vaccine research for fear of being held responsible for harm that they never caused, if such a vaccine were to go on the market. And when you inhibit new products, you pay a price in loss of jobs. Finally, strict liability is a very expensive kind of insurance. A large percentage of liability damage awards, including the cut taken by the lawyers, goes to litigation expenses, money that the victims never see.

If you judge that the benefits outweigh the costs, then strict liability is ethically justified.

PO:

Products. Harms. Lawsuits. Costs. Benefits. Compensation. Money. Are you a monotheist or a moneytheist?

Is it possible that all products are potentially harmful to the consumer? Remember the Buddhist monk who was confronted by a thief, demanding that he hand over his supplies? The monk greeted the thief, invited him in to take anything he wanted. The thief cleaned him out. A friend came by later to find the monk gazing at the moon in meditation. "How awful," the friend said, "the thief took everything." "No, he didn't," the monk replied. "I have my beautiful moon." Who is richer, the thief hauling

away the take from the impromptu garage sale giveaway,
or the monk enjoying his beautiful moon?

⟋The Amish are the richest people in the world. Their
home doubles as a living place, a church, a nursing home,
a retirement village. They don't pay or receive Social Security, since they already have social security. ⟋

ETHICAL EXPERIMENT:

Get rid of the harmful products in your life without having to sue anyone. Make a list of all your possessions.

There is an expression that people use – "the weight
of my possessions." Which are the products in your life
that weigh you down, that are a drag, that just take up
space, that require more care than they're worth, that you
always seem to be worried about, that are a drain on your
pocketbook, that you hang on to even though for the past
12 months you haven't used them?

You have other belongings that you delight in, that
free you up, that you love to use, that care for you more
than you have to care for them, that are empowering, that
you use with a light hand and a joyful heart.

Evaluate each of your possessions with a number
from 0 to 10. *Zero* represents those products in your life
that are an absolute dead weight, all the way up to *ten* for
products that enhance your life in a light and lively way.

On the number scale, draw a cutoff line representing
the level of harmful product that you won't put up with
any more. Get rid of these low-scoring harmful possessions.

You are a victim no more. This set of self-inflicted
torts is banished from your life.

SELF

19 Alcoholism: Disease or Moral Choice?

Step 1: "We admitted we were powerless over alcohol - that our lives had become unmanageable."

The Big Book

Step 1 actually teaches addicts that they are not responsible for what they put in their mouths, that they have no capacity to refrain from ingesting alcohol. Could it be that alcoholism is largely a result of this idea? . . . <u>Learned helplessness from Step 1</u> often can be a self-fulfilling prophecy. **The small book**[1]

The therapeutic view of evil as sickness, not sin, is strong in codependency theory. . . . Sickness, however, is <u>more marketable than sin</u>: readers who find it satisfying and useful to be diagnosed as victims of disease would probably resent being called evil.

I'm Dysfunctional, You're Dysfunctional[2]

What is the role of moral choice in addictive behavior? More specifically, is the addictive consuming of alcohol a disease, like cancer, for example, or is it a choice, like deciding to drink a glass of lemonade? If it is a disease, then alcoholism does not belong in the realm of the

---

1. Jack Trimpey, *The small book: A Revolutionary Alternative for Overcoming Alcohol and Drug Dependence* (Bantam Doubleday Dell, revised edition 1992), p. 35.

2. Wendy Kaminer, *I'm Dysfunctional, You're Dysfunctional: The Recovery Movement and Other Self-Help Fashions* (Random House Vintage Books, 1993), p. 18.

moral life. People do not morally choose to enjoy colon cancer. If by some miracle a colon cancer patient could be told, "If you decide not to eat oatmeal any more, your colon cancer will be cured and will never return," the patient would leap at making such a choice. But, alas, colon cancer is a disease, and is not susceptible to such a moral cure. Is alcoholism like cancer? Or can we indeed offer an alcohol addict a choice, "If you decide not to drink alcohol any more, your alcoholism will be cured and will never return"?

There is a sense in which colon cancer is a choice. If you don't eat enough fiber, you can increase your chances of getting it. But once you have this disease, the cure is not a moral choice. The cure lies in physical medical intervention, such as surgery. There is a sense in which alcoholism is a disease. Ethanol is a toxin. The ethanol swallowed into the body attacks the alcoholic's vital organs. But this toxin's assault on the body can be stopped by a moral choice: I decide not to swallow this poison any more. So does the alcoholic choose his poison, or is she the victim of a disease?

Two recovery systems give opposite answers to this question. Alcoholics Anonymous (AA) revolutionized the treatment of alcoholics by reframing alcoholism as a disease. Prior to AA, alcoholics would "take the pledge," "go on the wagon," and fall off the wagon, again and again and again. The medical community shunned treating alcoholics because their therapies were so futile. So their treatment fell to the clergy, who tried to use religion to boost their moral strength and willpower, for the most part with little success. AA changed all that, with the disease concept of alcoholism and the Twelve Step Program for recovery from (but not cure of) this disease.

The Rational Recovery (RR) system rejects AA's fatalism that the alcoholic is infected with a lifelong disease, and rejects also the lifelong group dependence and religious surrender exacted by AA as the price of recovering from and coping with this disease. Based on psychologist Albert Ellis' Rational-Emotive Therapy (RET), RR shifts the focus away from disease theory as irrelevant and onto choice, and advocates individual responsibility in place of group surrender, and the application of reason in place of religious surrender.

So the question we consider is: *Is alcoholism an incurable disease to be coped with only by religious surrender and group dependence?*

YES:

The charismatic Bill Wilson appeared on the scene at exactly the right time, the end of Prohibition, to found "a religion that is not a religion," Alcoholics Anonymous. The theology of this religion is contained in *The Big Book*, with its Twelve Step Program that has become the blueprint for the recovery movement from every imaginable addiction: gamblers, overeaters, narcotics, sex addicts, shopping addiction, and every imaginable variety of so-called "codependent" victims and abusers that populate daytime television talk shows. So the Twelve Step Program must be doing something right, though you may not want to go so far as to say: "If you do not participate in a 12-step program, your chance of staying clean and sober is 0%." The executive vice-president of the Betty Ford Center, who spoke these words,[3] exemplifies the very common "true believer" spirit that informs AA.

It was a stroke of genius to declare alcoholism to be a disease, albeit a disease discovered in church basements rather than in medical labs. This removes from the strug-

---

3.   Cited by Trimpey, *op. cit.*, pp. 241-242.

gling alcoholic the sense of guilt and moral failure resulting from the never-ending cycle of relapses, following
upon constant moral resolutions to reform. If this is a disease, the failures are not his fault. Self-esteem is restored.
The 12-step program rekindles hope in the alcoholic's
life. AA gives her a new family, who suffer from the same
disease as she does and so can understand and support
her. A holistic lifestyle plan is laid out for her, based on
self-honesty, and on seeking forgiveness to heal the relationships damaged by her addiction. Eventually the alcoholic (always "recovering," never cured) will be strong
enough to bring this message of faith to other sufferers
from this same disease.

The price of this recovery is a kind of Taoistic surrender of autonomy. It is a kind of trying by not trying. The
"New Year's resolution" kind of approach doesn't work.
Individual moral effort is supplanted by surrender to the
group's plan and support. Reliance on one's own strength
is replaced by surrender to a higher power. This power
knows how to guide me better than I can guide myself.
There is a religious faith quality to this surrender. I need
to put aside my critical mind, and let the program work
its power. "There's never been anyone too dumb to get
this program, but there's been a lot of people who were
too smart."[4] Criticism of AA dogmas is dismissed as stub-
born addictive resistance. Give up criticism. Accept that
you will never, never be cured. Recovery is a lifelong and
never-ending process. Your dependence on the group will
never end. Your identity will always be "recovering alcoholic."

In the past two decades, families and intimates of addicts have been sucked into the web of complicity through
the concept of codependency. Addiction does not occur

4.   *Ibid.*, p. 91.

and flourish in a vacuum. The intimate companions of the addict conspire to enable the addiction. The addict and the circle of family/friends are players in the same sick game. The addict is the scapegoat. But the "good" players in this game, by their emotionally dependent ties with the addict, their covering up, their rescue efforts, are enablers of the addiction. As the addict suffers from a chronic life-long disease, the codependent enablers also suffer from this correlative disease. Indeed, it seems that every dysfunctional behavior occurs in a social context, which is the dysfunctional group that makes the dysfunction possible. Some recovery professionals have estimated that 95% of American families are dysfunctional. Since nearly everyone is either sick or dysfunctional or an enabler of dysfunction, this makes the whole population of the United States into a potential patient pool for the recovery industry.

Clearly both AA and ACOA (Adult Children of Alcoholics) exist to help people assume responsibility for their own lives. But it is always in the context of allegiance to and dependence on the recovery groups, and the recovery project is lifelong. (Recovery groups are flexible in that they urge you to take what you can from the groups and leave the rest, but they do not brook criticism of the basic assumptions that it is fatal to go it alone, and that these diseases are incurable.]

NO:

RR shows a pathway to abstinence without the 12 steps, without the surrendering one's autonomy to a group or to a Higher Power. No religious conversion is required, no moral inventory, no cultic faith. The system is very narrowly focused on the undesirable behavior, putting alcohol in your mouth, and how to use your reason to stop doing that. Everybody has 100% control over pouring liquid in a glass, holding a glass, bringing it to one's mouth, and swallowing. No disease forces these actions. Suppose someone dying of AIDS were told, "Listen, you'll be cured if you never put alcohol in your mouth again." They'd agree in a minute and never look back. No "One day at a time." No "maybe." No "I'll try." "Thank you," they'd say. "That's it. I don't even want to look at alcohol again." What a small price to pay for a cure from a terminal disease. Alcohol addiction is terminal. And the cure is just that simple.

The key is to be just as rational about alcohol decisions as about other decisions in life. For example, if a thought, "I've gotta have a drink" comes to mind, ask, "If this thought is true, will it help me be safe, sober and more alive?" "If this thought is true, 'I gotta have a drink' – what is the evidence? Is it giving me the feelings that I want? Is it bringing me closer to my goals? Does it minimize my conflicts with other people?"

As I keep doing this, I see more and more clearly the irrationality of these thoughts, and become less and less likely to fall for them. And if I lapse and have one drink, there is no need to buy into AA's self-fulfilling prophecy that "I have no control over alcohol." There is no need to have another drink. I sleep it off, and learn for the next time. RR, based on Albert Ellis's RET, really isn't concerned about the cause of alcohol addiction, whether it is genetic, or psychological, or social conditioning, or a character flaw. Whatever the cause, you are not a victim of that cause. You are a rational human being in control of what you put into your mouth. If a five-year-old can refrain from stealing from a cookie jar, surely a grown man or woman can refrain from swallowing alcohol.

You don't need to be loved; you can give love. You don't need the group's esteem, just self-esteem. You don't need a higher authority; just listen to the voice of your own reason. RR equips you to live your life independently, without endless need for external support and guidance. In RR, you don't proclaim, "I am an alcoholic." That could be a self-fulfilling prophecy. There's so much more to life than the "struggle" to stay sober. If you define it as a struggle, then it becomes a struggle. RR leaves that struggle behind and moves on. As a nondrinker, you have new goals to reach, new challenges. That's the self-fulfilling prophecy of RR.

RR does not view the families and intimates of alcoholics as sick codependent enablers. Clearly family members are mutually dependent on each other. Some of the dependence is rational, and other dependence can be irrational and counterproductive. RET assists friends and families of alcoholics to sort out their dependent behaviors, to avoid the irrational dependencies, and to develop a rational emotive autonomy as the basis for independent decision-making. Neither addicts nor their families need look forward to a life sentence in the recovery movement. 95% of American families may be imperfect, but they are not all chronically ill with a lifelong disease. People can learn to rationally self-correct their imperfections over a period of time, and seek goals and meaning in life without shedding endless tears over their lost inner child.

PO:

Is AA rightly called a cult, even a religious cult? Who cares? Bottom line: Don't put alcohol in your mouth. If it takes a cult to get you to knock it off, then be glad you found a cult to save your life.

Are AA members like doctors in hospitals, who talk about the AIDS in Room 4, the cancer in Room 303, the broken hip on the fourth floor, with their constant refrain, "I am an alcoholic," wearing the label like a badge of honor? You are not your disease.

How about a new label: not, "I am an alcoholic," but "I am a non-drinker."

Why not drink yourself to death? People work themselves to death. That can be the downside of excessive hours on the job. The payoff is more income for family and children and advancement in career, and they make a moral decision for work at the price of health. People also smoke themselves to death. The upside of smoking is stimulation, sophistication and a defense against being overweight. So they make a moral choice to enjoy this habit. Health is not the be-all and end-all of moral values.

ETHICS EXPERIMENT:

Are you addicted to some hobby, pastime, substance, food, behavior, or person – an addiction that is interfering with your life? Give it up for a day. For a week. Can you just make up your mind, and do it? Well, do it.

20 Free Speech: The Right to Be Wrong

Every idea is an incitement.
                Justice Oliver Wendell Holmes[1]

My own book, **The Feminine Mystique,** *which helped to start the modern women's movement, was suppressed as pornographic in libraries in the Midwest. Why, I don't know. Its only passion was for the personhood of women.*   **Betty Friedan[2]**

The Internet, we smugly say, has become a means of circumventing the restrictive codes of Tyrannies. But the reverse of this coin is less attractive: it also allows an almost exclusive American contagion to ooze outwards, unstoppable, like an oil spill, contaminating everyone and everything in its path.
        Simon Winchester, "An Electronic Sink of Depravity"[3]

The legal right to freedom of speech is ever under siege. The U.S. Congress would ban "indecency" on the Internet. Some feminists would penalize distributors of pornography, even to adults, on the grounds that it constitutes violence toward women. Church leaders levy re-

---

1.   Gitlow v. New York 268 U.S. 652, 673 (1925) (dissenting), cited in Nadine Strossen (President of ACLU), *Defending Pornography: Free Speech, Sex, and the Fight for Women's Rights* (Scribner, 1995), p. 284.

2.   Betty Friedan, "Feminism" in *The Meese Commission Exposed: Proceedings of a National Coalition against Censorship, Public Information Briefing on the Attorney General's Commission on Pornography* (New York: National Coalition Against Censorship, 1987), pp. 24-25.

3.   *The Spectator* (February 4, 1995).

ligious sanctions on those who controvert issues of doctrine and law. Hate speech is banned on campuses.
Broadcasters and politicians, who venture a politically
incorrect observation, however casually, find themselves
out of work. These attacks on free speech raise the issue
of whether free speech is a human right. Do you have
the moral right to be wrong? Do human beings enjoy a
moral right to unfettered free speech.

So here is the question: ***Is there a moral right to freely
express oneself in whatever way one chooses in good conscience
to consenting adults, even though others consider this expression
provocative, evil, indecent, offensive, erroneous?***

YES:

Absolutely free speech is a moral right because it is a
practical necessity for leading a morally good life based
on reality and truth. Our weak and fallible minds do not
easily arrive at an adequate view of reality. We have to
painstakingly read and listen to many points of view; in
the political arena, disparate parties enter the fray, forg-
ing compromises as the partial truth of each is complemented by the alternative realities proposed by the others;
in the realm of gender, women from Venus soften the
sharp-edged views of men from Mars; in the generational
wars, the young with their keen, impatient present-mo-
ment sensibilities test their views against the quieter
deeper simplicities of elder wisdom. It is not an easy task
to gradually evolve our approximations of truth and virtue, and untrammeled free speech is one of the founda-
tions that makes this journey possible.

If we had infallible minds, with perfect mastery of
truth, and therefore could be always certain about the
right and proper thing to do, then the right to free
speech would be superfluous. It would give way to the

duty to speak the truth, that truth which is so elusive in the real world in which we live. In that ideal world where free speech would not be necessary, we would all know the truth perfectly and agree on it. In such a world, error would have no rights. There would be no right to be wrong because there would be no excuse to be wrong.

Would-be censors pretend to live in that world of absolute truth and certainty. Seated securely in their all-knowing judgement seats, they confidently decree which ideas and expressions are wrong and erroneous and, therefore, to be suppressed and censored, never to see the light of day. They try to determine what lesser minds and inferior groups may or may not think and say. And so books are burned, groups are disbanded, critics are fired, Internet sites are blocked.

The sad practical truth is that censors are not in possession of absolute truth. They may enjoy the political clout to silence those who offend them. But they can look forward to the day when others will acquire the political power to impose *their* opposing partial truths on the original censors. The alternative to free speech absolutism is "Might makes Right." If you have the right to silence others who offend you, you'll quickly find others silencing you for offending them. By tolerating others who offend, we help each other arrive at a fuller view of reality. By listening to painful alternative truths that we'd rather not hear, we cooperatively attain a richer grasp of truth. By acting on these fuller truths, we are enabled to live out a more comprehensive morality.

Free speech has its responsibilities and accountability. My words have consequences sometimes damaging and harmful. If I abuse my freedom of speech, to calumniate others, to destroy reputations, to provoke violence, society rightly penalizes me for the harm caused by my abuse.

When my speech overflows into harmful action, the remedy lies in the courts, with fines and prisons. If I offend others without harming them, the remedy is not to silence the speaker, but to counter the offender with speech of my own that shows where s/he is wrong. Free speech, even when offensive, is an instrumental value. It protects our right to unimpeded search for truth.

NO:

There can no more be a right to untrammeled free speech than there is a right to untrammeled free action.[4] Actions hurt as well as help. So there is no moral right to do anything whatsoever you please. The same goes for speech. Words are not mere sound waves impacting ear drums. Words come from people and embody the intentions of people. When I make a statement, I say this is true and the opposite is false. If someone believes the opposite of what I said, they may well be hurt and offended. A statement in favor of motherhood could be construed as demeaning of non-mothers. A statement in favor of apple pie could provoke environmentalists concerned about pesticides in apples. And most statements are much more provocative than defenses of motherhood and apple pie.

Speech matters. Speech intends to shape the world. To state the true excludes the false. To state the good excludes the bad. As Justice Holmes said, "Every idea is an incitement." Every statement about what is true and good could be seen as a clear and present danger to those whose ideas are being declared false and bad. If your

---

4.   Free speech is an incoherent concept, according to Stanley Fish, a chief proponent of the "reader response" theory of literary criticism. See his *There's No Such thing as Free Speech, and It's a Good thing, Too* (Oxford University Press, 1994), and his *Professional Correctness: Literary Studies and Political Change* (Oxford: Clarendon Press, 1995).

words mean anything at all, somebody somewhere is going to interpret them as "fighting words." This is why people incessantly gossip and judge and condemn the "stupid" views of those with whom they disagree. An idea is not an innocent bystander. Any idea could be perceived by someone or some group as a threat to act on that idea in a way that is objectionable. There is no clear line between speech and action. So the right to say anything I please can be plausibly seen as a threat to *do* anything I please, and that is unacceptable.

So how do we decide which speech is acceptable and which not? The same way we decide which actions are acceptable and which are not. In each case, society rightly weighs the benefits of permitting speech against the harms that speech may cause. Speech and politics inevitably go hand-in-hand. Free-speech absolutism is a high-sounding cloak for the unacknowledged agendas in the minds of the absolutists.

A student complains about the suppression of his magazine filled with hate speech against minorities. He now feels the censor in the back of his head when he writes. Reply: you are better off with a speech code in the back of your head than with the anti-ethnic degradation you had in the back of your head before. Then there is the slippery slope objection: if you ban hate speech today, tomorrow you'll be banning unpopular political reformers. Reply: all speech is restrictive; the political reformer seeks to restrict the status quo; when we speak to each other, we are engaged in a constant struggle to restrict others without being restricted ourselves; such is the nature of speech. Or consider complaints that religious leaders who cut off debates, say, about women's ordination in the Catholic Church, are "chilling free speech." Reply: all speech attempts to chill opposite speech; women's ordina-

tion proponents seek to chill and undermine those who
would deny women – the only question is, whose speech is
going to be chilled? Make sure it is not your own. The
bottom line: even free-speech absolutists don't want free
speech, they want *their* free speech.

PO:

I wonder if free-speech absolutists at a constitutional convention would support a charismatic speaker whose words
imminently threatened to end all free speech rights, once
and for all?

I wonder if high school students should enjoy free-
speech rights on a par with their elders, e.g., the right to
wear T-shirts emblazoned with bawdy and irreverent graf-
fiti, the right to form gay-straight alliances to openly discuss sexual orientation, the right to report in school
newspapers stories that reflect poorly on teachers and the
school.

Did you ever hear a Catholic priest in a sermon
against abortion honestly present the pro-choice side and
ask what people might learn from it?

Since meaning comes from the intention of the
speaker, speech is accountable to the communities for
which it speaks. A feminist who uses her academic classroom as a political platform could be censured for academic incompetence; a biologist who cites the Bible as
evidence for a scientific hypothesis could lose his credentials and credibility; a punk rocker who interrupted the
show to sincerely announce that she is "born again" would
be laughed off the stage."

"Congress shall make no law *abridging* speech," says
the First Amendment. It protects the speech you already
have. But it didn't give free speech to the slaves. And it
took over a hundred years to give it to women. What mas-

querades as free speech is really the right of the powerful to dominate the speechless. So argues feminist advocate Catharine A. MacKinnon.[5]

While the Bible is viewed primarily as a confessional theological source of doctrine and inspiration, it is also a dangerous literary political document. Among other atrocities, today it provides divine cover for attacks against homosexuals and for patriarchal violence against women. Do human beings, including women and homosexuals, have the right not to have their dignity undermined by destructive speech, even at the cost of banning such literary weapons? Should a gun ban be complemented by a Bible ban?[6]

Think back five years or so to a physical injury you might have had, a pain, a broken bone, a cut or a bruise. Does it still hurt today? Probably not. Now think back five years ago to someone who hurt you with their words. Does it still hurt? Probably yes. Free speech is dangerous.

ETHICS EXPERIMENT:

Are you being unjustly intimidated or forbidden to express your mind at work, or at school, or church? What would happen if you tested the limits of this censorship and expressed yourself? Try it and see.

---

5.   Catharine A. MacKinnon, in *Feminism Unmodified: Discourses on Life and Law*, see Chapter 16, "The Sexual Politics of the First Amendment," (Harvard University Press, 1987), pp. 206 ff.

6.   See Carol J. Adams and Marie M. Fortune (eds.), *Violence Against Women and Children: A Christian Theological Sourcebook* (Continuum Press, 1995). Provocative essays collected here take a fresh look at the Adam/Eve myth and women's subordination, at overly facile concepts of forgiveness, at the biblical concept of submission, at responses of Christian communities to abuse of women, and many other such themes.

21 When Does an Ecological Plus Become a Human Minus?

Designated as an endangered species in 1993 . . . the first and only fly to make the list, the Delhi Sands flower-loving fly, is sorely testing the federal commitment to saving near-extinct species. In this case the government is protecting a creature that spends most of its life underground, living as a fat, clumsy, enigmatic maggot.

"Why should a fly stop civilization?" asks an exasperated California state senator. . . . "I'm for people, not flies."[1]

(1) The [environmental] resource base is finite; (2) there are limits to the carrying capacity of the planet; (3) economic growth is not a panacea for [diminishing] environmental quality.[2]

Nature had to be devaluated to a state where it could be useful economically and technically. . . . But nature could only be devaluated if and when humanity detached itself from nature and ceased to feel part of

---

1.   Ruben Ayala, quoted by William Booth, "A Fly in the Ointment," *The Washington Post National Weekly Edition* (April 14, 1997), 9.
2.   K. Arrow et al., "Economic Growth, Carrying Capacity, and the Environment," *Science* (28 April, 1995). This is from a policy statement agreed upon by 11 leading economists and ecologists, as stated in the policy forum section of *Science*.

> *it. . . . The objectification of nature and the autonomization of the human subject go hand in hand.*[3]

Traditional ethics has generally failed to give an adequate framework for environmental responsibility. Relentlessly centered on the mind, body and spirit of human beings, traditional ethics drags the environment in by the back door. A dichotomy is set up between humans and the environment. What hurts the environment but helps humans tends to be justified. But if humans are hurt, then environmental responsibility kicks in.

RIGHTS OF NONHUMANS:

Does the nonhuman world, living and nonliving, have rights as well, a moral claim, a dignity that needs to be respected? Indeed, what justification is there for separating human beings from the environment at all? Only "environmental activists" raise such questions. Somehow we see ourselves as outside the environment and superior to it, or even as in charge of it and owners of it. So the rights of an endangered species of maggot get pitted against the rights of humans to enjoy the maggot's habitat. The endangered maggot has minimal political clout since we can do very well without it, thank you. The rain forest and the ozone layer have more clout, because without the former, humans may eventually have trouble breathing, and without the latter, humans become more vulnerable to the sun's carcinogenic rays.

---

3.   Barbara Noske, *Humans and Other Animals: Beyond the Boundaries of Anthropology* (London: Pluto Press, 1989), p. 53. The arrogance of men's systematic domination of women carries over into domination of nature, as if men could be separate from and superior to both. This insight is at the heart of ecofeminism's contribution to environmental ethics.

Such anthropocentrism becomes more and more un-
credible as science on a daily basis extends the frontiers of
the universe and of life itself in ways that even only 10
years ago we could scarcely imagine. Using the Hubble
telescope's "Deep Field Observations," we are able to witness galaxies forming from sub-galactic clumps near the
beginning of "time." We have come to realize that there
exist an estimated 50 billion galaxies. And that's just the
universe "out there."[4]

Back on earth, our vistas are extended in the opposite direction – the bottom of the ocean, just seven miles
from the surface of the earth. Here can be found 10 million new species. More than 90% of the species on earth
exist here in the deep. The existence of these species has
revealed how little we really know about the conditions
necessary for life. Just a few years ago, life appeared as
very fragile and rare – in need of photosynthesis within a
relatively narrow temperature range in order to survive. At
the sea's bottom, we see hydrothermal vent (think "hot
springs") animals growing without light under unimaginable pressures, using chemosynthetic processes, not photosynthesis. Life can begin and flourish under conditions
heretofore unimagined.[5] Life is not confined to the
unique fragile conditions of the earth's surface. The universe could be, and probably is, teeming with life.

From these perspectives, an anthropocentric ethics is
a poor and meager instrument indeed for assessing our
responsible place in this immense and intricate whole.
And even anthropocentric ethics looks good compared to

4.   F. Duccio Macchetto and Mark Dickinson, "Galaxies in the Young
Universe," *Scientific American* (May 1997), 92-99.
5.   See William J. Broad, *The Universe Below: Discovering the Secrets of the
Deep Sea* (Simon and Schuster, 1997), and also Richard Ellis, *Deep
Atlantic: Life, Death, and Exploration in the Abyss* (Alfred A. Knopf, 1996).

the economic yardstick commonly used to evaluate "rational" environmental decisions. It may well make economic sense to cut down redwood trees for lumber. Does it make human sense? Does it make ecological sense?

This chapter will not get into anthropocentric moral assessment or economic calculus to determine the rights of humans over and against the rights of various endangered species of flora and fauna. Instead we will outline some broader models that are currently offered as frameworks for environmental ethics.[6] You are invited to consider and evaluate these as you formulate your own view of the place of human beings in the total scheme of things, and arrive at the model that best serves responsible ecological decision-making.

Lets's consider in turn: *(1) Biocentric Ethics, (2) Ecocentric Ethics, (3) Deep Ecology, (4) Ecofeminism.*

(1) BIOCENTRIC ETHICS:

All of the models that we will consider see the environment as embodying inherent worth, value and dignity. The goodness of the environment is not merely instrumental. It is not to be considered good merely to the extent that it serves human needs. The environment is not merely good *for* something, it is good, period.

The biocentric model focuses on the intrinsic worth of all living things.[7] There is a community of life that in-

6.   For a clear and comprehensive look at the current state of the question in ethics and ecology, see Joseph R. Des Jardins, *Environmental Ethics* (Wadsworth Publishing Company; second edition, 1997). This book helped orient my thinking for this chapter in terms of these ecological models.

7.   For a good statement of the biocentric model and the duties that flow from it, see Paul Taylor, *Respect for Nature,* (Princeton University Press, 1986). For an early classic defending the moral and legal rights of nonhuman living things, see Christopher Stone's *Should Trees Having*

cludes mosquitoes and cows and creatures at the bottom of the sea. Human beings are members of this community on the same terms as all other living things. And all these living species, humans included, are interdependent. It makes no more sense to pit one species against another, trees against human beings for example, than it would to pit my stomach against my lungs. As interdependent parts of a single whole, when I affect the part, I affect the whole. An assault on trees is an assault on humans. An assault on my stomach will affect my lungs. Living things have dignity worthy of respect because each is a teleological center of life, with a direction and a goal, each pursuing its own good in its own way. Finally, humans are not inherently superior to other living things. Humans are not outside of and superior to the life community. They are codependent members of this community, not external masters of it.

Certain moral imperatives follow from this biocentric perspective. Most fundamentally, respect for living things entails the duty of nonmaleficence, "Do not harm." Hindus call this the virtue of *ahimsa,* the doctrine of non-harm toward all living things. So, don't hurt your family and friends. Don't harm your enemies. If you must eat animals, do so compassionately, gratefully, and low on the food chain. Many Buddhist retreat centers enjoin visitors not to kill insects, even mosquitoes. Eschew pesticides; they kill pests, and in the food they keep on killing. Eat organically, i.e., food produced in a way "that promotes and enhances biodiversity, biological cycles, and soil biological activity."[8] Non-harm entails noninterference. As far

---

Standing?: and Other Essays on Law, Morals, and the Environment (original edition Avon Books, 1974, subtitled "Toward Legal Rights for Natural Objects," reprinted by Dobbs Ferry, NY: Oceana Publications, 1996).

as possible, allow all organisms to pursue their own good, not manipulating or controlling their habitats in any way that would limit this development. And when we have harmed and have interfered, justice requires that we remedy the harm.

Critique: Two criticisms can be brought against this biocentric model. First, when the focus is on individual organisms and the protection of individual species, inevitably an adversarial relationship is set up among individuals and species. The good of one organism or species may well interfere with and even harm another organism or species. Must I put my child at risk of encephalitis by refraining from killing mosquitoes? The above ethical principles don't deal well with conflicts of interest among living things.[9] Secondly, the ethical principles seem to separate humans from the rest of nature. Should non-harm and noninterference be a one-way street in making environmental decisions? Aren't humans also a part of the biosystem and, therefore, deserving of not being harmed or interfered with by other species?

(2) ECOCENTRIC ETHICS:

Ecocentric ethics proposes a more holistic approach than that of the biocentric model. The focus is on ecological systems more than on individual living organisms, on the

8. This definition of organic agriculture is by the National Organic Standards Board, in an effort to forestall marketing abuse of the label "organic." See Jennifer Barrett, "Growing Pains," *Yoga Journal* (May/June 1997), 76.
9. For an excellent discussion of this issue, see "'Forum: The Benefits and Ethics of Animal Research," *Scientific American* (February 1997). Articles include: "Animal Research is Wasteful and Misleading," "Animal Research is Vital to Medicine," "Trends in Animal Research," and "Animal Research Forum."

forest more than on the individual trees. And consideration is given to the non-living as well as to the living components of these ecosystems. Forests, deserts, grasslands, wetlands and lakes involve total holistic habitats whose components interact and depend on each other in mutually beneficial ways. Such ecological wholes demand respect on their own merits. "Wilderness" makes its own moral claims. The "frontier" is not just potential real estate waiting to be tamed and developed.

Ecocentrism comes in many forms. Some conservationists, falling back on anthropocentrism, see wilderness as valuable because of the resources it provides for human use. Naturally occurring medicines can be found in the rain forest, and so the rain forest must be preserved. Others, like John Jay Audubon and Henry Thoreau, romanticized the wilderness as valuable in its own right because it is unspoiled by human predators. The imperative is to seal off wetlands and bird sanctuaries, for example, from human taint and pollution.

Critique: In criticism of ecocentric ethics, there remains that tendency to separate out humans from these ecosystems. In a truly holistic perspective, shouldn't humans be viewed as rightly interacting in an interdependent way in all of these ecosystems? Shouldn't humans and cacti alike be allowed to invade the desert and coexist there? Shouldn't wetlands and lakes make place for humans, just as humans make place and respect lakes and wetlands? A second and related criticism is that ecological ethics tends to view ecosystems in a static way, as if they must forever remain unchanged. The ethical focus is on preserving them in a kind of mythical pristine state. Smokey the Bear says trees should never burn down. The Endangered Species Act decrees that species must never go out of existence. But lightening continues to inflame the forests, volcanos continue to explode, causing islands to appear and disappear, species we never heard about continue to be born and to die on the earth's surface and in the ocean's depths, antibiotics attack viruses and viruses develop immunities to antibiotics. Should the focus be more on welcoming human beings into the responsible evolution of ecosystems rather than on preserving ecosystems as unchanged?

The *Gaia* model is a recent bold hypothesis for overcoming these criticisms. American biologist Lynn Margulis and British scientist James Lovelock suggest that ecosystems be understood as living organisms, and further that the whole earth be viewed as itself a living organism.[10] If living things have dignity worthy of respect because each is a teleological center of life, with a direction and a goal, one is impelled to accord respect and moral worth to the ecosystem, which is *Gaia*, if it operates in a similar way, like a living organism.

(3) DEEP ECOLOGY:

The Deep Ecology movement arises in opposition to what Arne Naess calls the "shallow ecology movement."[11] Shallow ecology is centered on the anthropocentric view of nature as the servant of human wants and needs, concerned with pollution and resource-conservation. Deep Ecology rejects the humans-in-environment model that tends to infect even ecocentric ethics, and flatly espouses a total-field, utterly nonanthropocentric model. Even

10. For example, James Lovelock, *The Ages of Gaia: A Biography of Our Living Planet* (Oxford University Press, 1988); Lynn Margulis and Dorion Sagan, *Slanted Truth: Essays on Gaia, Symbiosis, and Evolution* (Copernicus Press, 1997).

11. Arne Naess, David Rothenberg, *Ecology, Community and Lifestyle: Outline of an Ecosophy* (reprint edition; Cambridge University Press, 1990). See also Bill Devalls and George Sessions, *Deep Ecology: Living as if Nature Mattered* (Salt Lake City: Peregrine Smith Books, 1985).

more characteristically, Deep Ecology sees our environmental crisis as basically a philosophical crisis. It calls for a radical transformation of consciousness that will revolutionize current economics, ideology and culture. The dominant worldview must be replaced by an alternative "ecosophical" worldview. Ecosophy holds that nonhuman and human ecosystems have the right to flourish in all their richness and diversity. In spite of our dominant worldview, humans have no moral right to privilege or preference. In fact, the problem today is not that humans are being harmed by a polluted nonhuman world; rather it is that the nonhuman world is being harmed by the pollution that is human beings (especially in the excess of the "population explosion"). Nonhuman life, and human life and culture will flourish if there is a decrease in the human population. Such a reversal of population growth and such a turnaround in priorities away from the domination of the earth by human beings will require an ideological revolution. Quality of life in a sustainable environment must become the ideal, not a "higher standard of living" that is destructive and unsustainable. Deep Ecology challenges you to embrace a lower standard of living that is compatible with a higher quality of life.

This explanation of ecosophy has spoken of human versus nonhuman as if these were two ontological realms. Don't be deceived. There is no assumption that in a conflict of interests between human and nonhuman, that the human should prevail. In fact, the revolution called for by Deep Ecology is best understood and more readily embraced when these distinctions of realms disappear. Whether a plague of locusts, a plague of nuclear radiation, or a plague of human beings, all are equally hostile to a sustainable whole.

Deep Ecology also challenges us to let go of the dominant worldview's bias toward individualism. As the Buddhist would say (and Deep Ecology has resonance with "Eastern thought"), the individual is an illusion. Individuals are the point of intersection of processes of all kinds, physical, chemical, biological, conscious, superconscious. Ecosophy sees the processes as more real than the individuals who arise and fall away in these processes. Responsible environmental policy ensures the conditions necessary for these processes to continue in a sustainable way. You might, with the Hindus, view your individual identity as a "self"; but this is not ultimate. More fundamental is the "Self," the total sum of processes in which your "self" and my "self" come into being and fade away. The Self, not the self, is Deep Ecology's focus.[12]

Critique: A main criticism of Deep Ecology is that for all its pretensions to be universal, it has a very Western take on things. The dominant ideology that it criticizes is not an ideology shared by most of the world, especially in the underdeveloped and poorer nations. The strains on ecosystems imposed by the developed nations, even with their relatively smaller populations, are far greater than the strains imposed by the less-developed poor nations; the latter, in spite of their dense populations, live at a much more environmentally stable and sustainable level. The so-called dominant worldview criticized by Deep Ecology oppresses not only nonhuman ecosystems; it oppresses large human ecosystems in the less-developed world.

---

12. Devall and Sessions, *op.cit.*, pp. 66-67.

(4) ECOFEMINISM:

Androcentrism, not anthropocentrism, is the root cause of our ecological crisis, says ecofeminism. Anthropocentrism says we are too human-centered. That's not the problem. Androcentrism says we are too male-oriented; we are too immersed in patriarchal patterns of domination and hierarchy. The degradation of nature and of nations is rooted not so much in an abstract dominant philosophy as in unjust actions and policies of human beings against nature and against other human beings. Deep Ecology tends to blame the victim of these injustices, the poor who live in underdeveloped lands with their burgeoning populations. Don't blame the poor for their lack of education, for the exploitation of their labor, the plundering of their natural resources. In the face of such aggressions, perhaps the most rational and responsible choice available for the poor is to increase and multiply.

The Rise of Gender Feminism: There are many feminisms. A chief divide is between equity feminism and gender feminism. For equity feminism, male and female alike are first and foremost human. Cultural roles should not be linked to biological sexual identity. All roles should be open to all. Biology is not destiny. Gender feminism, on the other hand, accepts that women are different from men, equal, but separate. There are distinctive women's ways of experiencing the world and distinctive feminine moral sensibilities. Psychologist Carol Gilligan started this revolution.[13] There is a way in which biology is and should be destiny. This is the view that inspires ecofeminism.

---

13. Her classic, *In a Different Voice: Psychological Theory and Women's Development*, has been reissued in paperback by Harvard University Press, 1993.

Gilligan corrected the bias in moral development studies that used male experience as normative for humans. When finding that in resolving moral dilemmas, women seemed to reason differently from men, researchers like Lawrence Kohlberg had concluded that women's moral development was deficient, retarded and lacking in reasoning skills.

With Freud, Gilligan agreed that women and men differ in what they regard as ethically normative, but unlike Freud she maintained that women's ways are just as moral as men's.

MEN	WOMEN
abstract principles of justice	compassion and care
"what's the fairest thing to do?"	"who will be hurt least?"
seek autonomy, fear commitment	seek commitment, fear abandonment
masculinity defined by separation	femininity defined by attachment
protect the *rights* of others	*care* for others

Like Gilligan, Nancy Chodorow reinforces Freud's observation that men and women inhabit different moral universes. She says, "The basic feminine sense of self is connected to the world, the basic masculine sense of self is separate." This encourages the stereotype that women on the job and in politics operate on a different wavelength from men. Women in business are said to care primarily for people's feelings and personal ties, while men are said to be rational, logical, and task-oriented. Or, if women reigned in politics, there would be an end to wars.

Gender Feminism and Eco-Feminism: Ecofeminism coun-
teracts androcentric patterns of domination and exploitation by underlining women's affinity for nature,
women's sensibility of care and connection. There is a
resonance with women's *intuition* that something is
wrong with traditional morality; that intimacy and an
ethic of care are as life-affirming and more valuable
than an aloof ethic of justice, whose principled rationality
often results in injustice to real human beings in the real
world. Women take great care to approach matters con-
textually and to make the least hurtful holistic decisions.

Ecofeminism needs to deconstruct the ways in which
androcentric rationality reduces and objectifies nature the
way it reduces and objectifies women. Sarah Hoagland[14]
shows how "John beat Mary," becomes "Mary was beaten
by John" becomes "Mary was beaten" becomes "women
beaten" becomes "battered women." And battered women
becomes a disease, battered women syndrome. Nicole
Brown Simpson died of this syndrome. And the alleged
killer walks. And life goes on. Carol J. Adams[15] shows how
"Someone kills animals so I can eat their corpses as meat"
becomes "Animals are killed to be eaten as meat" becomes
"animals are meat" becomes "meat animals" becomes
"meat." What started as humans killing animals to eat
their corpses gets reduced to a food product, animal's nature: meat, Twinkies – same thing.

We are experiencing today a backlash of nature
against the arrogant androcentric efforts to dominate it.
Edward Tenner calls this the Frankenstein Effect.[16] He

---

14. *Lesbian Ethics: Toward New Values* (Palo Alto: Institute for Lesbian
Studies, 1988), pp. 17-18.
15. *Neither Man Nor Beast: Feminism and the Defense of Animals*
(Continuum, 1994), p. 102.
16. See his book, *Why Things Bite Back: Technology and the Revenge of
Unintended Consequences* (Knopf, 1996).

cites the immunization of viruses against antibiotics, computer operating systems that render computers inoperable, football protective helmets used as lethal weapons, low-tar cigarettes that encourage smokers to smoke more, and the Chernobyl meltdown that was triggered by a safety test. We become dominated by what we would dominate.

Critique: Equity feminists would criticize ecofeminism for making ecological responsibility into a gender thing. They would reject the gender-stereotyping by ecofeminists that pigeonholes women's nature as gentler, kinder, more caring, more sensitive.[17] Another line of criticism would challenge ecofeminism's diagnosis of the ecological crisis. Yes, androcentric attitudes of domination over nature are totally counterproductive. Care, connection, and cooperation need to be our keynotes. But let's postulate a just world where all are free to pursue happiness. Can the globe really tolerate the current ideology about happiness, as the American standard of living for all? It is not physically possible. Social justice needs to be wedded to Deep Ecology's mind change.

ETHICS EXPERIMENT:

The globe currently sustains six billion human beings. By the year 2030 (how old will you be?), this population is projected to almost double. American borders are somewhat porous now. By 2030, there is no way to prevent privileged nations from being overrun by hordes desperate for a place to live. Your decisions now will create, or not create a sustainable environment then. A world of 11

---

17. See Rita M. Gross's brilliant critique of gender feminism in *Buddhism After Patriarchy: A Feminist History, Analysis, and Reconstruction of Buddhism* (State University of New York Press, 1993), Appendix A, "Here I Stand: Feminism as Academic Method and as Social Vision."

billion people, with 11 billion cars, 11 billion color television sets, 11 billion computers, 11 billion private bed-
rooms, 11 billion handguns, 11 billion daily meat entrees
is simply unimaginable because impossible. A sustainable
environment in the year 2030 requires radical new patterns of communication, transportation, food production,
waste disposal, entertainment, sports, political structure,
shelter, reproductive behavior, policing, conflict resolution. The answers cannot be more of the same. Pick one
of these areas and devise a plan for the next century.
Make sure your plan cares for quality of life (which is not
necessarily the same as high standard of living, but it
could be if you cut down the population enough); make
sure it is sustainable, that it does not unrealistically stress
all the human and nonhuman ecosystems on which it
must depend and interact if it is to succeed. What first
step could you take in your own life today to make this
plan a reality?

22   Ethical Pluralism: Zero-Sum Game or Win-Win?

It is not enough to succeed. Others must fail.

Gore Vidal[1]

A woman and two little boys in their swimming trunks got on the hotel elevator I was riding, obviously on their way to the pool. She said to them, "So who's going to jump into the pool fastest?" And they said, "We both are!" I thought, "How long can they hold out?" The genuine alternative to being number one is not being number two. It's being able to dispense with these self-defeating rankings altogether.[2]

Everybody has the best seat!

Zen saying.

This book has presented ethical issues not as a religious ethics catechism – but as ethics for a pluralistic world, with diverse inquirers, some accustomed to guidance from absolutist catechisms, others with no sure guides, others searching alone or in dialogue with others. We search out an ethical path with intimate companions with whom, with all our differences, we try to forge viable family lives;

---

1.   Adam M. Brandenburger and Barry J. Nalebuff, *Co-Opetition: A Revolution Mindset That Combines Competition and Cooperation: The Game Theory Strategy That Is Changing the Game of Business* (Doubleday, 1996), p. 3.

2.   Alfie Kohn, "The Case Against Competition," *Noetic Sciences Review* (Summer 1990), p. 90, a talk based on his book, which won the National Psychology Award in 1987, *No Contest: The Case Against Competition* (Houghton Mifflin, 1986).

we work with professional colleagues carving out codes for treating clients with consistent accountability; as citizens in the political arena we hammer out compromises that will serve the common good; and internationally through dialogue and negotiation rather than war, we try to ensure the survival of the human race on earth. If there were one absolute ethics that could provide the way and the truth for all, the UN should mandate and enforce it immediately. But every truth claim begets a counter claim. A classroom of 20 students will find six different religions represented, and within each religion, several different orthodoxies, and 20 different philosophies and approaches to ethics underlying all the religions. So our approach in this book has accepted pluralism as a given.

The challenge has been to walk a path between relativism (one ethics is as good as another) and absolutism (my ethics is right, yours is wrong). Absolutism makes ethics a zero-sum game: I win, you lose. Relativism says there is no game, because there are no rules. Pluralism, with its carefully mutually respectful dialogue, attempts to approach ethics as a win-win game. This is not easy. Ethical disputes in American society are a war zone, with battles fought to the death, zero-sum: I must win, you must lose. The competitive ethos that informs our *laissez faire* capitalism informs every aspect of our life and thinking. The truest thing, it seems, that we can say of human nature is that it is "the war of everyone against everyone else," as asserted by Thomas Hobbes. Whether we are talking about jobs or education or income or justice or ethical truth, competition is the name of the game. This is a war. There must be winners and losers. The winners deserve to win; the losers are left behind. And all are better for having faced the challenge of the battle.

Is competition a true picture and a necessary part of human nature?[3] If the answer is yes, then ethics is a war, and we must not shrink from the battle, but engage all our energies to win. And it is right for pro-choicers, for example, not to compromise one iota with pro-life, and for governments to silence dissenters, and for churches to excommunicate the unorthodox. Psychologist Alfie Kohn has radically challenged the domination of this competitive paradigm. He defends the countercultural claim, that competition in any amount at all is always destructive. Mainstream culture denies this, and sees competition as a necessary dimension of human nature playing a constructive role. Finally, a third position has been suggested, called "Co-Opetition." Let's consider this issue of individual and society, competition and cooperation, zero-sum and win-win.

So we ask: *Is competition always destructive for human beings?*

NO:

Aggression is inborn in human nature. Thomas Hobbes pointed this out. Scratch the surface of an ostensibly socialized human being and you quickly get to the selfish competitive beast underneath. Competition is not only good, it is necessary. It is who we are. What looks like society is basically the war of everyone against everyone else. A little handgun, a Saturday night special, enables the weakest one among us to kill the strongest. Death is the great leveler. Competition is at the heart of what it means

---

3.   Taking issue with the Darwinian competitive survival of the fittest, increasingly biologists have zeroed in on the role of cooperation in evolutionary progress. See, for example, Matt Ridley, *The Origins of Virtue: Human Instincts and the Evolution of Cooperation* (Viking Press, 1997).

to be a human being. Each one of us is in a survival contest to amass as much material security as possible for ourselves, in a world where each other person is trying to do
the same. And of course, there is not enough for all. No
amount would ever be enough, even for a single person.
Ball players who make $5 million dollars a year go on
strike to make even more. Billionaires use their money to
defraud additional millions. Thus the war goes on.

So we pay police to protect us. We lock our cars
when we leave them, if only for a moment. We invest in
security systems. We don't walk the streets alone at night.
When groups of strangers approach us on the sidewalk,
we cross to the other side of the street. We indoctrinate
our children to fear and avoid unfamiliar people. In the
security of our own homes, we sense danger from the
computer screen on the Internet. From our own families,
we lock drawers and cabinets and closets and diaries. A
police strike is a signal to rob banks all over the city. A
natural disaster turns upstanding citizens into bandits,
looting the stores and robbing the bodies of the dead.

American society brilliantly exploits this trait of human nature by making competition the engine of progress
and success. We accept competition as a given. Fighting
on our own behalf in zero-sum games brings out the best
in us. We don't question Vince Lombardi's maxim, "Winning isn't everything; it's the only thing."[4] The loser of a
world boxing championship match is not praised as the
second-best fighter in the whole world; he is viewed as a
loser. Competition builds character by enlisting our ener-

---

4.   Interestingly, Lombardi himself regretted this quote, saying shortly
before his death, "I wish to hell I'd never said the damned thing. I
meant having a goal . . . I sure as hell didn't mean for people to crush
human values and morality." See James A. Michener, *Sports in America*
(Random House, 1976), p. 432.

gies to maximize our dominant position in this survival war. So students compete for the highest grades, athletes compete for places on the varsity, applicants compete for the best jobs and highest salaries, citizens compete for political office. In the relatively unstructured, hurly-burly world of democracy, it is competition that filters talents and brings the cream to the top.

Competition Systemic: Kohn distinguishes *intentional* competition from *structural* competition. Intentional competition is an individual's need to be #1. But much more fundamental is the systemic structural competitiveness built right into so many of our institutions. Like it or not, you have to compete to get into college, to make a living or to get a seat on a bus. This structural lesson starts early on. In school, competition is the name of the game. Students who cooperate on a test or a project are called cheaters. And the mandate to win is so strong that it becomes an imperative to win at all costs. People who win by getting away with fudging or breaking the rules are admired. They are expected to try anything in order to win. Even as I write this, a middle-aged couple were disqualified for trying to outwit the hidden cameras in the Boston Marathon so that they could win their age division in the race by driving, not running part of the way. They were caught two weeks later. But no one is shocked. "Nice try; better luck next time."

Competition of moralities: This constructive role of competition fuels our belief in the benefits that flow from the marketplace of ideas. We tend to view this marketplace as a continuation of the war, a competitive arena. Our confrontational judicial system becomes the model of the clash of ideas. Some ideas will win. Some will lose. Even our philosophical and ethical debates become a zero-sum game. It is in the political arena where these issues are most bitterly contested, where winners are most richly rewarded and losers ruthlessly destroyed. But that's OK. Because the winning ideas are by that very fact validated as the best ideas, the truth. The losing ideas which failed are by that fact viewed as false. In this model, ethical pluralism becomes a zero-sum game, with winners and losers, and "I'm right – you're wrong" kinds of assumptions.

This is the case in favor of competition's constructive role in human evolution. There are indeed excesses in this struggle of the fittest to survive. But competition is an essential part of human nature and plays a positive role. There is another view. Perhaps the costs of competition over cooperation are not worth the positive results that competition allegedly brings. Could it be that competition is learned, and can be unlearned? Could it be that competition is always destructive?

YES:

The Culture of Winning: Psychologist Alfie Kohn defends the position that competition is certainly not a necessary part of human nature, and that it is always destructive. It is almost impossible in American culture to entertain such a hypothesis. Like water for the fish, competition is the invisible environment in which we live and breathe. The problem is not so much the obsessive individual driven to be #1. Rather it is the institutions that systemically shape our behavior in ways that make competition seem inevitable. In American politics, for example, the one imperative is to win. This takes money. Huge cash sums are collected from powerful interests who, with a wink and a nod, expect favors in return and corrupt the political process. But everyone feels helpless in the face of these ill-disguised bribes – trapped in the need to win at all costs, so "everybody does it," and an alternative seems unimaginable. In athletics, the cheap shot, the spitball, the undetected foul are praised if they remain undetected. The need to win is their justification – competition thriving on the morality of "the end justifies the means." Again, an alternative to this ethos seems beyond our ability to comprehend.

This same morality flourishes in the world of business. Listen to the director of a business ethics center:

> As long as you have a business culture that puts people in impossible situations – "Your division has to grow 7% next year or else we're going to be No. 2 in the field, and if we are, you're going to be job-hunting" – you're going to have people shipping inferior goods, bribing when they have to, trampling workers beneath them and generally conducting themselves in the time-honored tradition: Results, and only results, count.[5]

The end justifies the means. We can't conceive of an alternative to beating out the competition in order to be #1.

Ethical Debates as Zero-Sum Game: Along with business and sports and government, must learning, too, be a zero-sum game? This same competitive ethos is the hidden agenda in the schools. And just like we talk about reforming health care by making it more competitive, we debate how to make our schools more competitive. Must debates about ethical issues and policies result in winners and losers? Human beings do actually live in cultures where cooperation, not competition, is the norm.[6] There is an alternative to the zero-sum game.

---

5.   Gary Edwards, quoted by Paul Wilkes in "The Tough Job of Teaching Ethics," *The New York Times* (January 22, 1989), p. 24F.

6.   See Ashley Montagu (ed.), *Learning Non-Aggression: the Experience of Non-Literate Societies* (Oxford University Press, 1978). Also, you can explore the myriad ways of being human in Fons Trompenaars, *Riding*

Granted, in ethical debates, there will always be point and counterpoint. There will always be thesis and antithesis. Each chapter in this book has turned on a question, to which some answer yes, and some answer no. For the ethical absolutist, the only question remaining is, will *yes* win over *no*, or will *no* win over *yes?* But the ethical pluralist, having engaged in point and counterpoint, looks forward to synthesis. True, there is conflict. Cooperation does not mean that conflict must be eliminated from human life. But conflict can find resolution. Each side can learn from the other. All parties are enriched by the synthesis arising out of the conflict.

In a zero-sum game, yes versus no quickly becomes we versus they. All of our moral debates take on the flavor of our adversarial legal system. Anne Strick comments in *Injustice for All:*

> We claim *righteousness for ourselves and require an "other," an opposite (religious, political, racial, national, sexual, name-it), a non-self who embodies evil. To that degree does blame become a basic behavior and revenge a solution. Such polarity not only implies superior-inferior; as it denies complementarity, it also invites battle. For superior tends to become pitted against inferior.*[7]

Identity politics, begun for the best of motives[8] to foster racial pride, sexual pride, gender pride, quickly becomes exclusivist. My identity is not only different from yours, but starts to be seen as better than yours. Apartheid

---

the *Waves of Culture: Understanding Diversity in Global Business* (Chicago: Irwin Professional Publishing, 1994).

7. *Injustice for All* (Penguin, 1978), pp. 83-84.

8. By underlining the uniqueness of minority identities, the mainstream "non-identity" was revealed to be just another identity, an identity that is predominantly male, white, Western, and middle-or upper-class.

starts to seem a good thing. Black pride becomes black separatism, for example. My identity enters into a contest with your identity, if only to become the #1 victim. My persecution is worse than your persecution, my holocaust is worse than your holocaust, my oppression is worse than your oppression.

Cooperation as Alternative: But competition isn't the only story. The trouble is that it is the most dramatic story. Cooperation doesn't make for good television ratings. Competition is not inevitable or natural. It just seems that way. Study after study shows that people learn less effectively when they are trying to beat others out than when they are working either alone or with others.[9] Learning is best approached like golf (a game in which you compete against yourself) or like a picnic (where you work together with others) than it is like tennis (a zero-sum game). This does not mean the advent of a sappy, smiley-face world of universal peace and harmony. Unique individuals in discussion and argument will always bring different ideas to the table. But you always know when the other is trying to beat you down and win, or trying to convince you of her view and listen for your reply. Conflict can be competitive and destructive, or it can be cooperative and enlightening. There is no eternal necessity to play a zero-sum game in ethics.

Human beings are inevitably self-interested. There will always be interest groups. But people can promote their interests cooperatively or competitively. Self-interest need not mean self-centered. I will cheerfully choose lamb chops from the restaurant menu because I like lamb

---

9.   Kohn, *No Contest, op.cit.*, pp. 46-48 cites 122 studies from 1924 to 1980 that showed that among every age group, in the vast majority of cases cooperation yielded better learning results than competition, or even than working alone.

chops. But I won't take the last three lamb chops from the buffet table before you have a chance to get any at all. I enthusiastically challenge your ideas, but not at your expense, not to defeat you, but in a dialogue where we both can learn.

PO:

Co-Opetition as Alternative: Ray Noorda, founder of the software company Novell, coined the term "Co-Opetition" to capture the dynamic relationship that exists between cooperation and competition.[10] The ideal of a competitive victory in which you survive to be #1 with the opposition destroyed makes sense only if you can imagine your competitive game to be the only game in town. But our interactions do not occur on neatly separate islands. Adopt a very practical holistic view of how your life is actually lived, and it quickly becomes apparent how in the big picture selfish competition is inevitably a losing game. Competition, the credo of American culture, is exposed as an illusion.

Co-Opetition is a recipe for making your unique contribution to the game which puts you into conflict with others who are different from you; but your contribution is made with a cooperative mind set, with a view to constructing a larger cooperative game with your opponent rather than reducing her or him to dust. Players in competition are simultaneously involved in many other games. Therefore you could be the overall loser if you compete, without "co-opetitive" awareness of the other games. For example, a wife could humiliate her husband with her superior reasoning, and win the logic game, but by that very

---

10. "You have to compete and cooperate at the same time," he said. *Electronic Business Buyer*, December 1993, cited by Brandenburger and Nalebuff, *op. cit*, who adopted "Co-Opetition" as the title of their book.

fact hurt herself in the family and marriage game. College admissions could be conducted strictly on S.A.T. scores, but the winners of the admissions game also are players in a pluralistic society, and could lose out on a multi-cultural education if S.A.T. scores result in a homogenous student body. A superstore could use a predatory pricing policy to drive a small competitor out of business, thereby losing out in the larger political game when it seeks a zoning variance for expansion. A pro-life zealot could give himself moral credit for murdering an abortion doctor, heedless of the cost exacted by this "victory" to make the wider society respect the seamless web of life.

There are games within games; it is so easy to win the battle and lose the war. "There is always a LARGER game."[11] John Donne's verse is a prescription for survival:

> *No man is an Island, entire of itself;*
> *every man is a piece of the Continent, a part of the main.*
>
> John Donne, *Devotions*

Competitive conflict is always destructive. One person must always lose. You are both players in other larger games, and in these games you will be playing with the enemy you created by your Pyrrhic victory. So in a purely competitive battle, even the winner becomes a loser.

Ethical pluralism understands the error of partial views. It is a fundamental law of ecology that you can't change just one thing. The universe operates holistically. Affect the part and you affect the whole.

---

11. Adam Brandenburger, *op.cit.*, p. 260.

ETHICS EXPERIMENT:

Test your view of human nature and ethics by playing the following version of *Prisoner's Dilemma*, a game based on this scenario:

> Two gang members are arrested for armed robbery. They are kept in solitary separate cells so they cannot communicate with each other. Without more evidence, the D.A. can only plea-bargain them each to one year in jail on a lesser charge. But using separate interrogation, he offers each of them a bargain. "Testify against your partner and you will go free, while your partner will serve three years for armed robbery." And there is a catch. If each one testifies against the other, both prisoners will serve two years in jail. So what do I as a gang member do? Can I trust my partner to be loyal to me, if I am loyal to him? Then we will serve only one year. But if I'm loyal and he's not, I get three years in jail, while he goes free. If we both cooperate with the police, we both serve two years. What is the rational thing to do? This is the Prisoner's Dilemma.[12]

Try this version of the game, which we will call *LIAR'S POKER.*

> *Directions:* "Win As Much As You Can"

> Pair off, and the two of you each toss a coin simultaneously. Peek and see whether you have heads or tails, but don't let the other see. Then tell the other person whether you have heads or tails. You can either lie, or you can tell the truth. Then show each other whether you really had heads or tails, i.e., whether you were lying or telling the truth. If it turns out you both were telling the truth, you each get $3. If one was telling the truth and

---

12. For a full discussion of this classical dilemma in terms of game theory and the dynamics of war and nuclear deterrence, see William Poundstone, *Prisoner's Dilemma: John von Neumann, Game Theory, and the Puzzle of the Bomb* (Doubleday, 1992).

*the other was lying, this is "sucker's pay-off": the liar
gets five dollars; the truth-teller [sucker] gets nothing. If
you both were lying, you each get one dollar. Use imagi-
nary dollars: keep score.*

*In summary, in each of 10 rounds, you either tell her
the truth or you lie. The scoring for each round is as
follows:*

*Truth – Truth: You each tell the truth. You each get
$3.*

*Truth – Lie: Sucker's payoff. Liar gets $5. Truth-teller
[sucker] gets nothing.*

Lie – Lie: You each lie. You each get $1.

Now: "Win as much as you can!"

*Play four rounds – keeping score. Then we'll pause for
a short discussion of strategy. Do not discuss strategy
during the first four rounds. Just play.*

*Round five is a "bonus round" – payoffs are tripled.
Play and score rounds 5, 6, and 7. Then pause to discuss strategy.*

*Round 8 is a bonus round: payoffs are multiplied by
five.*

*Round 10 is a bonus round: payoffs are multiplied by
10.*

Play and score rounds 8, 9, & 10.

Score sheet:

1._____ _____	5._____ _____ [X 3]	8. _____ _____ [X 5]
2._____ _____	6._____ _____	9. _____ _____
3._____ _____	7._____ _____	10. _____ _____ [X 10]
4._____ _____		

:totals

The game tests intricate dynamics between cooperation ("Be loyal to my partner") v. competition ("Betray

her for selfish gain"). Cooperate or compete? What are the best rules to play in order to maximize benefit? Game Theorists around the world have tested countless strategies for success. There is a growing consensus that the best strategy is "Tit for Tat." You maximize benefit by cooperating with your partner. But if your partner betrays you, in the next move you have to teach your partner a lesson and betray her back (Tit for Tat). Then go right back to cooperating again. Does it help you to know this? Play the game again and see.

It seems that competition will never be eliminated from human relations. But we benefit most when we compete under a dominant paradigm of cooperation. Businesses, too, are becoming more aware of their macro-interdependencies and are moving away from the dominance of the competitive paradigm.[13] As for ethics, we'll never be rid of the "pluralism" part of ethical pluralism. But we benefit best when our ethical diversity is incorporated into a cooperative world of mutual respect, mutual dialogue and mutual learning from one another.

---

13. James F. Moore, *The End of Competition: Leadership and Strategy in the Age of Business Eco-Systems* (Harper Business, 1997).

Bibliography of Cited Books

Adams, Carol J. and Marie M. Fortune (eds.). *Violence Against Women and Children: A Christian Theological Sourcebook*. Continuum Press, 1995.

Adams, Carol J. *Neither Man Nor Beast: Feminism and the Defense of Animals*. Continuum, 1994.

Anderson, Walt. *Reality Isn't What It Used To Be: Theatrical Politics, Ready to Wear Religion, Global Myths, Primitive Chic, and Other Wonders of the Postmodern World*. Harper Collins, 1992.

Arthur, John and Amy Shapiro (eds.). *Campus Wars: Multiculturalism and the Politics of Difference*. Westview Press, 1995.

Baker, Christina Looper and Christina Baker Kline. *The Conversation Begins: Mothers and Daughters Talk About Living Feminism*. Bantam, Doubleday, Dell, 1997.

Brace, C. Loring. In *Race and Other Misadventures: Essays in Honor of Ashley Montague in His Ninetieth Year*, edited by Larry T. Reynolds and Leonard Lieberman. General Hall, 1996.

Brandenburger, Adam M. and Barry J. Nalebuff. *Co-Opetition: A Revolutionary Mindset that Combines Competition and Cooperation: The Game Theory Strategy that is Changing the Game of Business*. Doubleday, 1996.

Brandt, Richard. "Cultural Relativism." In *Ethics in Business*, edited by T. Donaldson and P. Werhane. Prentice-Hall, Inc.; 2nd edition, 1983.

Broad, William J. *The Universe Below: Discovering the Secrets of the Deep Sea*. Simon and Schuster, 1997.

Cahill, Lisa Sowle. "Sex and Gender Ethics as New Testament Ethics." In *The Bible in Ethics: The Second Sheffield Colloquium*, edited by John W. Rogerson, Margaret Davies, and M. Daniel Carroll Rodas. The Sheffield Academic Press, Ltd., 1995.

Cerullo, Margaret and Marla Erlien. "Beyond the 'Normal' Family: A Cultural Critique of Women's Poverty." In *For Crying Out Loud: Women and Poverty in the U.S.*, edited by Rochelle Lefkowitz and Ann Withorm. The Pilgrim Press, 1986.

Coleman, S.S., Gerald D. *Homosexuality: Catholic Teaching and Pastoral Practice.* Paulist Press, 1995.

Coward, Harold. *Pluralism: Challenge to the World Religions.* Orbis Books, 1985.

De George, Richard T. "Ethical Dilemmas for Multinational Enterprise: A Philosophical Overview." In *Ethics and the Multinational Enterprise: Proceedings of the Sixth National Conference on Business Ethics*, edited by W. Michael Hoffman, Ann E. Lange, and David A. Fedo. Lanham, MD: the University Press of America, 1986.

De Bono, Edward. *De Bono's Thinking Course.* Facts on File Publications, 1985.

De Bono, Edward. *Po: Beyond Yes and No.* Simon and Schuster, 1972.

Des Jardins, Joseph R. *Environmental Ethics.* Wadsworth Publishing Co.; second edition, 1997.

Devalls, Bill and George Sessions. *Deep Ecology: Living as if Nature Mattered.* Salt Lake City: Peregrine Smith Books, 1985.

Donaldson, Thomas. *The Ethics of International Business.* Oxford University Press, 1989.

Dorick, Gwendolyn. *Friends Among Strangers: Personal Relations Among New York City's Homeless.* Ph.D. dissertation; Columbia University Department of Sociology, 1994.

Dworkin, Andrea. *Right Wing Women.* Coward-McCann, 1983.

Dworkin, Andrea. *Pornography.* Penguin: Plume book, 1989.

Edin, Kathryn. *Making Ends Meet.* Russell Sage Foundation, 1997.

Ellis, Richard. *Deep Atlantic: Life, Death, and Exploration in the Abyss.* Alfred A. Knopf, 1996.

Elshtain, Jean Bethke. *Public Man, Private Woman.* Princeton University Press, 1981.

Ephron, Delia. *Hanging Up.* Ballantine Books, 1995.

Eskridge, Jr., William. *The Case for Same Sex Marriage: From Sexual Liberty to Civilized Commitment.* The Free Press, 1996.

Exum, J. Cheryl. "The Ethics of Biblical Violence Against Women." In *The Bible in Ethics, op. cit.*

Fein, Ellen and Sherrie Schneider. *The Rules: Time-Tested Secrets for Capturing the Heart of Mr. Right.* Warner Books, 1996.

Fish, Stanley. *There's No Such Thing as Free Speech and It's a Good Thing, Too.* Oxford University Press, 1994.

Fish, Stanley. *Professional Correctness: Literary Studies and Political Change.* Oxford: Clarendon Press, 1987.

Fox-Genovese, Elizabeth. *Feminism Is Not the Story of My Life: how today's feminist elite have lost touch with the concerns of women.* Nan A. Talese, 1996.

Fox-Genovese, Elizabeth. *Feminism Without Illusions.* University of North Carolina Press, 1991.

Friedan, Betty. "Feminism." In *The Meese Commission Exposed: Proceedings of a National Coalition Against Censorship, Public Information Briefing on the Attorney General's Commission on Pornography.* New York: National Coalition Against Censorship, 1987.

Fuller, Jack. *New Values: Ideas for an Information Age.* University of Chicago Press, 1996.

Furchtgott-Roth, Diane, and Christine Stolba. *Women's Figures: the Economic Progress of Women in America.* Independent Women's Forum and The American Enterprise Institute, 1997.

Gallagher, Winifred. *I.D.: How Temperament and Experience Make You Who You Are.* Random House, 1996.

Gallop, Jane. *Feminist Accused of Sexual Harassment.* Duke University Press, 1997.

Gans, Herbert J. *The War Against the Poor: the Underclass and Antipoverty Policy.* Basic Books, 1995.

Gilligan, Carol. *In a Different Voice: Psychological Theory and Women's Development.* Harvard University Press; reissued 1993.

Glazer, Nathan. *We Are All Multiculturalists Now.* Harvard University Press, 1997.

Grandin, Temple. *Thinking in Pictures and Other Reports from my Life with Autism.* Doubleday, 1995.

Grant, Judith. *Fundamental Feminism: Contesting the Core Concepts of Feminist Theory.* Routledge, 1993.

Gross, Rita M. *Buddhism After Patriarchy: A Feminist History, Analysis, and Reconstruction of Buddhism.* State University of New York Press, 1993.

Gudorf, Christina E. *Body, Sex, and Pleasure: Reconstructing Christian Sexual Ethics.* The Pilgrim Press, 1994.

Haas, Robert. "Ethics in the Trenches." In *Business Ethics 95/96,* edited by John E. Richardson. Brown and Benchmark Publishers, 1995.

Harris, John. "The Political Status of Children." In *Contemporary Political Philosophy: Radical Studies,* edited by Keith Graham. Cambridge University Press, 1982.

Henderson, Verne E. "Ethical Criteria for Multinational Consulting." In *Ethics and the Multinational Enterprise, op.cit.*

Hillman, James. *Kinds of Power: A Guide to Its Intelligent Uses.* Currency/Doubleday, 1997.

Hoagland, Sarah. *Lesbian Ethics: Toward New Values.* Palo Alto: Institute for Lesbian Studies, 1988.

Hoberman, John M. *Darwin's Athletes: How Sport Has Damaged Black America and Preserved the Myth of Race.* Houghton Mifflin, 1997.

Holt, John. "Why Not a Bill of Rights for Children?" In *The Children's Rights Movement: Overcoming the Oppression of Young People,* edited by Beatrice Gross and Ronald Gross. Anchor Press/Doubleday, 1977.

hooks, bell. *Talking Back: Thinking Feminist, Thinking Black.* South End Press, 1989.

Huben, Peter W. *Liability: the Legal Revolution and Its Consequences.* Basic Books, Inc., 1988.

Humphry, Derek. *Final Exit: The Practicalities of Self-Deliverance and Assisted Suicide for the Dying.* Dell, 1992.

Ireland, Patricia. *What Women Want.* Dutton, 1996.

Kaminer, Wendy. *True Love Waits.* Addison-Wesley, 1996.

Kaminer, Wendy. *I'm Dysfunctional, You're Dysfunctional: The Recovery Movement and Other Self-Help Fashions.* Random House Vintage Books, 1993.

Keane, S.S., Philip S. *Sexual Morality: A Catholic Perspective.* Paulist Press, 1977.

Knitter, Paul. *No Other Name? A Critical Survey of Christian Attitudes Toward the World Religions.* Orbis, 1985.

Kohn, Alfie. *No Contest: the Case Against Competition.* Houghton Mifflin, 1986.

Kourany, Janet *et al.*, eds. *Feminist Philosophies.* Prentice-Hall, 1992.

Kuttner, Robert. *Everything for Sale: The Virtues and Limits of Markets.* Alfred A. Knopf, 1997.

LaFleur, William. *Liquid Life: Abortion and Buddhism in Japan.* Princeton University Press, 1992.

Lane, Robert. *The Market Experience.* Cambridge University Press, 1991.

Lehrman, Karen. *The Lipstick Proviso: Women, Sex, and Power in the Real World.* Anchor Books, 1997.

Lindblom, Charles E. *Inquiry and Change: the Troubled Attempt to Understand and Shape Society.* Yale University Press; reprint 1992.

Lindblom, Charles E. *Politics and Markets: the World's Political and Economic Systems.* Basic Books, 1977.

Lorde, Audre. *Sister Outsider.* Trumansburg, N.Y.: The Crossing Press, 1984.

Loulan, JoAnn. "Butch Mothers, Femme Bull Dykes: Dismantling Our Own Stereotypes." In *Dyke Life,* edited by Karla Jay. Basic Books, 1995.

Lovelock, James. *The Ages of Gaia: A Biography of Our Living Planet.* Oxford University Press, 1988.

Lugones, Maria and Elisabeth Spelman. "Have We Got a Theory for You! Feminist Theory, Cultural Imperialism, and the Demand for 'The Woman's Voice.'" In *Feminist Philosophies, op. cit.*

Luker, Kristin. *Abortion and the Politics of Motherhood.* University of California Press, 1984.

MacKinnon, Catharine A. "The Sexual Politics of the First Amendment." In *Feminism Unmodified: Discourses on Life and Law.* Harvard University Press, 1987.

248   *Bibliography*

Macklin, Ruth. *The Enemies of Patients.* Oxford University Press, 1993.

Maran, Meredith. *Notes from an Incomplete Revolution: Real Life Since Feminism.* Bantam Books, 1997.

Margulis, Lynn and Dorion Sagan. *Slanted Truth: Essays on Gaia, Symbiosis, and Evolution.* Copernicus Press, 1997.

Mason, Mary Ann. *From Father's Property to Children's Rights.* Columbia University Press, 1994.

McNeil, John. *The Church and the Homosexual.* Beacon Press; 4th edition, 1993.

Michener, James A. *Sports in America.* Random House, 1976.

Montagu, Ashley (ed.). *Learning Non-aggression: the Experience of Non-Literate Societies.* Oxford University Press, 1978.

Moore, James F. *The End of Competition: Leadership and Strategy in the Age of Business Eco-systems.* Harper Business, 1997.

Moore, Marianne Moody. *Case Studies in Business Ethics.* West Publishing Co., 2nd edition, 1996.

Morgan, Kathryn Pauly. "Women and the Knife: Cosmetic Surgery and the Colonization of Women's Bodies." In *Nagging Questions: Feminist Ethics in Everyday Life,* edited by Dana E. Bushnell. Rowman and Littlefield, 1995.

Morgan, Robin (ed.) *Sisterhood is Powerful.* Vintage Books, 1970.

Naess, Arne, and David Rothenberg. *Ecology, Community and Lifestyle: Outline of an Ecosophy.* Cambridge University Press; reprint edition, 1990.

Njeri, Itabari. *The Last Plantation: Color, Conflict, and Identity.* Houghton Mifflin, 1997.

Norris, Kathleen. *The Cloister Walk.* Riverhead Books, 1996.

Noske, Barbara. *Humans and Other Animals: Beyond the Boundaries of Anthropology.* London: Pluto Press, 1989.

O'Neill, Onora and William Ruddick (eds.). *Having Children: Philosophical and Legal Reflections on Parenthood.* Oxford University Press, 1979.

Paglia, Camille. *Vamps and Tramps.* Random House Vintage Books, 1994.

Pannikar, Raimundo. *Myth, Faith, and Hermeneutik.* Paulist Press, 1979.

Peddicord, Father Richard. *Gay and Lesbian Rights: A Question of Sexual Ethics or Social Justice?* Sheed and Ward, 1995.

Plaskow, Judith, "Transforming the Nature of Community: Toward a Feminist People of Israel." In *After Patriarchy: Feminist Transformations of the World Religions,* edited by Paula M. Cooey, William R. Eakin, Jay B. McDaniel. Orbis Books, 1991.

Pope Pius XI. *Casti Connubii.*

Poundstone, William. *Prisoner's Dilemma: John von Neuman, Game Theory, and the Puzzle of the Bomb.* Doubleday, 1992.

President's Commission for the Study of Ethical Problems in Medicine and Biomedical and Behavioral Research. *Defining Death.* Government Printing Office, 1981.

Purdy, Laura M. *In Their Best Interest? The Case Against Equal Rights for Children.* Cornell University Press, 1992.

Quill, M.D., Timothy E. *A Midwife through the Dying Process: Stories of Healing and Hard Choices at the End of Life.* Johns Hopkins University Press, 1996.

Quill, M.D., Timothy E. *Death and Dignity: Making Choices and Taking Charge.* W. W. Norton and Co., 1993.

Ridley, Matt. *The Origins of Virtue: Human Instincts and the Evolution of Cooperation.* Viking Press, 1997.

Robinson, Richard D. *International Business Management: A Guide to Decision-making.* The Dryden Press; 2nd edition, 1978.

Roiphe, Katie. *Last Night in Paradise: Sex and Morals at the Century's End.* Little, Brown and Co., 1997.

Rollin, Betty. *Last Wish.* Random House, 1996.

Scarezoni, Letha and Virginia Ramey Mollenkott. *Is the Homosexual My Neighbor?* Harper and Row, 1978.

Schumacher, E.F. *Small Is Beautiful: Economics as if People Mattered.* Harper and Row, 1973.

Sethi, S. Prakash. "Changing Rules of International Corporate Behavior." In *Ethics and the International Enterprise, op. cit.*

Shavelson, Dr. Lonny. *A Choice of Death: the Dying Confront Assisted Suicide.* Simon and Schuster, 1995.

Shrage, Laurie. *Moral Dilemmas of Feminism.* Routledge, 1994.

Singer, Andrew W. "Ethics: Are Standards Lower Overseas?" In *Across the Board.* The Conference Board, Inc. 1992.

Smith, Timothy. "The Church Corporate Responsibility Movement: Fifteen Years Later." In *Ethics and the Multinational Enterprise, op. cit.*

Sommers, Christina Hoff. *Who Stole Feminism? How Women Have Betrayed Women.* Simon and Schuster, 1994.

Sowell, Thomas. *Migrations and Cultures.* Basic Books, 1996.

Stone, Christopher. *Should Trees Have Standing?: Toward Legal Rights for Natural Objects.* Dobbs Ferry, NY: Oceana Publications, 1996.

Strick, Anne. *Injustice for All.* Penguin, 1978.

Strossen, Nadine. *Defending Pornography: Free Speech, Sex, and the Fight for Women's Rights.* Scribner, 1995.

Sullivan, William M. "Calling or Career: the Tensions of Modern Professional Life." In *Professional Ideals*, edited by Albert Flores. Wadsworth Publishing Co., 1988.

Superson, Anita, "Right-Wing Women: Causes, Choices, and Blaming the Victim." In *"Nagging" Questions: Feminist Ethics in Everyday Life*, edited by Dana E. Bushnell. Roman and Littlefield, Publishers, 1995.

Superson, Anita. "The Employer-Employee Relationship and the Right to Know." In *Ethics in the Workplace*, edited by Robert A. Larmer. West Publishing Co., 1996.

Taylor, Paul. *Respect for Nature.* Princeton University Press, 1986.

Tenner, Edward. *Why Things Bite Back: Technology and the Revenge of Unintended Consequences.* Knopf, 1996.

Thaler, Richard H. *The Winner's Curse: Paradoxes and Anomalies in Economic Life.* Free Press, 1992.

Tobias, Sheila. *The Faces of Feminism: An Activist's Reflection on the Women's Movement.* Westview Press, 1997.

Trimpey, Jack. *The small book: A Revolutionary Alternative for Overcoming Alcohol and Drug Dependence.* Bantam Doubleday Dell; revised edition 1992.

Trompenaars, Fons. *Riding the Waves of Culture: Understanding Diversity in Global Business.* Chicago: Irwin Professional Publishing, 1994.

Turkle, Sherry. *Life on the Screen: Identity in the Age of the Internet.* Simon and Schuster, 1995.

Velasquez, Manuel G. *Business Ethics.* Prentice-Hall; 2nd edition, 1988.

Vogel, David. "Is U.S. Business Obsessed with Ethics?" In *Across the Board, op.cit.*

Wilson, Midge and Kathy Russell. *Divided Sisters: Bridging the Gap Between Black Women and White Women.* Anchor Books, 1996.

Witt, Lynn, Sherry Thomas, and Eric Marcus (eds.). *Out In All Directions: The Almanac of Gay and Lesbian America.* Warner Books, 1995.

Wogaman, J. Philip. *Economics and Ethics: A Christian Inquiry.* Fortress Press, 1986.

Wogaman, J. Philip. "Reflections on Church Activism and Transnational Corporations." In *Ethics and the Multinational Enterprise, op.cit.*

Young-Bruehl, Elisabeth. *The Anatomy of Prejudices.* Harvard University Press, 1996.

Zimming, Franklin E. *The Changing Legal World of Adolescence.* Macmillan/The Free Press, 1982.

Zita, Jacqueline N. "Male Lesbians and the Postmodernist Body." In *Adventures in Lesbian Philosophy,* edited by Claudia Card. Indiana University Press, 1994.

Bibliography of Cited Articles

19th Century Marriage Manuals. *The New York Times* (June 2, 1996), E7.

Annas, George J. and Sherman Elias. "The Politics of Transplantation of Human Fetal Tissue." *The New England Journal of Medicine*, Vol. 320, No . 16 (April 20, 1989), 1079-1082.

Annas, George. "Pregnant Women as Fetal Containers." *Hastings Center Report* (December 1986), 13-14.

Arrow, K. et al. "Economic Growth, Carrying Capacity and the Environment." *Science* (April 28, 1995) .

Associated Press. "Damage Award for Retouched BMW" (May 10, 1997).

Bammam, M.D., Jacqueline. "A Neonatologist's Concern." *Update* (Loma Linda University Ethics Center), Vol 3, No. 4 (November 1987), 2.

Banister, Judith et al. "No Daughters Need Apply," *Washington Post National Weekly* (May 20-26, 1996) .

Barrett, Jennifer. "Growing Pains." *Yoga Journal* (May/June 1997), 76.

Blakely, Mary Kay. "Is One Woman's Sexuality Another Woman's Pornography?." *Ms* (April 1985), pp. 35-37, 46-47.

Bohren, Jan. "Six Myths of Sexual Harassment." *Management Review* (May 1993), 61-63.

Booth, William. "A Fly in the Ointment." *The Washington Post National Weekly Edition* (April 14, 1997), 9.

Brakman, Sarah-Vaughan. "Adult Daughter Caregivers." *The Hastings Center Report* 24, No. 5 (1994).

Bray, Anna J. "Why Have Tort Costs Exploded?." *Investor Business Daily* (January 20, 1995), A 1-2.

Brody. Elaine. "Filial Care of the Elderly and Changing Roles of Women and Men." Journal of Geriatric Psychiatry 19, No. 2 (1986): 177-178.

Capron, Alexander Morgan. "Anencephalic Donors: Separate the Dead from the Dying." *Hastings Center Report* (February 1987), 5-9.

Codling v. Paglia. 32 New York 2nd 330, 298 Northeastern 2nd 622, 345 New York Supplement 2nd 461 (1973).

Donaldson, Thomas. "Multinational Decision-making: Reconciling International Norms." *Journal of Business Ethics* 4 (1985), 357-366.

Fine, Alan. "The Ethics of Fetal Tissue Transplants." *Hastings Center Report* (June/July 1988).

Forum: The Benefits and Ethics of Animal Research. In *Scientific American* (February 1997) .

Fost, Norman. "Organs from Anencephalic Infants: An Idea Whose Time Has Not Yet Come." *Hastings Center Report* (November 1988), 5-10.

France, David. "This Doctor Wants to Help You Die." New York (January 13, 1997), 28.

Gallagher, Janet. "The Fetus and the Law – Whose Life Is It Anyway?." Ms (September 1984), 62-66, 134-135.

Gorman, C. "A Balancing Act of Life and Death." *Time* (February 1, 1988), p.49.

Greeley, Henry T. et al. "Special Report: The Ethical Use of Human Fetal Tissue in Medicine." *The New England Journal of Medicine,* Vol. 320, No. 16 (April 20, 1989), 1094-1095

Greenhouse, Linda. "Justices Listen to Arguments on Fetal Protection Policy." *The New York Times* (October 10, 1990), A20.

Hardman, Wendy and Jacqueline Heidelberg. "When Sexual Harassment is a Foreign Affair." *Personnel Journal* (April 1996), 91-97. Heaney, M.D., Robert P. "Sex, Natural Law, and Bread Crumbs." *America* (February 28, 1994), 12-16.

Henshaw, Stanley K. et a/. "A Portrait of American Women Who Obtain Abortions." *Family Planning Perspectives* 17:2, (1985) 90-96.

Horgan, John. "Seeking a Better Way to Die." *Scientific American* (May 1997), 100-105.

Johnson, Dawn. "A New Threat to Pregnant Women's Autonomy." *Hastings Center Report* (August-September 1987), 33-40.

Jong, Erica. "Fear of Flirting – Bob Packwood Meets Cotton Mather." *The Washington Post National Weekly Edition* (December 14-20, 1992).

Lehrman. Karen. "Truth in Feminism: Reflections on the way women really live vs. The way feminists say they ought to live." *The New York Times Book Review* (May 4, 1997).

Macchetto, F. Duccio and Mark Dickinson. "Galaxies in the Young Universe." *Scientific American* (May 1997), 92-99.

Mackenzie, Thomas, Theodore Nagel and Barbara Katz Rothman. " "When a Pregnant Woman Endangers Her Fetus." *Hastings Center Report* (February 1986), 24-25.

MacKenzie, Debra. "Third World Kidneys for Sale," *New Scientist* (March 28, 1985) and "Embryos to Lipsticks?," *New Scientist* (October 10, 1985).

Mahawald, Mary B. Jerry Silver, and Robert A. Ratcheson. "The Ethical Options in Fetal Transplants." *Hastings Center Report* (February 1987) . 9- 15.

Menard, Louis. "Everybody Else's College Education." *The New York Times Magazine* (April 20, 1997), 48.

Miller, Laura. "Oppressed by Liberation." *The New York Times Book Review* (May 11, 1997).

Nolan, Kathleen. "Genug ist Genug: A Fetus is not a Kidney." Hastings Center Report (December 1988). Nussbaum, Karen. "Education Doesn't Cut the Pay Gap." *Mesa Tribune* (November 14, 1991), A1, A7.

Pellegrino, M. D., Edmund D. "Professional Ethics: Moral Decline or Paradigm Shift?." *Religion and Intellectual Life* Vol. lV No. 3 (Spring 1987), 21-39.

President's Commission for the Study of Ethical Problems in Medicine and Biomedical and Behavioral Research. "Defining Death." U.S. Government Printing Office, 1981, 36-41.

Raines, Lisa J. and Stephen P. Push. "Protecting Pregnant Workers." *Harvard Business Review* (May-June 1986), 29.

Roberts, M. "Understanding Rita." *Psychology Today* (December 1986), 20; 14.

Robertson, John A. "Rights, Symbolism, and Public Policy in Fetal Tissue Transplants." *Hastings Center Report* (December 1988), 5-12.

Samuelson, Robert. "A Question of Freedom." *The Washington Post National Weekly Edition* (April 28, 1997), 5.

Sciolio, Elaine. "The Army's Problems With Sex and Power." *The New York Times* (May 4, 1997), 4E.

Shewmon, Alan D. "Anencephaly: Selected Medical Aspects." *Hastings Center Report* (February 1988), 11 -19.

Slade, Margot. "Sexual Harassment Stories from the Field." *New York Times* (March 27, 1994), Section 4.

Stevens, Edward. "A Bill of Rights for Adult Daughter Caregivers." *Regis Today* (Winter/Spring 1995) .

Stryker, Jeff. "A Bedside Manner for Death and Dying." *The New York Times* (Sunday May 19, 1996), p. E3.

Tasso. *The Sun: A Magazine of Ideas* (May 1991), 40.

Thorn, E. "Trade in Human Tissue Needs Regulation." *Wall Street Journal,* (August 19, 1987), p. 3.

Transplant Policy Center Ann Arbor. "Anencephalic Infants as Sources of Transplantable Organs." *Hastings Center Report* (November 1988), 28-33.

Tversky, Amos and Daniel Kahneman. "The Framing of Decisions and the Psychology of Choice." *Science* 211 (January 30, 1981, 453-458.

U.S. Bishops. "Catholic Framework for Economic Life." *Woodstock Report,* (March 1997), 9.

Walters, James and Stephen Ashwal. "Organ Prolongation in Anencephalic Infants." *Hastings Center Report* (February 1988), 19-27.

Walters, James W. "Anencephalic Organ Procurement: Should the Law be Changed?." *BioLaw: A Legal and Ethical Reporter on Medicine, Health Care, and Bioengineering* (December 1987) Vol 2, No. 9, S:88-S:89.

Wilkes, Paul. "The Tough Job of Teaching Ethics." *The New York Times* (January 22, 1989), 24F.

Wilike, M.D., J.C. and Dave Andrusko. "Personhood Redux." *Hastings Center Report* (october/November 1988).

Winchester, Simon. "An Electronic Sink of Depravity." *The Spectator* (February 4, 1995).